DESTROYERS

DESTROYERS

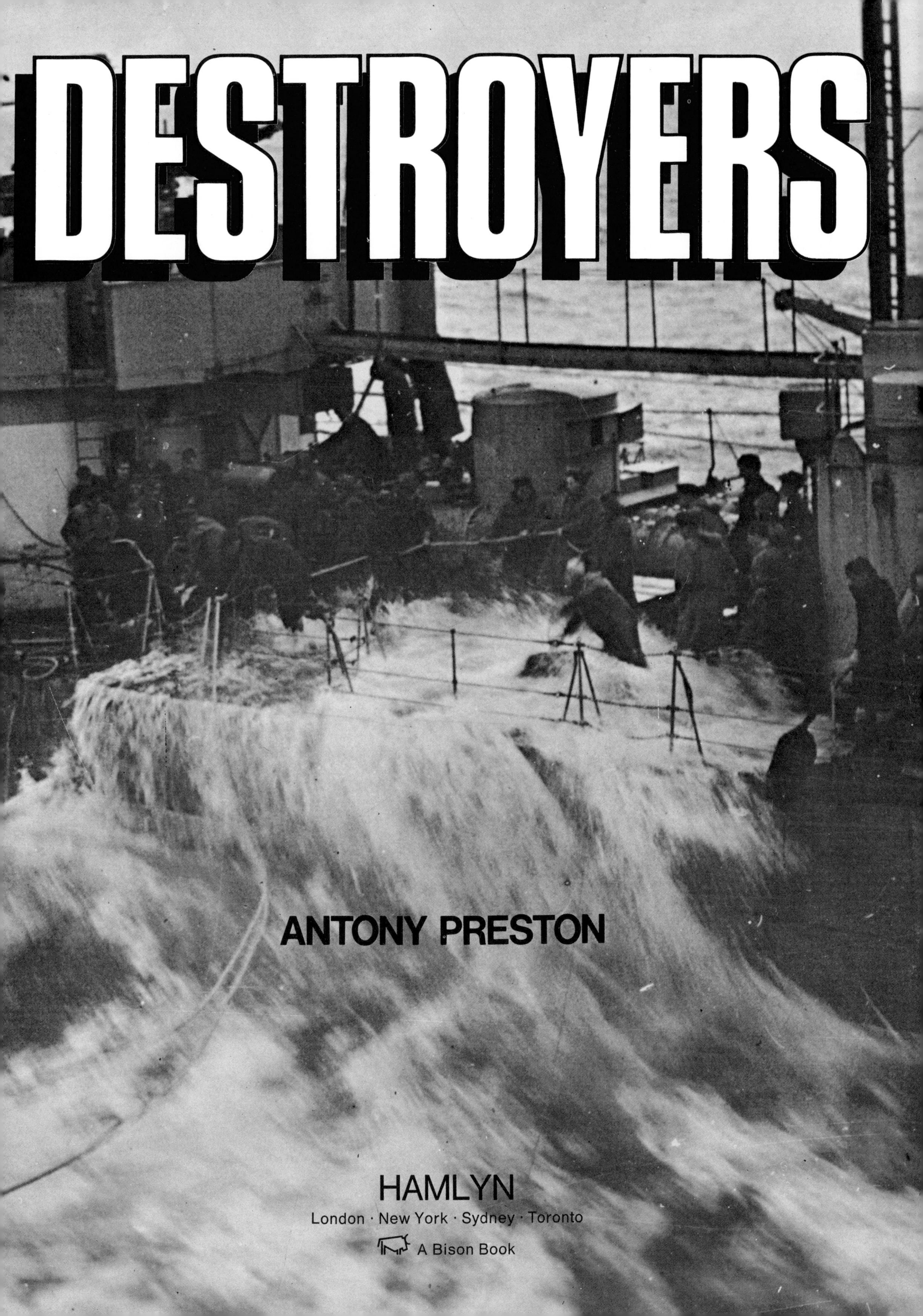

ANTONY PRESTON

HAMLYN
London · New York · Sydney · Toronto
A Bison Book

This book was designed and produced by
Bison Books Limited
4 Cromwell Place,
London SW7

Published by
The Hamlyn Publishing Group Limited
London · New York · Sydney · Toronto
Astronaut House, Hounslow Road
Feltham, Middlesex

ISBN 0-600-32955-0

Printed in Hong Kong

Second impression 1978

CONTENTS

The Early Destroyers

No warship can match the reputation, the glamour or the achievements of destroyers. If a single word could describe their qualities it might be 'style', for they were handsome, indispensable and above all, hard-working. From being a novel type of vessel built for only one task, in the space of 80 years the destroyer became an all-purpose ship, escorting the fleet, attacking with torpedoes, sinking submarines, landing troops or bombarding shore positions.

To understand the origins of the destroyer we must go back a century to the time when a British engineer in Fiume was experimenting with a new weapon. Robert Whitehead had been approached by a retired Austrian naval officer called Luppis who had invented a strange device which he hoped might have some effect on naval warfare. What Luppis had built was a small self-propelled boat which could be guided from the shore by two wires. His intention was to guide the explosive-filled boat into the side of a warship but the quick mind of Whitehead seized on a much more useful development of the idea.

Whitehead could see that the guiding wires had to go, and that if the 'boat' could be induced to travel underwater in a straight line it could sink a ship with much greater ease. For once progress was rapid; Luppis carried out his experiments in 1866 and in the same year Whitehead produced a vehicle which could travel submerged 200 yards at 6.5 knots. Two years later he demonstrated two models with guncotton warheads to the Austro-Hungarian Navy, and in 1870 he took them to England to demonstrate them to the Admiralty. They were named 'torpedoes', after an electric ray which stuns its prey. The name had first been used by David Bushnell for what we now call mines, and it continued in use for all underwater explosive devices for some years.

The Admiralty was most impressed by the hundred or more firings of the Whitehead torpedo in September–October 1870 and immediately bought the rights. But it was to be another four years before a ship existed capable of firing the torpedo. This was HMS *Vesuvius*, an experimental 90-foot craft, but the first warship *designed* to fire the torpedo was HMS *Lightning*, launched and completed in 1877. She was armed with a bow launching tube for a single Whitehead torpedo and was little more than a large steam launch. She aimed the torpedo by steering herself at the target, but she was capable of steaming at 19 knots in calm weather and her 14-inch diameter torpedo could run for 600 yards at 18 knots. This was a very high performance for any ship in the 1870s, and the British Admiralty felt justified in ordering more 'torpedo boats' of the same type. The first 11 were ordered from the same builder as the *Lightning*, the Thames-side firm of John I Thornycroft, but a further eight were ordered from seven different firms to see if they could make any improvements and to evaluate the characteristics of these novel craft.

Soon after the new ships were ordered it was decided to give them all numbers, and so the *Lightning* became HM *Torpedo Boat No 1*. She and the others were put through a number of exercises to test their abilities but their role was restricted to the defence of harbours for the moment. They were too small to do anything more than dart out of a harbour to fire their torpedoes at a blockading or attacking enemy squadron. Any attempt to use them offensively was out of the question as they were too narrow, too small and too lightly built to take the pounding of a voyage in the open sea. Nevertheless the destructive power of the Whitehead torpedo made a profound impression on the leading navies, for in both France and Great Britain the first rumblings of a revolution in naval technology could be felt. The French, having ignored the Whitehead torpedo when it first appeared, began to take notice when they saw the British experimenting with torpedo boats. What appealed to the French was the torpedo boat's apparent

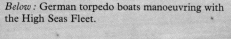

Below: German torpedo boats manoeuvring with the High Seas Fleet.

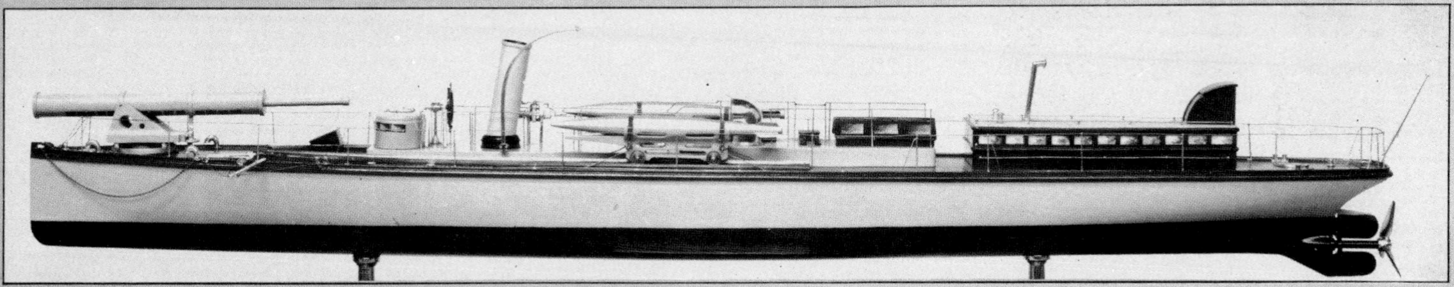

Top: Four British 'torpedo boat destroyers' are completed in Palmer's shipyard at Jarrow.
Above: The ancestor of the destroyer, HMS *Lightning*, the first torpedo boat. Two 14-inch Whitehead torpedoes were carried to be fired from the bow tube.

Above: The Italian destroyer *Audace* takes the water 4 May 1914 at Livorno. She was sunk in collision in August 1916 in the Ionian Sea.

ability to destroy the largest warships with a single devastating shot. Ever since the Napoleonic Wars had seen the destruction of their large fleet the French had been looking for a weapon to offset Britain's overwhelming superiority at sea; first it had been the Paixhans explosive shell in the 1820s, then it had been armour in the 1850s, but each time the British had outsmarted them by adopting the innovation themselves. This time the British appeared to have taken the lead in developing a weapon of stealth, and it was unthinkable that the French could allow themselves to fall behind.

In fact the French had very nearly beaten the British to the punch, for they ordered their *Torpilleur No 1* in 1875, but she did not enter service until a year after the *Lightning*, and was followed by six more. The French swallowed their pride and ordered three from British yards, two of them from John I Thornycroft. By 1880 30 torpedo boats had been completed and another 30 were being built. The success of the two leading British firms, Yarrow and Thornycroft, meant that other navies were also buying torpedo boats, and within a short while the navies of Austria, Chile, Greece, Germany, Italy, Japan and Scandinavia all had them. The British would have been happy to let the torpedo boat develop at a slower pace, for both the boats and their torpedoes were still at a primitive stage of development. But the French continued building them and between 1881 and 1885 a further 44 boats were ordered, bringing the total to 104. Under pressure from anxious naval officers and politicians the Royal Navy replied by launching another ten in 1885–86. But the Admiralty realized that the answer to the torpedo boat could not be merely more torpedo boats, and at the same time started to look seriously at the problem of finding an antidote.

One solution was to build a 'torpedo ram', an armoured ship with, it was hoped, enough speed to drive off torpedo boats and also a reinforced ram bow and torpedoes of her own to allow her to go on to sink enemy ships. The only one built, HMS *Polyphemus*, was a hopeless failure as she was slower than the torpedo boats. Gatling and Nordenfelt machine guns firing solid shot up to one-inch diameter were introduced, but these proved unable to stop torpedo boats and they had to give way to heavier quick-firing guns. Torpedo nets, rigged in a gigantic crinoline around a ship, offered some measure of protection while she was at anchor, but if she tried to steam at any speed the nets were swept away. The basic problem was that the rate of fire of big guns was too slow and the torpedo boat was too small a target to be picked up easily at night or in poor visibility.

What was needed was another vessel which could chase the torpedo boat at the same speed or better, with guns to sink her. A leading British shipbuilder, J Samuel White, designed and built at his own expense a larger torpedo boat, called the *Swift*. She was 25 feet longer than the existing Thornycroft and Yarrow boats, and although she was rather slower the novel form of the hull aft gave her greater manoeuvrability. Her greater beam allowed for the heavy armament in those days of six 47mm quick-firing guns and three torpedo tubes; she marked a clear step forward. The Admiralty was suit-

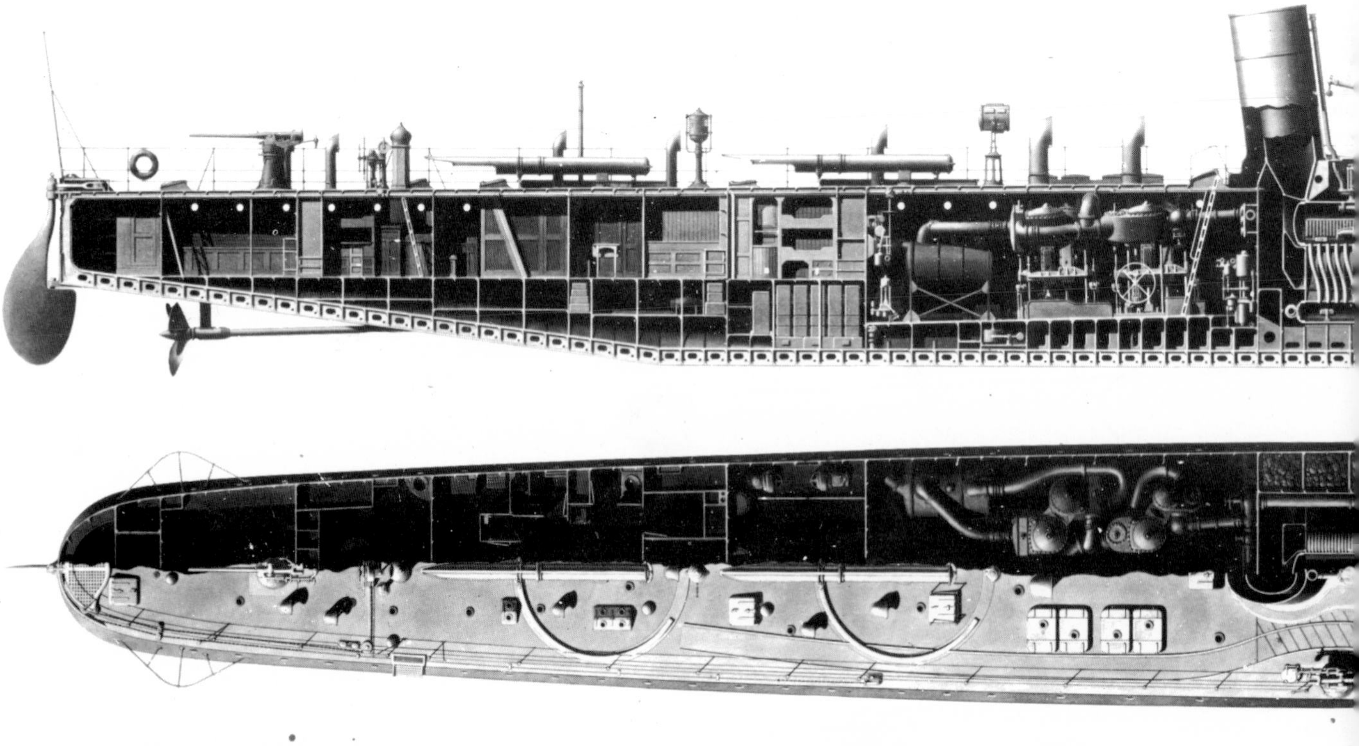

ably impressed and bought her immediately as *Torpedo Boat No 81*. She inspired a new idea, that of the 'torpedo boat catcher', an even larger vessel armed with guns and torpedoes. Four of the new craft were ordered to a design drawn up by the Director of Naval Construction, and HMSs *Rattlesnake*, *Grasshopper*, *Sandfly* and *Spider* joined the Fleet in 1887–88.

In April 1887 the brand-new *Rattlesnake* started a long-awaited series of experiments with 18 torpedo boats. During the next two weeks she did her best to catch her small enemies, but failed miserably. She was unfortunate in that lightweight high-speed steam machinery was still in its infancy, and her hull was too lightly built. In a flat calm she could catch the torpedo boats, although a margin of only two knots was not enough to be decisive and the vibration was nearly unbearable. In any sort of seaway her speed immediately fell off but the torpedo boats did no better, and the experiments showed that daylight attack would be suicidal. The speeds of larger warships had been rising steadily since the mid-1870s, and now they were only some four knots slower than the torpedo boats. In a full power trial held at the end of these 1887 experiments, the fastest speed achieved by a torpedo boat was only 16.75 knots, not enough to give immunity to gunfire. Nor was the machinery reliable enough; nearly half the boats broke down during the 88-mile run.

Although a further 13 'catchers' of an improved *Rattlesnake* type were ordered in 1889 nobody expected much from them, for even though they were faster, the speed of torpedo boats had risen from a theoretical 20 knots to 24 in ideal conditions (ie, without armament in smooth water). It was proving very hard to produce a small, fast craft which was also robust enough to carry the guns needed to sink a torpedo boat. Even when private firms were invited to install their boilers and machinery in Navy-designed hulls in a further series of 'catchers' laid down in 1891–93, they were too slow and too frail for the job. The Admiralty was very worried, for by this time the French Navy had 220 torpedo boats, some of the latest capable of a reported 27.5 knots; Russia had built 152, Germany 143 and Italy 129 boats. The state of tension existing between Britain and France made war a possibility and, as the Russians would almost certainly join the French, the Royal Navy's 186 torpedo boats would be opposed by a total of 372 French and Russian boats.

Above: The British first-class torpedo boat No 93 shows a clear resemblance to early destroyers but she is smaller and carries lighter guns.

The Admiralty decided to cut its losses and seek the help of private torpedo-boat builders, reasoning that they were the likeliest people to be able to find an antidote to their own product. In 1892, shortly after becoming Third Sea Lord and Controller of the Royal Navy, Rear-Admiral J A Fisher asked Alfred Yarrow, the head of Yarrows, to study the problem and draw up a specification for a ship capable of destroying torpedo boats. Yarrow immediately visited the French shipbuilders and submitted a detailed report which became the basis for a directive from Fisher to the Director of Naval Construction. There were only two conditions: a speed of at least 27 knots and a powerful gun armament. The DNC, Sir William White, recommended that the specification be put out to private tender,

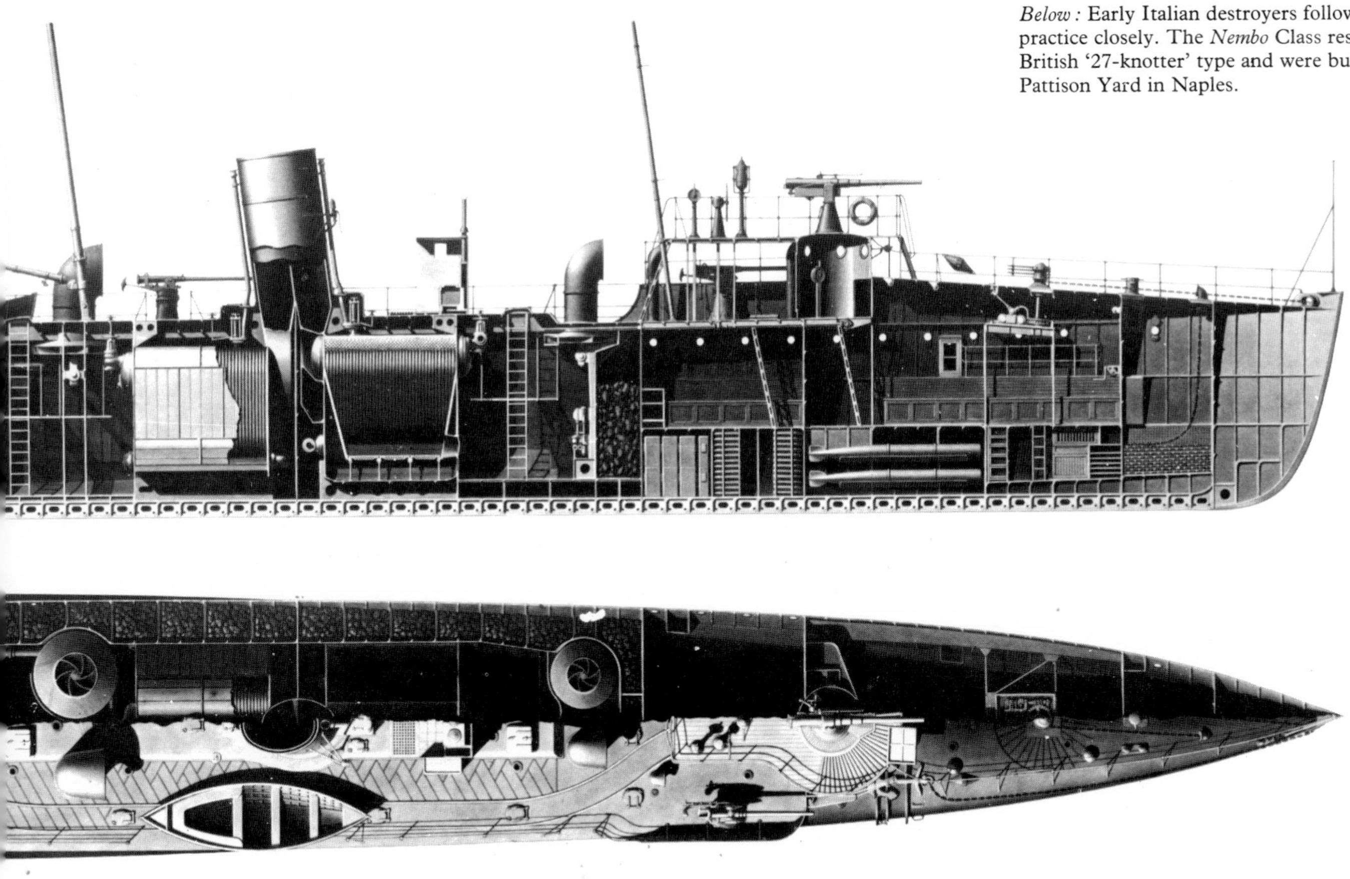

Below: Early Italian destroyers followed British practice closely. The *Nembo* Class resembled the British '27-knotter' type and were built at the Pattison Yard in Naples.

Above and left: HMS *Daring* was typical of the early '27-knotter' destroyers with five quick-firing guns, a twin 18-inch torpedo-tube on deck and a single 18-inch in the bow.

for as he put it, 'the Royal Dockyards had failed to build a satisfactory vessel'. The only people who could give the right amount of attention to the design of hulls and machinery were those firms which had specialized in torpedo boats.

No time was lost, and four ships were ordered on 27 June 1892, two from Yarrow and two from Thornycroft. The official term was still 'Torpedo Boat Catcher' but on 8 August for the first time the phrase 'Torpedo Boat Destroyer' appeared in official correspondence, marking the start of the destroyer story.

Below: The early destroyer builders were given great latitude in the details, as long as they met the basic specifications. The British firm of Palmer's Shipbuilding and Iron Company liked lots of funnels and so HMS *Viking* became the only six-funnelled destroyer in the world.

The term had been used earlier, in the 1880s, but never officially, and henceforward it was to be used exclusively for the new type of warship, usually shortened to TBD.

The first torpedo boat destroyer to be completed was HMS *Havock* in October 1893, and with the disastrous failure of the 'catchers' in everybody's mind, her trials were watched with considerable apprehension. Nobody needed to worry, for she reached her designed speed of 26 knots easily and behaved well in a seaway with only slight vibration. Manoeuvrability was good, and in the Annual Manoeuvres in 1894 the *Havock* showed her seaworthiness by staying at sea for 24 hours without any difficulties. She quickly showed her mettle by catching two 'enemy' torpedo boats, then next day she caught the 'catcher' *Speedy*, overtook her and circled around before leaving her standing. Her armament of one 76mm gun and three 47mm guns was backed up by three 18-inch torpedoes so that she could also attack enemy ships.

Nobody could call these prototype destroyers comfortable, and it was soon noted that no crew member could get undisturbed rest, even in fine weather. The construction was flimsy as the hull weight had to be kept down; the plates 'panted' and allowed dribbles of water to find their way into the mess-decks. With no attempt at air-conditioning or lagging of the bulkheads there was constant 'sweating' and condensation, and the stokers had to wash on deck. Even the officers did not have cabins to themselves, and had to sleep in cushioned seats around the ward-room. The Admiralty was anxious to recruit the cream of personnel to man the destroyers and so the inducement of 'hard-lying money', an extra pay allowance for difficult conditions, was introduced. There was a new spirit of adventure in the Royal Navy, and ambitious young officers seized the chance to escape from the irksome round of duties aboard big ships. For the lower deck as well, there was the compensation of the more relaxed discipline of a small ship's company and the chance to acquire professional qualifications. It was the beginning of that undefinable special quality which marked the 'destroyerman' in all navies during the next 80 years. It is not surprising to see the names of future admirals among the commanders of the early destroyers, for decisiveness and a good deal of nerve were often required. Many years later the writer 'Taffrail', otherwise known as Captain Taprell Dorling, recalled that it was impossible to disguise the fact that one's ship had been in a collision as the bows had a nasty habit of folding like a concertina. Which was not surprising, since the plating was only 0.125-inch thick, the same as heavy cardboard. Before the hull was painted it was possible to see the outline of the frames and stringers, like wet burlap stretched over a frame.

In spite of these problems the first four TBDs more than proved their worth. As soon as the *Havock*'s preliminary trials showed how good the design was, more were ordered, and by September 1894 a total of 40 TBDs were in hand. They were known as '27-knotters', from the specified contract speed, and they were followed by 28 '30-knotters' in 1896. None of them could get within a knot-and-a-half of these speeds in service, but neither could the torpedo boats, and the destroyers were much more weatherly. The wisdom of giving the destroyers a heavy torpedo armament was soon demonstrated, and it became the standard tactical doctrine to destroy hostile torpedo boats with guns before going on to attack the hostile main fleet as torpedo boats. Although torpedo boats continued to be built in the RN for another few years, by 1900 it was taken for granted that the TBD had usurped their function and made them obsolescent.

The advent of the *Havock* and her sisters was watched with some interest from across the English Channel. The French knew that the TBD could make a large part of their enormous fleet of

torpedo boats useless, but all they could do was follow the British lead and build their own TBD or *contre-torpilleur*. Just like the Admiralty the *Conseil de Travaux* admitted its own inadequacy and approached the most distinguished French torpedo boat designer, M Augustin Normand, to design a suitable type of ship. Normand submitted designs for a *torpilleur de haute mer* of 244 tonnes and an *aviso-torpilleur* of 403 tonnes, but the design which was accepted was his so-called '300-tonne' *torpilleur d'escadre* type. The prototypes of the *Durandal* Class were roughly the same size as HMS *Havock*, and although they had more powerful machinery they displaced more and so their effective speed was no higher. The *Durandal* ran her trials in the summer of 1899, and she was followed by another 54 ships of similar type during the next eight years.

The German Navy had followed the lead given by the British and French in building torpedo boats, but in one respect had already made the first move towards the destroyer. In December 1886 the Schichau shipyard at Elbing launched the so-called 'division boat' *D.1*, a 230-ton enlarged torpedo boat, whose job was to act as the leader for torpedo boat flotillas. In fact the last of the series, *D.10*, was launched in October 1898 by Thornycroft at Chiswick, and was very similar to the contemporary '27-knotters' being built for the Royal Navy. A year later the first of a new enlarged or 'high seas' type of torpedo boat, the *S.90*, was launched by Schichau. She was armed with three 50mm guns and three 45cm (17.7-inch) torpedo-tubes, and in November 1899 she ran a three-hour trial. With 65 tons of coal on board she maintained 26.4 knots, and was able to maintain 12–14 knots for 12 hours. Incidentally, the Germans were the only navy to continue the practice of numbering destroyers rather than naming them. A distinguishing letter indicated the builder: S – Schichau, V – Vulcan, G – Germania, etc.

The American Civil War had seen tremendous development in underwater warfare with submarines and mines being used by the Confederates and experiments with spar torpedoes had continued in the 1870s, but it was not until 1886 that Congress could be persuaded to award funds for the building of the first Whitehead torpedo boat. Named the USS *Cushing* after the officer who led an attack against the Confederate ram *Albemarle* in 1864, she was launched in January 1890 by the Herreshoff Manufacturing Company of Bristol, Rhode Island. She displaced only 105 tons and had a speed of 22.5 knots, and she was followed by a further 13 vessels authorized between 1890 and 1896.

The US Navy was the first of the front-line navies to use torpedo boats in war, and in view of the great faith in their abilities expressed it was a salutary lesson learned in the Spanish–American War of 1898. All in all the results were disappointing. There was no opportunity to attack the Spanish Fleet, and with only six boats at sea they could have achieved very little. For want of anything better to do they went on patrol duty, a task which soon showed up their unreliability and flimsiness. The Engineer-in-Chief described the condition of some of the torpedo boats as 'horrible', with burnt-out boilers, broken cylinder covers and jammed pistons and valves. Much of this was caused by the lack of trained engineers, for the only way to get good performance out of the machinery was to nurse it. Continuous steaming soon wore out the crew, for the motion was violent and the accommodation cramped. There were no refrigerators and even the drinking water became contaminated by rust or seawater. There was also the danger of being scalded to death by high pressure steam in the tiny boiler-rooms or of watchkeepers being washed overboard from the open platforms which served as bridges.

Like other navies the USN tried to improve the type by looking at foreign designs, and the war with Spain loosened

Above and below: The yacht *Turbinia* was the test-bed for the Parsons steam turbine (top right). The first warship to be driven by the new method of propulsion was the ill-fated destroyer *Viper* seen here on trials at 36 knots.

the purse-strings enough to allow the building or purchase of a series of boats of Normand, Schichau and Yarrow design. Although no more successful than their foreign contemporaries they paved the way for the transition to the destroyer, and gave US shipbuilders and designers useful experience. The torpedo boat with her lightweight steel hull and light, high performance machinery, pushed the 'state of the art' to its limits, and even if she did not fulfil all her promise in service she was pointing the way to the future.

The relative failure of the large torpedo boats *Farragut*, *Stringham*, *Goldsborough* and *Bailey* authorized in 1896–97 led to the ordering of a class of 16 destroyers under the 1898 programme. Four distinct types were built, three to private builders' designs and one to plans drawn up by the Bureau of Construction and Repair. The private builders adopted the 'turtleback' forecastle used in the old torpedo boats and in the first foreign destroyers, but in the Navy designed group this was replaced by a raised forecastle. This was a great improvement, for it made the destroyer a better sea-boat. The bow did not tend to bury itself in a seaway so easily, and therefore the boat could maintain speed for longer. As a bonus the high forecastle provided better accommodation forward and more deck room for the crewmen working the anchors and mooring wires.

Back in England, the Admiralty, although satisfied that the large number of destroyers built between 1893 and 1900 had provided the answer to the torpedo boat threat, was aware that improvements could be made. The triple- and quadruple-expansion reciprocating engines used up to now had reached their limit, although there were constant improvements in boilers. In 1897, at Queen Victoria's Diamond Jubilee Fleet Review a novel craft had appeared, the steam yacht *Turbinia*. She was powered by a revolutionary new type of engine, the Parsons steam turbine, and her turn of speed had been greater than any existing destroyer or torpedo boat. The stunt had the desired effect and the Royal Navy was ordered to build a turbine-driven destroyer, the *Viper*. A second boat, the *Cobra*, was built as a speculative private venture by one of the leading British shipbuilders, while the Parsons company built a third, to be called the *Python*. All three were very similar to the latest '30-knotters', and so offered a simple basis of comparison.

The trials of HMS *Viper* were an outstanding success. In November 1899 she ran for an hour at 36 knots, a speed well in excess of anything achieved by previous destroyers. What was even better was the absence of the terrible vibration which made life aboard the older destroyers so unbearable, and the reduced wear and tear. Although consumption at low speed was heavy, fast running used less coal than was used in most existing destroyers. The fact that the *Viper* was wrecked only

Above: The *Zulu,* one of the 'Tribal' Class, the first oil-fired destroyers is seen here in 1914.

18 months after being completed would have meant nothing, but just one month later the *Cobra* broke in half while on her way south to receive her armament. There was nothing to connect the two accidents, but inevitably the steam turbine was blamed by public opinion. In the case of the *Cobra* it was even suggested that the 'immense' power of her turbines had torn her apart, whereas the official enquiry came to the conclusion that structural weakness had caused the long hull to fracture after prolonged working in rough seas.

Fortunately the Admiralty did not stop its experiments with turbines; all that happened was that less publicity was given to the purchase of the *Python*, now known as the *Velox* to avoid the apparently unlucky snake-names. Two of the next class of destroyers and one torpedo boat were also to be turbine-driven. The *Velox* was never as successful as the *Viper*, but the turbine was soon established as a success, not only in destroyers but also in larger warships as well.

The new destroyers marked a big change in policy. In January 1901 new requirements were drafted; the size should not exceed that of the existing boats and the speed specified in the contract would have to be achieved at full load. It was no use asking for speeds which could not be realized in service, and if destroyers were to spend more time at sea their habitability would have to be improved. Many improvements suggested by experience with the '30-knotters' and by reports from Germany about the latest Schichau designs were incorporated in the new class before they were ordered. They were known as the 'River' Class, and they marked the evolution of the destroyer into a genuine fleet escort, capable of accompanying the Fleet to sea in all weathers. Eventually 37 were ordered between 1902 and 1905, and they proved a great success.

The most obvious difference in the 'Rivers' was the high forecastle, much like the US Navy's *Bainbridge* Class, but there were other internal differences. The contract speed was reduced to 25.5 knots, and this gave the designers the leeway needed to incorporate more strength into the hull structure. Officers had separate cabins for the first time, and, unheard of luxury, the Captain had a heating stove. In each cabin a hip bath was stowed overhead, but the mess-decks had only wash-basins. The crew spaces allowed 20 inches of seating per man, and 18 inches of hammock space, although some men slept on cork mattresses spread on top of the lockers. If this was regarded as palatial, one can imagine what it had been like before.

The 'River' Class answered the Royal Navy's requirements more than adequately, but it was not long before another big change was made. The driving energy of Sir John Fisher as First Sea

Below: HMS *Goshawk* and the 1st Destroyer Flotilla in a line ahead circa 1912.

Lord was soon turned from dreadnoughts and battlecruisers to destroyer design. In November 1904 he demanded that the next class should be capable of 33 knots and use oil fuel. This resulted in the 'Tribal' Class, but in many ways this was a retrograde step. Fisher's infatuation with maximum speed meant that some of the strength of construction which had made the 'River' Class so successful had to be sacrificed. Although oil had much to recommend it as a fuel for destroyers, not least because it reduced the number of stokers, the 90 tons carried made the 'Tribals' very short on endurance. In service they proved fragile and under-armed, in short, typical products of Fisher's ill-considered interventions in the sphere of ship design. They made their designed speed, but were always a liability. It was said of them that they even used oil when at anchor. The *Afridi* and *Amazon* once used 9.5 tons each merely raising steam for a three-mile journey to a fuel depot and back.

Another Fisher-inspired abortion was the *Swift*, which doubled the displacement of destroyers in an attempt to give them sufficient size to take over the scouting duties of cruisers. Fisher wanted a destroyer capable of 36 knots, but the 2000-ton *Swift* failed to reach this speed on trials, and had to be accepted after making only 35 knots. Yet, Fisher leaked to the Press the figure of 39 knots for his 'ideal ship'. She could never have taken over the duties of a cruiser for despite her great size she was flimsily built and wildly uneconomical. In Fisher's eyes she could do no wrong, and long after her faults had been made obvious he bombarded anyone prepared to listen with talk of more 'Super-*Swift*'s' as the warships of the future.

The departure of Fisher from the Admiralty had a beneficial effect on British destroyers. In 1909–10 the *Beagle* Class joined the Fleet, robust 1000-tonners good for 27 knots. Instead of the oil fuel of the 'Tribals' they were coal-fired, but to compensate they were armed with the much more powerful 21-inch torpedo. Although the next class reverted to oil fuel the main characteristics of British destroyers were now established, and they continued a logical process of step-by-step improvement until 1914.

Other navies were inevitably affected by British developments. The first destroyers built for the US Navy since the *Bainbridge*s were the five *Smith* Class, authorized in 1906–07, followed by 21 *Paulding* Class in 1908–10. They were handsome craft, with three or four funnels, depending on the builders, and they were known as the 'flivvers'. They adopted steam turbines, and the *Paulding* was the US Navy's first oil-fired destroyer. The Germans, having set the pace earlier with large torpedo boats, were slow to match the growth in size of British destroyers; the boats built between 1906 and 1911 ran to about 760 tons. Although turbines were introduced, only a few destroyers were given a single oil-fired boiler, as the German Navy preferred coal-firing. This meant that when steaming fast at night the funnel-tops gave a telltale glow which could be seen by a hostile ship.

The French, having once dominated the scene, seemed to lose interest in the subject of destroyers, and when they belatedly realized that the little '300-tonne' boats were quite outclassed they seemed to have lost their touch. Between 1906 and 1914, when other navies' destroyers were becoming more uniform, more robust and faster, the French produced a series of eccentric designs of poor performance. The first to have turbines were the *Voltigeur* Class, built in 1908–10, but they had a clumsy three-shaft arrangement, with turbines on the outer propeller shafts and a triple-expansion engine on the centre shaft. In the *Bouclier* Class of 1909–13, size rose to 800 tonnes to match foreign developments, but the hulls proved to be too weakly constructed, and by the time all the various faults were corrected the extra weight took four knots off their speed.

In the North Sea the British and Germans were watching one another rather than the French or anyone else, and tactics were steadily changing to match the improvements in destroyer capabilities.

Below: Italian coastal torpedo boats of the PN type lay a smokescreen. These 120-ton ships were built between 1910 and 1913 and operated in the Adriatic Sea in World War I.

In the German Navy the torpedo was still regarded as the prime weapon, and the latest large torpedo boats had four 50cm (19.7-inch) torpedo-tubes. The British, whose main object was to protect their battle fleet, gave their destroyers a heavier gun armament and only two 21-inch torpedo-tubes, to make it easier for them to drive off the enemy's destroyers and torpedo boats. This divergence of policy was deliberate, for although the British destroyers were intended to attack an enemy fleet with torpedoes the experience of the Japanese at the Battle of Tsushima had shown that the only positive results had been obtained when their torpedo craft approached to very close range.

To get the maximum value out of destroyers they were employed in large groups or flotillas, the British having 20 destroyers in each, divided into five divisions. Each division was led by a Commander, but the other boats were commanded by lieutenants or lieutenant-commanders. To handle the administration and signalling, as well as to provide extra gunpower for emergencies, the flotilla was led by a fast scout cruiser. In the years before World War I destroyer speeds outstripped those of light cruisers by such a margin that they had to be replaced by specially designed 'flotilla leaders' which were larger destroyers with sufficient accommodation for the flotilla-commander, known in the RN as Captain (D), and his staff. Under normal conditions one division would be stood down for boiler cleaning and for the routine six-monthly refit, during which the bottom would be scraped and repainted to prevent a reduction in speed. Minor repairs were undertaken by the flotilla's depot ship, usually an old cruiser stationed at the port or anchorage most convenient for the flotilla's operating area. During the routine refit half the ship's company at a time was given leave. The remaining 16 boats were on duty, one division having steam up, a second at one hour's notice and the other two at three hours' notice. During World War I the six-month cycle was reduced to four months to allow for the greater wear and tear of constant steaming, and to ensure that more destroyers were operational. The German flotilla organization was similar but there were 11 torpedo boats in each flotilla, led by a light cruiser, and the refit and boiler-cleaning cycle was shorter.

Above: A crowded deck of an Italian destroyer. These 'Generali' Class boats were similar to wartime construction but were not completed until 1921–22.
Below: A British 'I' Class destroyer rests in Sheerness Harbour, September 1914. Behind her is the destroyer depot ship, the old cruiser *Blake*.

The major problem in developing adequate tactics was communications. It must be remembered that radio was in its infancy, and ship-to-ship communication was limited to flag signals or Morse lamp. The time taken to transmit a simple signal, such as the bearing of the enemy, took as much as half an hour by the time it was passed to all 20 boats from Captain (D) and acknowledged as understood. The weakness had been noted as far back as the 1887 Manoeuvres, when it was concluded that the best tactical formation was a division of eight, but in 1914 it was felt that the larger number of officers carried by the leaders had overcome the problem. The Germans, with only 12 boats to a flotilla, were better placed, but in practice smoke and spray often made signals hard to distinguish, and it was almost impossible to guarantee that a flotilla of destroyers could react quickly to a change in the tactical situation.

Above: HMS *Lance* is launched at Woolston on 25 February 1914. In August 1914 she fired the first shot of the Naval War, and that gun is still in existence in the Imperial War Museum, London.

As the British and German nations pursued their collision course, their flotillas put into practice recent developments. By 1914 the range for a daylight attack had risen to 2000 yards, from the virtually suicidal range of 400 yards, thanks to the greater range of torpedoes. It was widely assumed that the only way to attack a hostile fleet was to work ahead of the enemy's line; it would then be possible to turn down on the enemy line at full speed, firing torpedoes across its line of advance. As the enemy's inevitable response would be to turn away, the ideal counter would be to have a second flotilla ready to attack on the other quarter, so that whichever way the battleships turned, they would be caught. This might have worked with a tactically inept fleet like the Russians' at Tsushima, but it was hardly likely to succeed against a determined opponent. No matter how much faith the experts might place in the torpedo, the fact remained that a massed daylight attack was a chancy affair. The two navies were poised for the first large-scale naval war in a hundred years, and their destroyers and torpedo boats were to be the principal striking weapons.

Destroyers in World War I

Both sides had assumed that there would be a big sea battle in the North Sea within days of the outbreak of war. In fact nothing of the sort happened, for neither the British nor the Germans were prepared to risk their capital ships in a reckless manner. Instead it was left to the light forces to contest the possession of the North Sea, mainly with mines and torpedoes. The first shot of the naval war was fired appropriately enough by the British destroyer *Lance* on 5 August 1914, a unit of the 3rd Flotilla, which had been recently formed with the latest class of destroyers, and led by the light cruiser *Amphion*.

On receipt of a report that a steamer had been seen 'throwing things overboard' the 3rd Flotilla weighed anchor and left Harwich. At midday they sighted smoke, and the *Lance* and *Landrail* gave chase. The steamer hoisted the German ensign, and was quickly stopped and sunk by the two destroyers. She turned out to be the auxiliary minelayer *Königin Luise*, and she had been caught only 13 hours after the declaration of war. The *Amphion* led her destroyers back to Harwich, but early next morning she ran into the minefield laid by the *Königin Luise*. A mine blew away the cruiser's forecastle, and 20 minutes later a second mine detonated the forward magazine. The destroyers escaped because of their light draft, but the disaster showed that mines were to be a much bigger threat than had been thought possible. As the war progressed minefields were to be laid in the North Sea, denying large areas to both sides.

Destroyers played a major part in the first big operation of the war, a raid on the German outposts off Heligoland, which led to the Battle of the Heligoland Bight on 28 August. It involved the submarines at Harwich as well as the destroyers, and the plan was to use an outer patrol line of submarines to decoy the German torpedo boat patrols out to sea, where they could be trapped by the Harwich force destroyers and their light cruiser leaders. Both sides had a lot to learn. First, the British betrayed their intentions by sending too many radio messages, and then poor staffwork at the Admiralty prevented the two commodores, Keyes and Tyrwhitt, from being told that the Admiralty had decided to send more powerful reinforcements, in the shape of a light cruiser squadron and four battle-cruisers. The Germans, on the other hand, were caught completely unawares, and their heavy units were lying in the Jade River, without steam up and unable to cross the bar until high tide. It had not occurred to the German High Command that the British would send such strong forces into the Bight, almost within range of the guns on Heligoland, and their light forces were at a disadvantage.

At about 0700 the *Laurel* opened fire on the German *G.194* and within an hour 32 British destroyers and the light cruisers *Arethusa* and *Fearless* were in action with the torpedo boats guarding the German inner patrol line. Destroyer gunnery could never be very accurate, and although the range fell to 7000 yards the haze meant that the heavy fire was largely ineffective. Suddenly the cruisers *Stettin* and *Frauenlob*, which had been lying at anchor off Heligoland and had raised steam when they heard the gunfire, ar-

Left: Commodore Reginald Tyrwhitt (right) led the Harwich Force of light cruisers and destroyers in many surface actions in the North Sea.

rived on the scene. They took on the *Fearless* and *Arethusa*, and were able to silence the *Arethusa* with 35 hits. The British destroyers left the cruisers to fight it out, and concentrated on punishing the torpedo boats *D.8* and *T.33*, which had found themselves caught up in the battle. The *Fearless* and her destroyers managed to trap the *V.187*, which went down fighting, with her ensign flying.

The *Arethusa* had been badly knocked about, and although the sweep should have been over, at 1030 her destroyers were still standing by while she stopped to make urgent repairs to her machinery and guns. Every minute that passed made it more likely that German reinforcements would appear from the Ems and Jade. When the first of these appeared, the cruiser *Strassburg*, she was mistaken for a much larger cruiser, and Commodore Tyrwhitt signalled to Vice-Admiral Beatty and his battlecruisers, 'Respectfully submit that I may be supported. Am hard pressed.' But long before any help could arrive the destroyers would have to face heavy punishment. Just as the *Laurel* turned away after firing her torpedoes a salvo of 10.5cm shells hit her. One hit in the engine-room killed four men and injured others; a second hit near the forward four-inch gun killed most of the crew and another wrecked the after-funnel and wounded her captain. Her next astern, the *Liberty*, lost her captain and signalman when a shell burst behind the bridge, and the last in line, the *Laertes*, was hit in the boiler-room.

Suddenly the cruiser *Mainz* shuddered as one of the British torpedoes hit her. In total darkness with every piece of glass between decks smashed, the ship began to sink slowly by the head. She had already been set on fire, and the arrival of the first British reinforcements, a squadron of light cruisers, sealed her fate. The *Arethusa* was still limping home at ten knots, and it seemed that she might yet be cut off and sunk, as the German reinforcements were arriving. But suddenly five large ships came into sight from the West. They were Admiral Beatty's battlecruisers, the *Lion*, *Princess Royal*, *Queen Mary*, *Invincible* and *New Zealand*, steaming at full speed, with dense clouds of coal-smoke billowing from their funnels. Heading between the burning wreck of the *Mainz* and the *Arethusa* the big ships turned their guns on the *Köln* and brought her to a stop. Then the luckless *Ariadne* blundered out of the mist and crossed the *Lion*'s bows, to be shattered by repeated hits. Pausing only to finish off the *Köln*, the battlecruisers drew off to cover the light forces' withdrawal.

Below: In 1914 the French Fleet had the principal responsibility for patrolling the Mediterranean but increasing German and Austrian pressure forced the Allies to reinforce it. These Japanese destroyers, seen at Corfu in April 1917, were part of a massive increase in light forces used to protect Allied shipping.

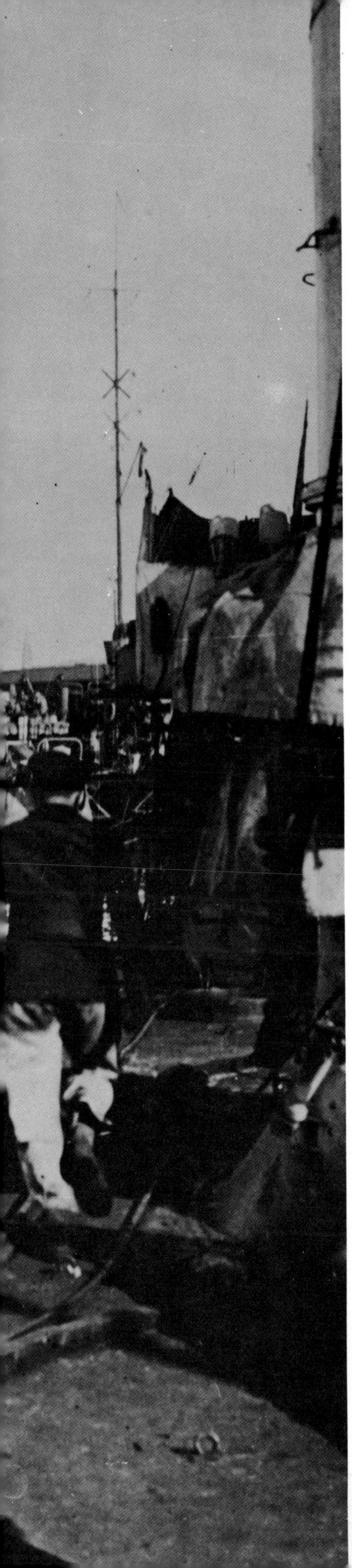

It had been a risky action, but the risks had been justified by the bold handling of the British destroyers, which had repeatedly held off light cruisers and had saved the *Arethusa* from being captured or sunk. It was to be the last major destroyer action for nearly two years, but the Harwich Force in particular was to be embroiled in many skirmishes with the opposing German cruisers and destroyers through the next four years. However much time the big ships on both sides might spend in harbour, the destroyers were constantly in action. The Harwich Force became more and more important as the chief offensive squadron in the North Sea, well placed to intercept raids by German surface ships and to mount offensive patrols in the Southern North Sea.

The other important squadron was the Dover Patrol, which initially comprised the 'Tribal' Class. They were based on Dover to guard the vital cross-Channel supply route between Britain and France. As the armies on the Western Front expanded, an ever-increasing number of troops had to be transported across the Channel, accompanied by vast quantities of war material such as coal for French industry and ammunition for the guns. In the first weeks, when German troops swept through Belgium, the Dover Patrol destroyers showed how adaptable they were by joining in the bombardments of the German right flank. In October 1914 a scratch force of old battleships and gunboats mustered off the coast of Belgium with French destroyers to lend much-needed fire support to the Allied armies.

The Swedish explorer and author, Sven Hedin, was a correspondent with the German Army, and was eating breakfast with staff officers in the Hotel Majestic on the sea front. Suddenly the destroyer *Crusader* appeared, steaming parallel to the shore. Hedin's companions were astounded at the insolence of the British, who were evidently reconnoitring the harbour to see if any torpedo boats were there. Two small field guns were ordered up to drive off the intruder, but as soon as the first shots were fired the destroyer turned to port, her guns flashed, and what had been one of the most elegant restaurants in Europe was blasted into ruins. The Germans soon mounted heavy guns to put a stop to this form of harassment, to which the British replied by building monitors with ex-battleship guns for long-range bombardment, and escorting these ungainly craft to and from Dover became another commitment for the destroyers.

The cross-Channel convoys were a tempting target for raids by German torpedo boats, particularly when the Germans were able to establish forward bases at Zeebrugge and Ostend. Fortunately for the Allies the Northern French port of Dunkirk was still in their hands, and it became an equally useful forward base. The normal precautions against a raid were to have a few destroyers with steam up at Dunkirk, usually four lying in the Downs, an important anchorage for ships being examined for contraband in the shelter of the Goodwin Sands, and a further force of destroyers in Dover harbour at ten minutes' notice for steam. Some idea of the problem, and also the size of target presented, is indicated by the fact that the average number of cross-Channel sailings was about 700 each year. Between August 1914 and December 1917 nearly six million troops were carried in addition to some 120,000 East–West transits of the English Channel. During the same period a further 800,000 casualties were brought back from France. Yet, in all this time only one hospital ship was mined and an empty transport was sunk by German torpedo boats. The casualties were all sustained by the warships and small patrol craft.

To achieve this degree of safety called for incredible exertions on the part of the Dover Patrol. Although destroyers were often seconded temporarily from the

Left: German torpedo boats in harbour in March 1917. Coal-fired boilers made for sooty decks.
Below: The British flotilla leader *Swift* at Dover after her successful action in the Channel in 1917. The gun on the forecastle was later removed.

Harwich Force, the burden rested mainly on the dozen 'Tribal' Class. Their routine was to have steam up, either in harbour at ten minutes' readiness, or at sea, for 17 days in succession. A three-day boiler cleaning followed, and every four months a three-week refit followed. During the duty period, officers and men remained on board and the captains could only count on one night's sleep in four. Admiral Bacon, who commanded the Dover Patrol, was a martinet who prided himself on driving his men, and he came near to working his subordinates to breaking point. The result was that efficiency was reduced and the likelihood of disaster increased. Lookouts were more likely to miss the telltale shape or possibly mistake a friendly vessel for an enemy one. In all, 12 destroyers including two of the 'Tribals' as well as one of the older torpedo boats were sunk in the English Channel. When the *Nubian* was torpedoed in a night action in October 1916 it was decided to repair her using the bow-section of the *Zulu* which had previously been severely damaged by a mine. The resulting hybrid was renamed HMS *Zubian*, and repaid the efforts lavished on her by sinking a U-Boat in 1918.

The most famous action of the Dover Patrol occurred on the night of 20 April 1917, when two large destroyers intercepted a force of German torpedo boats in the Channel. The flotilla leader *Swift*, which had been rearmed with a six-inch gun forward, and the ex-Chilean leader *Broke* were patrolling off Dover when they heard firing off Calais and saw gunflashes. When shells began to fall on Dover they knew for certain that another raid was in progress; they steered for Calais, but took care not to be drawn away from what they rightly interpreted as the enemy's objective, the large collection of shipping which was sheltering in the Downs. In fact two large torpedo boats had bombarded Calais to draw off the patrols while four more had slipped in to bombard Dover before joining forces again.

About seven miles East of Dover the *Swift* and *Broke* sighted six vessels steaming fast off the port bow in the opposite direction. The strangers opened fire and the two British boats replied immediately. The *Swift* put her helm hard over to ram, but Commander Peck and his staff on the bridge were dazzled by the flash of the six-inch gun and she passed just astern of the German line, firing a single torpedo as she went. Commander Evans, astern in the *Broke*, held his fire to allow the torpedo director a clear moment to aim. This torpedo or the one fired by the *Swift* a moment earlier, hit the *G.85* full amidships in a huge plume of smoke and spray. Evans, seeing his intended victim hit, altered course to ram the next torpedo boat astern. It was the *G.42*, and she tried frantically to escape, with sparks pouring from her funnels as her captain called for maximum speed. But he had left it too late, and with a screech of grinding steel the *Broke*'s bow tore into her thin side plating and flung her over on her beam ends.

It must have been a nightmare scene,

Below: German 'A' Class torpedo boats at sea off the Flanders Coast.

Above: Commander Edward Evans, Captain of the flotilla leader *Broke* rose to become a colourful Admiral.

with the *Broke*'s guns pouring shells into *G.42* at point-blank range. Several of the German seamen had clambered onto the forecastle of the British destroyer, and an improvised party of the survivors of the forward gun crews assuming that they were boarders, armed themselves with rifles, bayonets and cutlasses. A murderous fight took place, at a range at which even the officers on the bridge were using their personal side-arms. The *Broke* herself was in danger, for a box of four-inch cordite cartridges was burning, and illuminating her in a lurid red glow. One of the surviving German torpedo boats slid past out of the darkness and fired shells indiscriminately into the inferno. In seconds the *Broke*'s decks were running with blood, as a quarter of her crew were killed or wounded by 10.5cm shells.

With her bows still locked into the hull of the dying German torpedo boat she was a sitting target until the unknown torpedo boat disappeared. Painfully she ground her way clear, leaving the after-part to sink. She tried to follow the *Swift*, which was in full pursuit of two enemy torpedo boats, but a shell had damaged the main steam pipe and soon she was losing feed-water to the boilers, so she steamed slowly back to the scene of the action. The *Swift* was soon back, for she had also been damaged severely by shellfire, and could not maintain full speed. It had been a brief and bloody engagement, but two large torpedo boats had been sunk and it effectively put an end to raids from the Flanders torpedo boat flotillas for the time being. Both Commanders were awarded the DSO, and 'Evans of the *Broke*' rose to become a colourful Admiral in later years.

By a strange coincidence the sister of the *Broke*, HMS *Botha*, played a nearly identical role in an action in the Channel a year later. On the night of 20 March 1918 she and HMS *Morris* were lying in the Dunkirk roadstead with the French destroyers *Capitaine Mehl*, *Magon* and *Bouclier*. As was normal with the Dover Patrol all five destroyers lay at their moorings with slips on their cables and steam up. At about 0345 next morning they heard gunfire to the north, which suggested that the Flanders torpedo boats were shelling the left flank of the British land forces between La Panne and Dunkirk. The *Botha* and her consorts immediately slipped their cables and headed for the gun flashes. By this time destroyers were being issued with starshell, which provided the necessary illumination at night. In the glare from one of her

Above: HMS *Broke* (left) and her sister *Botha* (right) were building for Chile in August 1914.

Left: A torpedo-hit usually inflicted serious damage on the flimsy hull of a destroyer. Despite losing its bow, this German boat limped back to port.

Below: The Germans built the small 'A' Class torpedo boats to operate off the Flanders Coast. These four are seen at Zeebrugge in May 1918.

starshells the *Botha*'s look-outs spotted a line of dark shapes on the port bow. As soon as an incorrect reply was received to her recognition signal the *Botha* put over her helm to attack with torpedoes at a range of 600 yards. The five destroyers opened fire with all guns which could bear, and the startled German line replied. The *Botha* was hit by a shell which cut an auxiliary steam pipe, and as her speed began to drop, Commander Rede quickly decided to ram the fourth German ship in the line rather than risk missing with torpedoes. His victim was the small torpedo boat *A.7*, and with hardly any shock the *Botha*'s bow sliced through her with a shower of sparks. The two halves floated away on either side, and the *Botha* swung round to try a second ramming against the next in line. But speed was dropping fast, and all she could do was pour a heavy fire into the torpedo boat *A.19* as she passed.

The *Botha* found herself in a dense smokescreen, and as it lifted one of the French destroyers mistook her for a German and fired a torpedo into her port side.

Fortunately it exploded in a full coal bunker, which cushioned the effect to the extent that the destroyer did not sink, and when the other destroyers returned they were able to take her into tow, after sinking the remains of *A.19*. It was on this occasion that one of the French destroyers suffered a boiler explosion and signalled in plain language, 'Can go no more, boiler go bang'.

Mention has already been made of the versatility of destroyers, and this was shown dramatically at the Dardanelles. There was little or no chance for destroyers to fulfil their proper role in this campaign, for the small Turkish Navy was penned up above the Narrows behind five minefields. The destroyers concerned were the *Beagle*s and a number of the old 'River' Class which had been brought back from China in August 1914. After the failure of the bombardments between 19 February and 12 March 1915, when the trawler-minesweepers found the current too strong to allow them to sweep for mines, it was decided to equip nine of the *Beagle* Class as minesweepers. With 12,000 horsepower they would have no difficulty in stemming the fast current which sweeps down the Straits, while they could use their high speed and

Above: In August 1914 the Germans ordered a new class of 1200-ton destroyers (*zerstorer*) which used turbines ordered by the Russians.

Left: The Royal Navy built a special base for the Grand Fleet destroyers at Port Edgar in the Firth of Forth. In these 'pens' they could berth alongside piers with piped water and electrical power which allowed running repairs to be implemented.
Right: British 'M' Class destroyers in rough weather escort the 2nd Battle Squadron of the Grand Fleet.
Below: The destroyer *Wolverine* keeps a watchful eye on 'W' Beach at Gallipoli. Under her famous Captain Andrew Cunningham, she served a record commission lasting from 1911 to 1918.

manoeuvrability to reach the sweeping position and to withdraw afterwards, with less risk of being hit by the Turkish guns. Which sounds good in theory, but nothing could be more nerve-racking than to be in a destroyer, linked by a sweep wire to another destroyer and forced to maintain a steady course at 12 knots, with shells falling all around. The *Wolverine* was hit on the bridge by a 10.5cm shell which burst on the starboard engine-room telegraph and killed the captain, the coxswain and a midshipman. Two other destroyer-sweepers were hit as well, and the attempt finally failed as it proved impossible to reach the crucial minefields in the Narrows. The concentration of guns was too heavy, and as the destroyers advanced up the Narrows they became more vulnerable.

The destroyers had to take on another role, that of amphibious transports, when the Allied Expeditionary Force was landed on the Gallipoli Peninsula. At Gaba Tepe seven destroyers, their decks crowded with troops and towing more men in the transports' boats, had to land their troops as close to the beach as possible. This put them within range of machine guns and small-arms ashore, and casualties were heavy among the men clustered without shelter on their decks. Once the troops were ashore the destroyers had to provide fire support in addition to their normal screening of the transports and warships lying off the beaches. After the loss of two battleships to a U-Boat in May the battleships and cruisers were withdrawn, and until the arrival of specially designed bombardment vessels from England, the burden of providing 'on-call' support fell largely on destroyers.

Two destroyers were stationed on the left flank at Cape Helles, and similarly there were two at Anzac Beach. Except for short periods the destroyers at Helles were the *Wolverine* and *Scorpion*, while the *Chelmer* and *Colne* were at Anzac. It must be remembered that destroyers had virtually no means of directing gunfire other than spotting the shellbursts, but this did not stop them from using indirect fire. HMS *Blenheim*, the depot ship at Mudros, heard that the destroyers had tried cutting the cordite charges in half, to allow the four-inch gun to be used as a howitzer, and within 24 hours provided a range-table for four-inch half-charges. The destroyer put herself close to one of three moored buoys, and registered on her target from there, with rounds of deliberate fire. As soon as the observation officer ashore signalled 'OK' ten rounds of rapid fire followed, and this method could even be used at night, with an aiming light displayed by the troops ashore at the extreme end of their front-line trench. The captain of HMS *Scorpion* throughout this time was Commander Andrew Cunningham RN, and he established a record which has never been broken, by commanding her for seven years from 1911 to 1918.

But the destroyer's most valuable contribution in World War I was her unexpected efficiency as an anti-submarine craft. Until specially designed escorts were built only the destroyer had the speed, manoeuvrability and armament to sink a submarine before she submerged.

Another advantage was the shallow draft of the destroyer, which meant that a torpedo needed to be set for an abnormally shallow run to have any chance of sinking her. Although she could hope to score a crippling hit on the conning tower the surest way was to ram, and HMS *Badger* attacked *U.19* in this way as early as 24 October 1914. On this occasion the U-Boat escaped with severe damage, but a month later the *Garry* sank *U.18*. As a result all the new destroyers under construction were fitted with a doubling at the foot of the stem to act as a 'can opener'.

Ramming was no good against a submarine which had already submerged, and soon a variety of contraptions were produced, such as the 'modified sweep'. This was a 200-foot indicator loop which could be towed across an area in which the U-Boat was believed to be lurking, and if the indicator needle showed that something had fouled the sweep a string of charges could be fired electrically. The 'lance bomb' was an explosive charge on the end of a pole, intended to be hurled downwards onto the deck of a U-Boat, but as it required the U-Boat to lie obligingly alongside the destroyer it was seldom used. The provision of hydrophones in 1917 at last gave destroyers a sensor which could *locate* a submerged submarine, but the most potent weapon

Top: A US destroyer escorts a convoy in 1917.
Left: HMS *Onslow* was one of many Grand Fleet destroyers equipped to tow a kite balloon. These unwieldy gas-bags provided reconnaissance until shipboard aircraft became available in numbers.
Below: HMS *Laforey* follows a hospital ship into the crowded anchorage at Mudros just before the Gallipoli landings in March 1915.

of all was the depth-charge, which could be pre-set to explode at varying depths. The first sinking by a destroyer using depth-charges was on 4 December 1916 when the *UC.19* was sunk by HMS *Llewellyn.* Initially the depth-charges were dropped from the stern but in 1917 throwers were produced, and these enabled depth-charges to be fired on either beam.

The threat from submarines had not been taken seriously in the early weeks of the war, but after several large ships had been torpedoed it was realized that no formation of ships should move anywhere without an escort of destroyers. After the inconclusive Battle of the Dogger Bank early in 1915, in which the destroyers had little to do but finish off the battered German cruiser *Blücher*, their work became almost entirely monotonous patrol work. Not only monotonous but exhausting, and the need to accompany the Fleet to sea in all weathers soon took its toll in the shape of exhausted crews and damaged boats. There was the ever-present danger from mines and the risk of collision between ships manoeuvring at high speed in fog or darkness, without lights or radar. Out of 67 British destroyers lost between 1914 and 1918, collisions accounted for 18 and another 12 were wrecked.

The great trial of strength between the British Grand Fleet and the German High Seas Fleet eventually came at the end of May 1916. The Battle of Jutland was the first and in a sense the only test of the theories of destroyer tactics, for both sides had large numbers of torpedo craft, 80 British destroyers and flotilla leaders and 62 German torpedo boats. The battle divided itself into two distinct parts, the day action on 31 May, in which the rival torpedo craft duelled with one another in vain attempts to take the pressure off their capital ships, and the night action on 31 May–1 June, in which the British destroyers faced the entire German Fleet alone.

It was two German torpedo boats, the *B.109* and the *B.110* which unwittingly started the battle. At about 1600 they were ordered to examine a small Danish steamer, and while they were doing this two British light cruisers were on the same mission. Shots were fired and both groups returned to their main body with the message 'Enemy in sight'. A fierce action developed between Admiral

Above : German torpedo boats wallow in heavy seas. The *Marineamt's* insistence on low freeboard and small dimensions resulted in poor seakeeping, a failing which continued for another 20 years.

Beatty's battlecruisers and the German battlecruisers under Hipper, and when the British lost HMS *Indefatigable* and the flagship *Lion* was badly hit, the destroyers were ordered to attack to relieve the pressure. At almost the same time 15 German torpedo boats were ordered to attack the British capital ships, as Hipper's line was coming under heavy fire. A fierce action developed in 'no man's land' between the two battle lines, in which the British *Nestor* and *Nomad* and the German *V.27* and *V.29* were crippled and left in a sinking condition. But the British destroyers' heavy gun-armament enabled them to keep the German boats off, and forced them to fire their torpedoes at too great a range to score any hits. The British destroyers fired their torpedoes at a range of 5000–7000 yards, and although most were dodged by a timely turn away by Hipper, one from the *Petard* exploded against the armour of the *Seydlitz*, tearing a hole 13 feet by 39 feet in her side. Although taking in water, she was able to keep her place in the battle line; the first destroyer action of Jutland must be considered a draw.

In the next phase of the day-action the two battlecruiser forces fell back on their main fleets. Visibility was deteriorating, partly because of haze but mainly from the dense clouds of coal smoke from the scores of coal-burning ships present. Both commanders were holding their light forces in check, knowing that a general fleet action was imminent, but this did not prevent HMS *Onslow* from attacking the cruiser *Wiesbaden* on her own initiative. Lieutenant-Commander John Tovey (a future Commander-in-Chief of the Home Fleet) decided that the damaged cruiser was a 'target of opportunity' and approached her. Suddenly he saw enemy ships looming out of the haze and realized that his destroyer was only 8000 yards from Admiral Hipper's battlecruisers. Tovey was unperturbed and turned to fire his four torpedoes at them, but just as the first torpedo leapt from its tube a heavy-calibre shell hit the *Onslow* in the boiler-room. With steam billowing from No 2 boiler-room and her speed dropping rapidly, the *Onslow* limped past the *Wiesbaden* and fired a torpedo at her, which exploded under the conning tower. Then Tovey saw a line of battleships, Admiral Scheer's High Seas Fleet, deploying into action, and decided that the destruction of one destroyer was worth the chance of scoring a torpedo-hit. Although making only ten knots and listing heavily the 1000-ton *Onslow* crawled across the empty expanse of sea and launched her last two torpedoes at a range of 8000 yards.

It would be pleasing to report that such heroism was rewarded by at least a torpedo-hit on a battleship, but both the *Onslow*'s torpedoes missed, and her hit on the *Wiesbaden* did not prevent that sorely battered ship from continuing the fight later. The destroyer eventually came to a dead stop. For a time it looked as if she might be sunk by the German ships, which were within gun range, and her anxious crew had a grandstand view of an action between the battleship *Warspite* and the head of the German line, but the battleships swept on and ignored her. She was eventually taken in tow by her fellow-destroyer HMS *Defender*, which had the dubious distinction of having an unexploded 12-inch shell in the ashpit of one of her boilers. The two cripples fell in with the damaged *Warspite*, making her

Above: The fore-funnel and bridge of HMS *Walker*, a brand-new 'V & W' boat runs trials late in 1918.

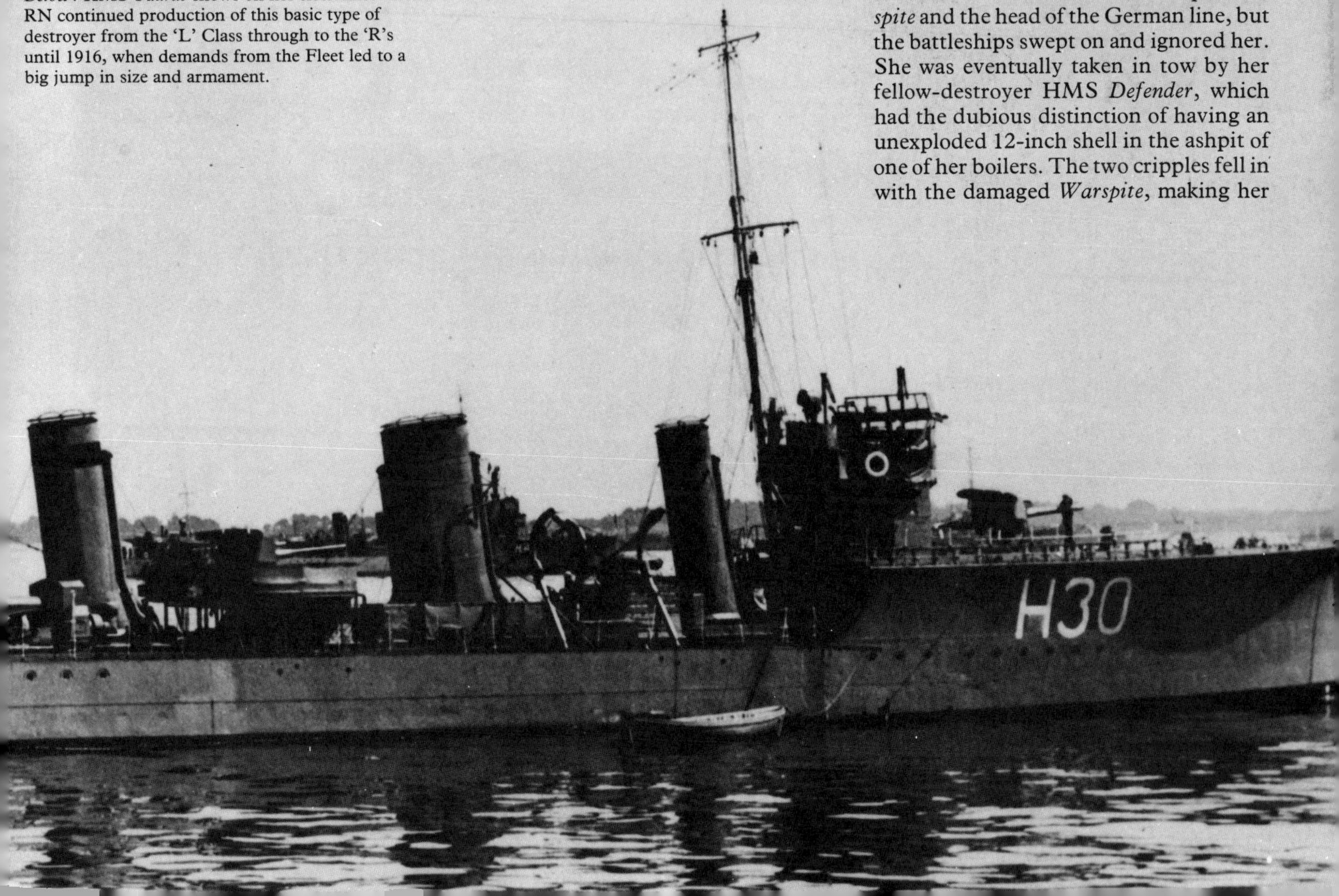

Below: HMS *Taurus* shows off her sleek lines. The RN continued production of this basic type of destroyer from the 'L' Class through to the 'R's until 1916, when demands from the Fleet led to a big jump in size and armament.

way back to Rosyth, but the big battleship dared not loiter to help the destroyers, and left them. After a nightmare journey across 350 miles in a rising sea the two ships arrived safely. Both captains received the DSO, Tovey for his gallant attack and Commander Palmer of the *Defender* for his outstanding seamanship and determination.

Meanwhile the Grand Fleet was deploying into action, and Admiral Jellicoe, the Commander-in-Chief, pushed his three battlecruisers *Invincible*, *Indomitable* and *Inflexible* to support Beatty's ships. Escorting these ships were four destroyers, led by Commander Loftus W Jones in HMS *Shark*. The *Shark* and *Acasta* attacked a German light cruiser and a battlecruiser with torpedoes, but the divisional leader was badly damaged by gunfire. Refusing a tow from the *Acasta*, Loftus Jones was preparing to abandon ship when two German torpedo boats appeared. Although only the midships four-inch gun was still working the crippled *Shark* fought back until she was hit by a torpedo. A handful of men, including the desperately wounded captain escaped on a raft, but during the night he and eight others died, leaving only six survivors out of a ship's company of 77 officers and men. The *Acasta* narrowly escaped the same fate, but she was totally disabled, and lay in the path of the Grand Fleet as it swept into action. Later that night she was given a tow by another destroyer and managed to make port.

Top left: HMS *Badger* approaches the wreck of the battlecruiser *Invincible* to pick up survivors clinging to a raft (centre), during the Battle of Jutland.
Centre left: The *Tipperary* was the fourth unit of the class of flotilla leaders taken over from Chile by the British in 1914–15.

As darkness fell the fleet action died away, leaving the British apparently well placed between the High Seas Fleet and its bases. The capital ships were grouped into cruising formation once more, to provide a more compact defence against a night attack by torpedo boats, which was expected. Admiral Jellicoe stationed his destroyers five miles astern of the main fleet, partly to screen his big ships against such an attack and also to give them the opportunity to attack the enemy fleet if it should pass to the South on its way home. But these destroyers had very little idea of the whereabouts of many of their own fleet, let alone the enemy, apart from the knowledge that the battle fleet was five miles ahead. In the confusion of the fighting that had just ended the staff had overlooked the fact that the destroyers had no way of knowing whether they were attacking friend or foe. If they flashed the recognition signal they could expect to be lashed by gunfire, and if they fired first they ran the awful risk of sinking one of their own ships. The truth of the matter was, of course, that no-one had ever imagined such a large number of destroyers gathered together, and so little concrete information about everybody's position. These miscalculations were to have disastrous results.

To summarize briefly, the High Seas Fleet decided to take its chance in a night action, and try to drive its way through the screen of destroyers. In this decision Scheer had been helped by two strokes of good fortune: an intercepted signal told him that the destroyers were well astern of Jellicoe's fleet, and a rash visual exchange of the night challenge and reply between two British battlecruisers at dusk had been partially read by a German light cruiser. The first piece of information gave Scheer the assurance that he was only facing light forces, against which the German night-fighting organization had more than a fair chance of success, and the second meant that British ships would be dangerously unsure in those vital opening minutes of night action, whereas the Germans would know immediately that they had been challenged by an enemy ship.

The first clash came at 2205, when the 11th Flotilla was challenged by ships which gave the first two letters of the challenge for the day, followed by two incorrect letters. Before anyone could decide what to do, searchlights were unmasked by the cruisers *Hamburg* and *Elbing*, followed by a withering fire. The light cruiser *Castor* fired back, and she and two of her destroyers each fired a torpedo, but the rest of the flotilla held their fire, convinced that a mistake had been made. The torpedoes missed and the two hostile cruisers disappeared into the darkness as rapidly as they had appeared.

The leader *Tipperary* and her 4th Flotilla had seen the gun flashes and searchlights of the *Castor*'s action, and so were alerted. This was not enough, for as soon as the *Tipperary* challenged what she mistook for a force of friendly cruisers, she was blasted by gunfire. The 4th Flotilla had in fact run into the head of the German battle fleet, and the puny destroyers were about to take on dreadnoughts 20 times their size. The *Spitfire* swung to starboard to avoid the blazing wreck of the *Tipperary*, but her captain was blinded by the searchlights, and failed to see the ram bow of a big ship looming overhead. To avoid being cut in

Below: Destroyers of the 11th Flotilla escort battleships of the Grand Fleet. Front to rear: HMS *Marmion*, *Marne*, *Prince Kempenfelt*, and *Morning Star*.

Left: The port mine-rail of HMS *Walker*. The British made extensive use of destroyers for high-speed minelaying in the Heligoland Bight and off the Flanders U-Boat bases.

half he chose to collide with his opponent, port bow to port bow, and the *Spitfire* ground down the side of the other ship. The big ship's forward turret swung round and fired a salvo at her, but the destroyer was so small that the shells roared overhead; even so, the blast was enough to flatten the bridge and demolish the mast and fore-funnel. When the *Spitfire* drew clear she had on board 20 feet of steel plating and part of some anchor gear wedged into her mess-deck. Lieutenant-Commander Trelawny thought that the enemy 'light cruiser' was probably not a new ship because of the thick paint, but his opponent was actually the dreadnought battleship *Nassau*, displacing 20,000 tons and armed with 12 11-inch guns.

The German ships were not having it all their own way, and the head of their line was thrown into confusion as a result of the British destroyers' torpedo attacks. The *Elbing* was one of a number of cruisers which were forced to weave through the battleships in an attempt to dodge the torpedoes, and while doing this she was rammed by the *Posen*. Then the *Rostock* did the same, and was caught by a torpedo as she squeezed through astern of the *Westfalen*. One destroyer, tormented by the dazzling searchlights, fired her puny four-inch guns at them; a 25-lb shell burst on the bridge of the battleship *Oldenburg*, killing or wounding most of the bridge personnel. The giant ship was turning at the time, and she continued to career wildly until the wounded Captain Höpfner managed to crawl to the wheel himself and bring her back under control. But the 4th Flotilla had been destroyed as a fighting formation without being able to stop the High Seas Fleet's breakthrough. Four destroyers had been sunk and four more seriously damaged, while 390 officers and men had been killed, and 72 wounded.

The next obstacle in Admiral Scheer's path was a mixed force of destroyers, mainly the 13th Flotilla, and some from the 9th and 10th Flotillas. Although casualties were not as heavy as in the 4th Flotilla, the German battle-line once again smashed its way through, damaging the *Petard* severely and literally blowing the *Turbulent* apart with gunfire, without suffering any loss. Then the 12th Flotilla attacked, and this time one of the torpedoes found its mark. Suddenly the pre-dreadnought battleship *Pommern*, in the 2nd Squadron, was illuminated by a flash which spread along her waterline. She heeled over, torn apart by a series of further explosions, and quickly disappeared in flames as her ammunition detonated. All 844 men were lost.

Jutland showed that the power of destroyers had been overrated. Although both Commanders-in-Chief had repeatedly turned away rather than face torpedo attacks, the gunfire of defending cruisers and the battleships themselves had been sufficient to drive off daylight attacks. At night destroyers had found it very difficult to operate against a well co-ordinated defence. There were 252 ships present at the battle, and of these only the German *Seydlitz* and the British *Marlborough* were damaged by torpedoes in daylight, while night attacks had only accounted for two light cruisers and the old *Pommern*.

For many years the experience of Jutland was to dominate destroyer tactics in all navies, which is why the fighting has been described at some length. What the British learned was that, above all, a group of destroyers must be given as much information as possible about the dispositions of both friendly and hostile ships. The second lesson was that the flotillas were too big, as had been pre-

dicted as long ago as 1887. The large flotilla was retained for the time being as an administrative unit but for tactical purposes it was broken down into divisions. Both sides had favoured black as the ideal colour for destroyers, to reduce the chance of being picked out at night, but this had proved to be false, as black stood out clearly. Although the Germans retained black for a while longer, immediately after Jutland the British flotillas began to change to the light grey already in use in larger ships.

Little could be done to improve communications from destroyer-to-destroyer, as flag signals or Morse lamp were still the only means, but the practice of having a half-leader in each division went some way to curing the worst problems. There was to be no second meeting between the British and German Fleets, and the growing need to divert destroyers to hunting U-Boats meant that any serious revision of destroyer tactics had to be deferred. One useful point had emerged from Jutland; a mine laid by the minelaying flotilla leader *Abdiel* had damaged the battleship *Ostfriesland* on her way home, and in the second half of 1916 more destroyers were converted. The

Above: The flotilla leader *Anzac* commemorated the gallantry of Australian and New Zealand soldiers at Gallipoli and in 1919 was transferred to the Royal Australian Navy.

20th Flotilla operated on the East Coast of England, and made frequent trips to lay mines in the Heligoland Bight and off the Flanders U-Boat bases. Destroyers proved ideal for this work, their speed enabling them to reach the area and get clear under cover of darkness.

It has already been explained just why destroyers were effective against sub-

Below: HMS *Pigeon* lying at Harwich in 1917.

Above: The *Allen* (DD.66) at Queenstown in 1917–18. The last of her class to survive she remained in service until 1945.

marines, but it was not until the second unrestricted U-Boat campaign of 1917 that destroyers became indispensable as escorts. Hitherto formations of warships had always moved with their screen of destroyers, but now merchant ships needed escorting as well when convoys were introduced in May 1917. It must be remembered that every destroyer released for convoy escort had to be taken away from fleet work. When the United States entered the war the US Navy was asked to send destroyers as the most urgent priority, and a Japanese offer to build destroyers for the French Navy and to send eight of their own to the Mediterranean was gratefully accepted.

On 24 April 1917 six destroyers of the US Atlantic Fleet, the *Wadsworth*, *Conyngham*, *Porter*, *McDougal*, *Davis* and *Wainwright* weighed anchor and left American waters for Europe. They were the first massive reinforcement sent by

Above: The *Belknap* (DD.251) runs her full speed trials after the Armistice.
Below: The first flotilla of US destroyers under Commander Joseph K Taussig USN arrives at Queenstown on 4 May 1917. The leading destroyer is USS *Davis* (DD.65).

the US Navy, and they were to prove crucial. A total of only 26 destroyers had been authorized between 1911 and 1914, and it was out of this group that the first reinforcements for Europe were drawn. In the interim a new type of destroyer was laid down, based on the 1913–14 designs but with a flush deck from bow to stern to give greater longitudinal strength in place of the conventional raised forecastle. The first class was a group of six experimental boats which tried out various types of machinery, but as soon as the need for vast numbers of destroyers was made known in 1917 two standardized types were selected. No fewer than 111 of the *Wickes* Class were built, followed by 162 of the similar *Clemson* Class. Although the last 50 of this giant programme were not completed at the Armistice, the rate at which the others were built meant that they were all in time.

Giving a foretaste of what US shipyards could do in World War II, the construction of these 'flush-deckers' broke every record in the book. The *Ward*

Above: The *Ward* (DD.139) was one of the first flush-decker destroyers. Like the *Allen* she survived until World War II and fired the shot at Pearl Harbor which sank a Japanese midget submarine.

Above: Destroyers were never spacious as can be seen from these two US destroyers at their Queenstown base in the South of Ireland. Spare parts for the four-inch gun are being shaped on the portable blacksmith's forge in the foreground.
Below: One of the big 1200-ton German destroyers, *V.99*, is seen on builder's trials, without her torpedo-tubes.

(DD.139) was commissioned in 70 days, having been launched after only 17.5 days, and the *Reid* commissioned after only 45.5 working days of building. In all 85 US destroyers served in Europe in 1917–18, including six of the old *Bainbridges*, which travelled 12,000 miles from the Philippines to Gibraltar.

The US destroyers saw considerable action, although most of their work was the same routine patrolling and escorting which was the lot of British and French destroyers during the same period. In November 1917 the *Fanning* (DD.37) and *Nicholson* (DD.52) sank *U.85* off Queenstown (now Cobh) in Southern Ireland. The *Jacob Jones* (DD.61) was torpedoed by *U.53* while on passage between Brest and Queenstown a month later. Her captain, Lieutenant-Commander D W Bagley, bore a name already distinguished in the US Navy, and he played an important part in keeping the dazed and injured survivors alive in freezing weather. In a rare example of chivalry, *U.53*'s commander Kapitän-Leutnant Hans Rose, signalled the position of the *Jacob Jones*' boats to Queenstown before leaving the scene.

One of the most courageous acts was that of the *Shaw* (DD.68), which was escorting the British liner *Aquitania*, carrying over 7000 troops. As the destroyer zigzagged close to the convoy her helm jammed, and she found herself heading straight for the side of the *Aquitania*. Commander William Glassford realized that he had a choice between slicing into the liner's thin side and possibly drowning thousands of troops, or altering speed so that his destroyer was the victim instead. With great courage he rang down for 'full speed astern', and he and his men waited for the awful seconds as the 45,000-ton *Aquitania* bore down on their 900-ton destroyer. When the crash came the *Shaw* was cut in two just forward of the bridge, with 12 men killed and 15 injured. Although her oil fuel caught fire the crew stayed aboard to fight the fire and finally got the machinery running again. Miraculously she did not sink, and was eventually repaired and recommissioned.

In World War I destroyers changed rapidly from being small, specialized craft to a warship type which was an integral part of the fleet. No other type proved so adaptable to the changes brought about by submarine and mine warfare, and no other type saw so much action. In every navy destroyers were hard-worked and indispensable. Valuable lessons had been learned about design and methods of employment, but above all a tradition of bravery, skill and determination had been forged in battle.

Above: At the end of World War I US destroyers were based at Brest to escort troops to France. *Left to right:* the *Little* (DD.79) and *Jarvis* (DD.38) lie alongside the four-stacker, *Burrows*.

Twenty Years of Peace

When World War I ended not only destroyer tactics but the destroyers themselves were in the throes of a revolution. We have seen how the orthodox ideas about torpedo attack had been discredited at Jutland in 1916, and a period of re-assessment started as soon as the victorious navies returned to a normal peacetime footing. This meant for all fewer destroyers than before 1914, for the world was a poorer place after 1918 and fleets were considerably reduced.

Destroyers were much bigger and could therefore be better armed than before. In April 1916, two months before Jutland, the British had ordered the first of a new type of flotilla leader, known as the 'V' Class. To allow higher speed in bad weather the hull was made bigger and the freeboard was raised, while the provision of reduction gears for the steam turbines gave more economy. The guns were carried much higher, with the second and third guns carried a deck higher on deck-houses forward and aft. In this position they were clear of the spray which blanketed the forecastles of existing destroyers, and as the bridge was further back and higher it too suffered much less from spray. Only five of these leaders were ordered at first, but in June 1916 rumours reached the Admiralty of powerful new German destroyers, and as a quick and effective reply it was decided to duplicate the new leader-design, but as an ordinary fleet destroyer without the special accommodation for the Captain (D) and his staff. The first 25 were ordered in June–August 1916, followed by a further 25 in December, and from the initial class-letters they became known as the 'V & W' Class. During the night attacks at Jutland many destroyers had missed opportunities because they carried too few torpedoes, and so the 'W' Class were armed with two sets of triple torpedo-tubes. The new destroyers were treated with some caution as they marked a big increase in size and topweight with their guns carried so high above the waterline, but in service they proved so successful that in January 1918 an upgunned version was ordered. This was the 'Modified W' Class, with 4.7-inch guns firing a 45-lb shell in place of the 32-lb shell fired by the four-inch gun in the 'V & W' boats, and it made them even better. To lead such powerful destroyers called for bigger flotilla leaders than the 'V' Class, and these were two groups known as the *Scott* and *Shakespeare* Classes, 1550-ton craft armed with five 4.7-inch guns and six 21-inch torpedo-tubes. For some years after World War I these were regarded as the most powerful destroyers in the world.

The Italian Navy had also increased

Above: The starboard rails and mine-chute of HMS *Vehement* shows how destroyers laid mines. The mines and sinkers were winched aft and dropped clear of the propellers.

Above: Destroyers required docking from time to time, as fouling below the waterline reduced their speed. This is HMS *Vampire* in 1918 before she went to Australia.
Below: HMS *Verulam* runs trials in 1918 – one of the new 'V & W' Class which set a new standard in gunpower and seaworthiness. This layout was copied by many navies.

the size of its destroyers. In 1913 they had begun three *esploratori* or 'scouts' known as the *Allessandro Poerio* Class. Although they displaced no more than 911 tonnes they were armed with six four-inch guns and four 18-inch torpedo-tubes and had a speed of 32 knots. They were followed by the similar but considerably larger *Carlo Mirabello* Class, built in 1914–17. These 1780-tonne vessels were intended to fulfil the role of a light cruiser, and the design had actually been scaled down from a 5000-tonne light cruiser. But with a six-inch gun forward, seven four-inch guns and a speed of 35 knots they were much closer to the destroyer category. As the British had found with the *Swift* and *Viking* in 1916, a six-inch gun was too heavy for a destroyer, especially as the weight forward tended to bury the forecastle in a seaway; by 1918 all three had an armament of eight four-inch guns. In 1921–22 three vessels of the *Leone* Class were laid down, and they set the pattern for future Italian developments. They had a long forecastle and were armed with four twin 4.7-inch gun mountings and two sets of twin 21-inch torpedo-tubes.

The Italian Navy's rival was the French Navy, and when the Chamber of Deputies authorized a long-term modernization in 1922 the big Italian scouts were very much in mind. Twelve destroyers or *torpilleurs* were authorized plus a further six *contre-torpilleurs* or large destroyers. Experience with high-speed turbines had not been happy up to 1914, and even the planned building of a destroyer with British Parsons geared turbines had been deferred because of wartime shortages. This destroyer, the *Enseigne Gabolde*, was finally completed in 1923 but she was only a small 900-tonner with relatively low power. As part of the booty awarded to France under the Treaty of Versailles eight German destroyers were handed over. The largest of these was the 2000-ton *S.113*, armed with four 15cm (5.9-inch) guns, and she had machinery of more than twice the power of the *Enseigne Gabolde*. The others were all 900-tonners completed late in World War I, but they also helped to bring French ideas of destroyer design up to date.

The *S.113* and her Vulcan-built half-sister *V.116* represented a belated attempt by the German Navy to produce destroyers as opposed to torpedo boats. This change of policy had been influenced by the big *G.101* Class built in 1914 for Argentina and the *B.97* Class built in 1915 around turbines ordered for Russian destroyers. To mark the jump in size they were known as *zerstörer*, and for the first time they approached British destroyers in size and armament. But none of these boats could match the British 'V & W' Class for weatherliness, and the 15cm gunned craft were particularly deficient in this respect. The shell

Left: Italian destroyers never adopted superimposed guns, preferring to increase gunpower with twin gun mountings. This is the *Turbine* in the 1930s.

Above: The 'Navigatori' Class were large flotilla leaders built in 1927–30. Although designed for ultra high speed, they proved top-heavy and deficient in seakeeping.

was too heavy for easy handling and the fire control provided was too crude to achieve results which justified the extra weight of the guns. To make things worse the machinery was unreliable and excessive topweight caused bad rolling. Nevertheless, the French *Amiral Sénès* (ex-*S.113*) and the Italian *Premuda* (ex-*V.116*) and *Cesare Rossol* (ex-*B.97*) were well suited to the less boisterous waters of the Mediterranean, and gave their new owners satisfaction. Fortunately we have a comparison between the German *B.98* and a British 'V & W', which occurred when HMS *Vivien* was escorting the *B.98* in a Force 6–7 wind and rough sea in mid-1919. The *Vivien* worked up from 10 to 20 knots, but at 15 knots the German boat was shipping so much water that her bridge personnel could not read a signal ordering her to ease down. Aboard the *Vivien* only No 1 gun was affected by spray, whereas all four of *B.98*'s guns were blanketed by repeated waves.

Whatever influence the big Italian and German designs may have had on destroyer development, the outstanding influences in the years after 1918 were the British 'Modified W' and *Shakespeare* Classes. The French copied the layout of superimposed single guns and centre-line torpedo-tubes for their new destroyers, and these features found their way into many destroyers built for minor navies. Only the Italians remained faithful to the old disposition, but they tried to com-

Below: A new duty for destroyers was to act as 'planeguard', picking up pilots who failed to land on carriers. Here, the *Westminster* accompanies HMS *Courageous* in April 1930.

Left: In 1931 Canada took delivery of two new destroyers. HMCS *Saguenay* and *Skeena* obtained distinguished records in the Battle of the Atlantic.
Top right: Builder's trials always showed destroyers at their best. This is HMS *Diamond* in 1932.
Centre right: HMS *Grafton* (seen here in June 1936) was typical of the standard British 'A to I' type built in 1926–36.
Below: If a destroyer was driven too hard in steep seas she could easily begin to leap out of the water as HMS *Walker* is doing here. Speed then had to be reduced to avoid structural damage.

H89

pensate by adopting twin gun mountings. The British, not unnaturally, were content to improve on the 'Modified W', but the only important change was to mount quadruple tubes. Following the building of two prototypes in 1924–26 a series of basically similar destroyers was started. They were built at the rate of eight per year, with a leader for each group, and each group had a distinguishing class letter. They ran through nine classes and so they were known as the 'A to I' Classes, handsome two-funnelled boats with four guns, eight torpedo-tubes and a sea speed of 30–31 knots. The Admiralty's policy was to build for its own fleet's requirements, without being unduly influenced by foreign designs, on the grounds that numbers were more important than individual quality. It was a time of great financial stringency, and the Royal Navy was only too aware of the political pressures against any form of re-armament, so the main requirement was the greatest numbers of destroyers for minimum cost.

In the United States there was even less willingness to consider the building of new destroyers. The enormous number of flush-deckers completed between 1917 and 1922 gave the USN a surplus of destroyers. This was not a good thing, as it inhibited the improvement of destroyer design at a time when rapid progress was being made abroad. The speed with

Below: In 1930 the British government cut the naval programme in half as a unilateral gesture of disarmament. The four ships of the 'C' Class which resulted did not fit into the RN's flotilla system and so they were transferred to Canada in 1937–39. The *Fraser* was formerly HMS *Crescent*.

Above: The Japanese 2nd Class destroyer *Aoi* steaming at 35 knots (minus guns) on trials. Most of these small destroyers served as escorts in World War II.

Above: When the US Navy started to build destroyers again in 1930 they followed the lead given by the British in the 'A to I' Class but with heavier armaments. USS *Perkins* (DD.377) is seen here in June 1937.

Above: USS *Cassin* (DD.372) in February 1937. She was to be a Pearl Harbor casualty.

which the flush-deckers had been built precluded any sophistication, and it was generally agreed that they were greatly inferior to their foreign contemporaries. The machinery was not very efficient, and they needed four boilers to produce the same power as the three-boiler 'V & W' boats. Allowing one funnel for each boiler produced a distinctive silhouette but it was expensive in deck space, and forced the designers to site the midship's four-inch guns and the torpedo-tubes on either beam. The tactical drawback of this layout was that only half the torpedo armament could be brought to bear in action, unless it was possible to guarantee that a squadron of flush-deckers could be brought into action first on the port side and then on the starboard side.

Many schemes were put forward to remedy these defects, but the US Navy was beset by the same financial problems as the Royal Navy. Keeping them going was all that could be done, and many expedients had to be adopted. Many were laid up in reserve, and some of these were partially 'cannibalized' to provide spares for those in better condition. The term 'Mothball Fleet' did not have the same meaning as it does today, and there was none of the expensive 'cocooning' and maintenance which preserves warships today. Rust and sea air corroded wiring, and as each year went by the effectiveness of the old destroyers declined.

A large design had been produced in 1919 by the Bureau of Construction and Repair, incorporating most of the latest British ideas, but this was shelved. Even the destroyers authorized by Congress in 1916 (DD.348–355) were not laid down until 1932. They were very similar to the British 'A to I' Classes, with a high forecastle and two funnels. But in other respects they incorporated features which improved their fighting power. For one thing, the US Navy had the five-inch/38 calibre dual-purpose gun with its excellent Mark 37 fire control system. This gun was to become the standard medium calibre weapon of US warships and it performed sterling service for 30 years.

The Americans and British might feel that they could allow destroyers to develop logically, in response to their own tactical and strategic requirements, but this state of affairs did not last for long. The French and Italians could be ignored but not the Japanese. The ambitions which had been kindled by her victory over Russia in 1904–05 had been fuelled by the profits made during World War I, and the virtual extinction of the German Navy after 1918 left the Imperial Japanese Navy as No 3 in the world. A combination of fear of the United States and a need to expand to acquire the strategic raw materials needed by her industries led the Japanese to try to achieve a balance of military power. But the Washington Treaty restricted the IJN to a 3:5 ratio in relation to both the USN and RN, and so the only way to close the gap was to improve the *quality* of each class of warship.

The policy of qualitative superiority applied across the board but it showed to greatest effect in Japanese destroyers. Up to 1923 design had been influenced first by British and then by German ideas. But in 1923 orders were placed for five destroyers of a new 'Special Type'. These were to be the first of the famous *Fubuki* Class, and they were like no destroyers yet seen. They were enormous, nearly 390 feet long and displacing 1750 tons, and 50,000 horsepower geared turbines gave them a theoretical smooth-water speed of 38 knots. Years before any other navy, the *Fubuki*s introduced a twin five-inch gun, and three of these Model A mountings gave them greater firepower

Below: The *Porter* Class were built to the maximum tonnage allowed in answer to the Japanese *Fubuki* Class. USS *Selfridge* (DD.357) is seen as completed with her low-angle five-inch guns and quadruple 1.1-inch AA guns.

than many light cruisers. The mounting was completely enclosed, making it not only weatherproof but gasproof as well. The torpedo armament was equally formidable, nine 24-inch tubes in three triple banks.

After ten of these craft had been ordered several improvements were incorporated in a second group of ten. They were given the Model B five-inch gun mounting, with 70° elevation to allow it to function as the world's first dual-purpose surface/anti-aircraft gun. It is easy to understand why these super-destroyers caused such a stir in naval circles when they appeared, and their striking appearance heightened their reputation. With tall funnels, high bridgework and massive gunhouses they looked far more impressive than any contemporary destroyers.

In 1933 a further improvement was made to the *Fubuki* Class, but this change was not evident, and its significance for the Americans was to remain a closely guarded secret until World War II. This was substitution of the Type 90 compressed-air torpedoes by the terrible 'Long Lance' Type 93. This monster was driven by liquid oxygen, a fuel with much greater thermal efficiency, and so it had much greater range and speed. Whereas a conventional 21-inch torpedo had a range of 8000–10,000 metres at 30–32 knots, the Long Lance Model 1 travelled 40,000 metres at its 'slow' setting of 36 knots; at 42 knots it ran for 30,000 metres, and at 49 knots it could still reach 22,000 metres. The increase in diameter to 24 inches in the Type 90 had already increased the weight of warhead to 500kg, whereas contemporary US and British torpedoes had 300–320kg warheads. The Long Lance was rugged and immensely destructive; a single hit could break a cruiser's back, and possession of it gave Japanese destroyers a wide margin of superiority in a torpedo attack. Another important asset was the provision of nine spare torpedoes, carried in the deck-houses. As a final bonus, the oxygen bubbles dissolved easily in sea water, and so the Long Lance left no telltale wake to assist an enemy ship in dodging a torpedo attack.

Above: Japanese Destroyer Division 29 lie alongside one another in 1926. The destroyers are numbered 13, 11, 17 and 15, but two years later became *Hayate*, *Oite*, *Yunagi* and *Asanagi*.

So far the story of Japanese destroyers has been one of dazzling success, but in 1935 disaster struck. In September of that year the Fourth Fleet was caught in a typhoon, and several destroyers suffered severe structural damage. The 'Special Type' destroyers came off worst despite their size, and the *Hatsuyuki* lost her bows. The Japanese designers had overreached themselves, and examination showed that the great weight of the bridge, five-inch gun houses and torpedo-tube shields had made them dangerously top-heavy. In 1935–37 many changes were made; superstructure was lightened, the hull was strengthened and given extra ballast, and the reload torpedoes were reduced from nine to six. Inevitably a great deal of weight was

Above: The *Jarvis* (DD.393) was one of a new class of single-funnelled destroyers built 1935–37.

added, over 250 tons in all, and top speed dropped to 34 knots. The *Fubuki*s were still formidable destroyers, but the 1935 typhoon had shown Japanese designers that they could not defy all the precepts of naval architecture with impunity.

The US Navy answered the *Fubuki* design by ordering eight large destroyers of the *Porter* Class (DD.356) in 1933. They were the first US destroyers designed to meet the need for squadron leaders, and although they had DD-numbers were often rated as DLs. They were some 500 tons bigger than the *Farragut* Class and approximated to the *Fubuki*s in size. A more realistic approach by US designers resulted in a heavier displacement than in the Japanese boats and guns were mounted at the expense of torpedo-tubes. The *Porter*s introduced the twin five-inch gun in US destroyers, but this early model of enclosed mounting did not have sufficient elevation to be of much use against aircraft, just like the Japanese Model A five-inch. Anti-aircraft fire was provided by two quadruple 1.1-inch mountings, one abaft 'B' five-inch gunhouse and firing over it, and the other on the after superstructure. Heavy tripod masts fore and aft gave them a handsome profile, but they proved an expensive luxury when the time came for additional weapons. To take advantage of the heavy gun battery, two fire control directors were provided, one forward and one aft, and in this respect they were better equipped than any other destroyers afloat, but with the heavy masts, the second director was extravagant with topweight.

The heavy torpedo battery in Japanese destroyers had not gone unnoticed, and in the following classes of US destroyers the number of tubes was increased. The *Mahan* Class (DD.364) were given three banks of quadruple 21-inch, one on the centre-line and the after pair winged out. This was a regression to the layout which had caused considerable criticism in the 'flush-deckers', for beam tubes were liable to weather damage, and could not

Below: The *Shirayuki*, second of the *Fubuki* Class, is ready to put to sea from Kure in May 1929.

always be trained in rough weather. But the risks were accepted as there was no other way of countering the nine-tube armament of the Japanese destroyers. In the *Gridley* Class (DD.380) of 1934 the idea was taken a step further, with four quadruple banks, all beam-mounted. A destroyer, like a submarine, was limited by the number of torpedoes she carried, and the immense distances in the Pacific meant a long haul to replenish the torpedoes if too small a number were embarked. Even so the next group of squadron leaders, the *Somers* Class of 1934 were found to be carrying too much topweight, and the *Sampson* group reverted to triple banks of tubes to rectify this.

Finding deck space for all these torpedo-tubes was a problem, and in the *Gridley* Class the solution was to trunk the boiler uptakes into a single funnel. Boilers were becoming more efficient too, and the next group had three instead of four with no reduction in power. Similar improvements were made in Japanese destroyers, but they retained the two-funnel layout. In the *Ariake* Class of 1931 an important change was made; although all Japanese destroyers had hitherto carried spare torpedoes, in this class the reloads were carried in the superstructure on the weather deck. In effect this doubled the torpedo armament as the tubes could be reloaded in less than 15 minutes. The technical superiority was matched by attention to tactics, and the Japanese took great care to perfect their night fighting. With reloads it was possible to fire one set at the beginning of an action, before a gun-action commenced; with a second set loaded there was no greater degree of risk than in foreign destroyers. Another tactic was to retire at high speed behind a smoke-screen after firing the first salvo of torpedoes; any enemy warships rash enough to think that the Japanese destroyers were escaping would be met by the same destroyers returning to the attack with their tubes reloaded.

It was left to the French to take the destroyer to its upper limit. They had been very impressed by the ex-German *Amiral Sénès*, but even as early as 1917 the Naval Staff had drafted a requirement for a destroyer armed with six 138.6mm (5.5-inch) guns, six torpedo-tubes, a speed of 35 knots and a radius of 3500 miles. Under the 1922 Programme six of the *Jaguar* Class were ordered, 2126 tonnes and armed with five 130mm guns, and they were followed by a further 18 of larger design. They set a new standard for good looks, with three or four funnels and big rakish hulls. They were known as *contre-torpilleurs* or 'destroyers of destroyers' to distinguish them from the smaller French destroyers also being built. There seemed to be considerable value in building these super-destroyers as the Italian Navy was making a name for its very high-speed cruisers of the 'Condottieri' type. Speeds of 37 knots and even 42 knots were being claimed for Italian six-inch gunned cruisers, and at the time it seemed that nothing could match these ships except an ultra-fast destroyer. As things turned out the Italian shipbuilders were a trifle over-enthusiastic in their claims, as the cruisers had run trials without guns or even gun turrets aboard, but the claimed performance of these and other Italian ships had all their likely opponents worried. Of course, it must be noted that the claimed speeds were never realized in action.

In January 1930 a new Fleet Law authorized the building of a further six French *contre-torpilleurs*, to be even bigger and faster than before. The reason, incidentally, for ordering destroyers in batches of six was that French tactics called for divisions of three boats. The new class was to be called *Le Fantasque*, and a truly fantastic group they turned out to be. Into a hull displacing 2610 tonnes was packed 74,000-shaft horsepower, to give a theoretical speed of 37 knots. Against these figures the armament seemed a little weak, only five single 138.6mm guns and nine 53.3cm torpedo-tubes, but it was comparable to many other destroyers of the day. But the big surprise came when the *Fantasques* ran their trials, for they mysteriously developed 27 to 50 per cent more power than the design called for. Not so surprisingly, this resulted in very high speeds, 40–42 knots on an eight-hour trial and 42–45 knots for an hour. This was a staggering achievement, and constitutes a record which has never been beaten by a steam-powered ship. The questions which have not been answered, however, are: how much did this cost the French Navy to achieve, and how did the designers manage to go so far over the specified power? In other words, the normal competitive tendering procedures and contract penalties must have been waived or drastically modified. In the US

Below: In December 1931 the new *Fubuki* Class destroyers were reorganized from four-boat to three-boat divisions, as a result of the limitations of the London Naval Treaty. The *Sazanami* leaves Yokosuka probably early in June 1932.

or Royal Navies such a discrepancy would have resulted in the dismissal of the head of the Engineering Branch.

Under the Versailles Treaty the German Navy had only been allowed to build small torpedo boats, and so the old distinction persisted. When Hitler denounced the Treaty, work began on new *zerstörer*, and as might be expected, they matched the growth in size in other navies. As before, numbers were used, not names, and *Z.1-22* displaced 2200–2400 tons. They had a layout of guns similar to the French *contre-torpilleurs* but adopted a 127mm (five-inch) gun. Speed was emphasized, but the machinery was a disappointment. High-pressure steam was used, but so many problems were encountered that their engineer officers wryly referred to the power-plant developing 'rickets'. The decision to use only their Z-numbers was rescinded, and they were given the names of destroyermen who had distinguished themselves in World War I.

The life in destroyers, whatever the navy, was different from service in any other type of ship. The cramped conditions meant an inevitable degree of discomfort, and in the older destroyers few facilities were provided. But this had its advantages, for there was less room for the spit and polish routine of bigger warships. The world which existed between the two world wars has vanished, and with it a way of life for navy-men that seems unbelievably remote from today. Both the British and the Americans kept their destroyers busy on what were vaguely defined as 'peacekeeping' duties in the world's trouble spots, principally

Top: Destroyer Squadron 2 of the Second Fleet with its flagship in Shibushi Bay on 6 April 1939. *Left to right:* *Naka* (cruiser flagship), *Amagiri, Asagiri, Yugiri, Oboro, Akebono* and *Ushio.*
Above: Destroyer Squadron 1 in Shibushi Bay on 15 March 1939. *Front to rear:* *Hatsuharu, Wakaba, Yamakaze, Suzukaze, Kawakaze, Umikaze,* and *Sendai* (cruiser flagship).
Right: The *Friedrich Ihn* (*Z.14*) was armed with five 12.7cm guns and eight 53.3cm torpedo-tubes.
Below: The *Tiger* was a 933-ton German torpedo boat built before the Treaty restrictions were lifted.

China and the Mediterranean. Destroyers were cheaper to deploy and generated less political heat than, say, a battleship or a cruiser squadron. Another advantage was that a squadron of destroyers could patrol a large area. In the early 1920s an Anglo–American agreement allowed US destroyers on the China Station whereas the British had submarines, but in 1927 the continuing disturbances and anti-foreign riots in China led the British to send a flotilla from the Mediterranean, and a year later a flotilla was brought out of reserve to allow the Mediterranean boats to return to their proper station.

Although the term 'Cold War' was unheard of, naval vessels spent a lot of their time getting involved in crises. Several US destroyers operated in the Mediterranean and Black Sea in 1919–20, assisting the relief agencies which were trying to cope with the famine, disease and chaos left by the recent war. Some even sailed up the Danube, and in 1922 the *Bainbridge* (DD.246) performed a particularly heroic rescue of 482 people from the burning French transport *Vinh-Long* in the Sea of Marmora. On 8 September 1923 the 14 destroyers of DesRon 11 were carrying out a 24-hour test run from San Francisco to San Diego. The squadron leader *Delphy* (DD.261) fixed her position that night at about nine miles off Point Arguello, but at about 2300 she passed through a fog bank and ran aground at 20 knots. Within minutes the *S P Lee* (DD.310), *Young* (DD.312), *Woodbury* (DD.309), *Nicholas* (DD.311), *Fuller* (DD.297) and *Chauncey* (DD.296) were also aground. The immediate cause

was a misinterpreted radio compass bearing but almost certainly the squadron had been set off course by abnormal currents caused by the great Tokyo earthquake the week before. All seven were written off as total losses, the biggest single peacetime accident to befall any navy.

British destroyers were also involved in the aftermath of war, and in 1922 the 3rd Flotilla had to be sent out hurriedly from England to Smyrna to cover the evacuation of the Greek Army, which had just been thrashed by the Turks in Asia Minor. The irony of it was that the destroyermen were nearly as hungry as the Greek soldiers, for they had come out from England so hurriedly that there had been no time to take on stores. Christmas was spent at Mudros, where so many destroyers had once been based in 1915, and a depot ship was sent there to look after them. The broadside messing system, whereby each mess bought its own food allowance and then had it cooked, was clearly not equal to the strain of a prolonged cruise away from base. To complicate matters the older boats had no refrigerators. The canteen messing system was introduced shortly afterwards, and solved many of the problems; a canteen manager was responsible for keeping a stock of food, and could buy fruit and vegetables ashore as the opportunity arose.

Living conditions aboard the older destroyers were spartan by anybody's standards, although much improved over pre-1914 destroyers and torpedo boats. In the British 'V & W' boats water for the galley was pumped up by hand from the fresh-water tanks to a small storage tank on the upper deck. In peacetime a wing fuel tank could be cleaned out and filled with water, to alleviate the almost inevitable water shortage which arose after a few days at sea. Salt water was used for flushing the 'heads' (WCs), and it was the responsibility of the 'captain of the heads' to ensure that the gravity tank for flushing was full each morning. Stokers and seamen had a wash-place under the break of the forecastle, six washbasins over a trough, and open to the elements. An officer had the luxury of a circular tin bath, which was normally lashed to the deckhead of his cabin, although flotilla leaders had the unimaginable luxury of a full-size bath-tub. Reading was not encouraged on the mess-decks, and the only lighting was from oil lamps. Even the ward-room and officers' cabins were not well lit, and the Admiralty's parsimony insisted on 'Pipe Down' at 2200. This was cunningly circumvented by wiring up a secondary lighting circuit to run off the 20-volt batteries used for the fire-control circuits, but it was so dim that it had to be augmented by oil lamps. But they were cosy, particularly on a winter's night, with the stove glowing. Leather armchairs, usually with their back legs shortened to make them more comfortable were arranged casually, and a shelf ran around the bulkhead and the ship's side, just the right height for putting down a gin glass (the RN never having been administered by Josephus Daniels).

Right: The iron deck of a destroyer could be a dangerous place in rough weather as seen in this photo of HMS *Venetia*.
Below: USS *Anderson* (DD.411) runs trials in 1939. The *Sims* Class was developed from the *Gridley* and *Benham* Classes, and became the basis for future classes.

Right: Triple torpedo-tubes were introduced in the British 'W' Class in 1918 but were superseded by quadruple and quintuple mountings as destroyers grew larger.

422

L36

F

Left: The USS *Mayo* (DD.422) of the *Benson* Class was completed in 1940, part of the large US programme of shipbuilding initiated to regenerate employment. The two widely separated funnels betray the fact that the machinery is arranged on the unit system, with alternate boilers and engine-rooms.
Centre left: The British response to large destroyers building abroad was the handsome 'Tribal' Class, built in 1936–38. HMS *Nubian* was armed with four twin 4.7-inch guns but had only four 21-inch torpedo-tubes.
Bottom: HMS *Eskimo*, another 'Tribal' seen in February 1939. 'B' gunshield is painted in red, white and blue for aircraft recognition while serving on the Non-Beligerency Patrol in the Spanish Civil War. The 'F' pendant number was changed to 'L' in 1939 and then to 'G' in 1940.

Nor was life on the lower deck unhappy, despite the sparseness of the fittings. Life on the Mediterranean Fleet destroyers was particularly popular. The climate was healthy, and in a happy, well-run ship it was not unknown for the 1st Lieutenant to arrange a 'banyan party' ashore, in other words a picnic followed by water-polo for those energetic enough. The Royal Navy always encouraged rowing regattas and boxing, both in the flotillas and in an annual Fleet competition. In the regattas there were many events, Stokers' Whaler, Communications Dinghy, etc, and competition between ships was fierce.

Life on the China Station could be more eventful than elsewhere, for the country was torn by strife, with local warlords, the Peking Government and later Chiang Kai-shek, the Communists and the Japanese fighting like jackals over a carcass. The main contribution they could make was to provide landing parties to protect foreign lives and property, and when the British 3rd Flotilla arrived at Hankow in 1927, the nine boats spent eight months moored off the Bund without weighing anchor once. This was exceptional though, and most destroyers enjoyed a more varied existence. Every year there were manoeuvres, when battle tactics could be practiced with other warships. Right through to the 1930s massed destroyer attacks were still the vogue, refinements of what had been tried at Jutland, with destroyers racing in line towards the 'enemy' battle fleet, or making smoke to cover 'friendly' ships against torpedo attack. Everything was done at high speed, which required superb seamanship and steady nerves.

Contrary to popular belief torpedo-tubes could not be swung round rapidly, and so the tubes were cranked to one of three bearings on either beam, 70°, 90° or 110°; when the torpedo-sight on the bridge came onto the target, the tin 'fishes' were fired with a small 'ripple' to reduce the risk of one hitting another. Angling the gyro allowed torpedoes to be fired on the run-in, and so reduced the time the destroyer had to be exposed to hostile gunfire. Even with this refinement daylight attack was becoming suicidal, unless the attackers could take advantage of poor visibility. Gunfire was still the main weapon against other destroyers, but the lively motion in any sort of seaway meant that their gunnery could never be of a high order.

As the world inched towards war after 1936 every navy became acutely aware of its lack of destroyers. The British at last responded to the challenge of the super-destroyer by building 16 of what were to become the famous 'Tribal' Class, and

Above: Many merchant vessels were mined and even torpedoed by 'mystery' (Italian) submarines during the Spanish Civil War. The British destroyer *Hunter* was damaged by a mine on 13 May 1937.

Above: Before the introduction of radar, smoke-screens were frequently used to conceal movements from an enemy force. Destroyers made smoke in two ways: by dropping cannisters of chlor-sulphonic acid astern and by changing the mixture of oil and air in the boiler furnaces.

Above: USS *Roe* (DD.418) seen at anchor off New York, 13 June 1940.
Below: The small German torpedo boat *Iltis* lifts her bow clear of the water for a third of her length.

followed them with a series of sturdy single-funnelled boats. The US Navy followed the British lead in refusing to be drawn into the race to produce a super-destroyer, and settled for the successful and attractive *Benson* Class, 1620 tons, five five-inch guns and ten torpedo-tubes. The large destroyers of the Axis Navies were to be matched by smaller but more numerous destroyers. When war broke out in September 1939 the Royal Navy had 79 old destroyers (many suitable only for anti-submarine escort), 113 modern destroyers and a further 44 under construction. France could add another 78 destroyers, of which 32 were *contre-torpilleurs*, and another 27 being built. Against this force the *Kriegsmarine* could only muster 22 destroyers, 20 torpedo boats and a further 25 large destroyers and torpedo boats being built. This serious imbalance was offset by the certainty that the bulk of the French destroyers would be committed to watching the Italian Navy, which could add 38 old destroyers and 84 new boats to the Axis strength. But when the Italians decided to choose their moment to enter the war a considerable portion of their light forces would be similarly tied down on escort duty, convoying troops and supplies to North Africa.

The war which was about to begin would prove yet again that there were not enough destroyers, and those that served were to perform harder service than their designers had ever dreamed. They were also to win for themselves even greater laurels and acclamation than they had 20 years earlier.

GERMAN DESTROYERS

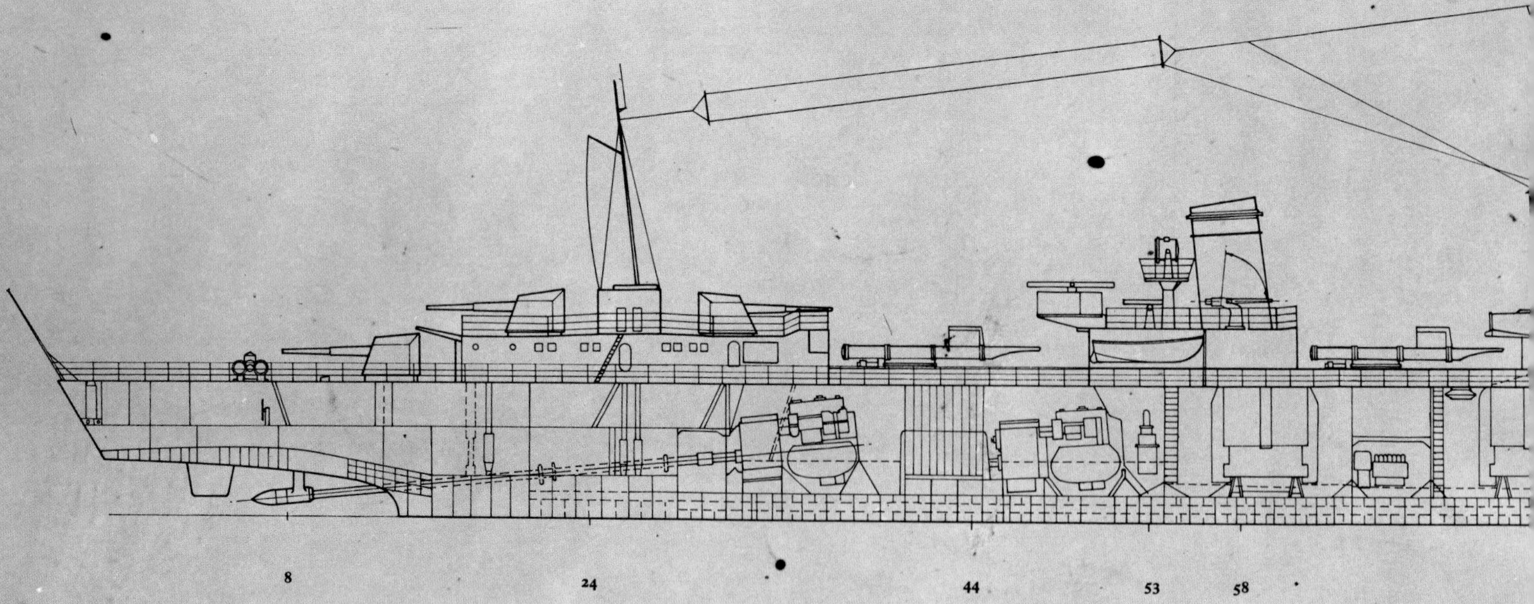

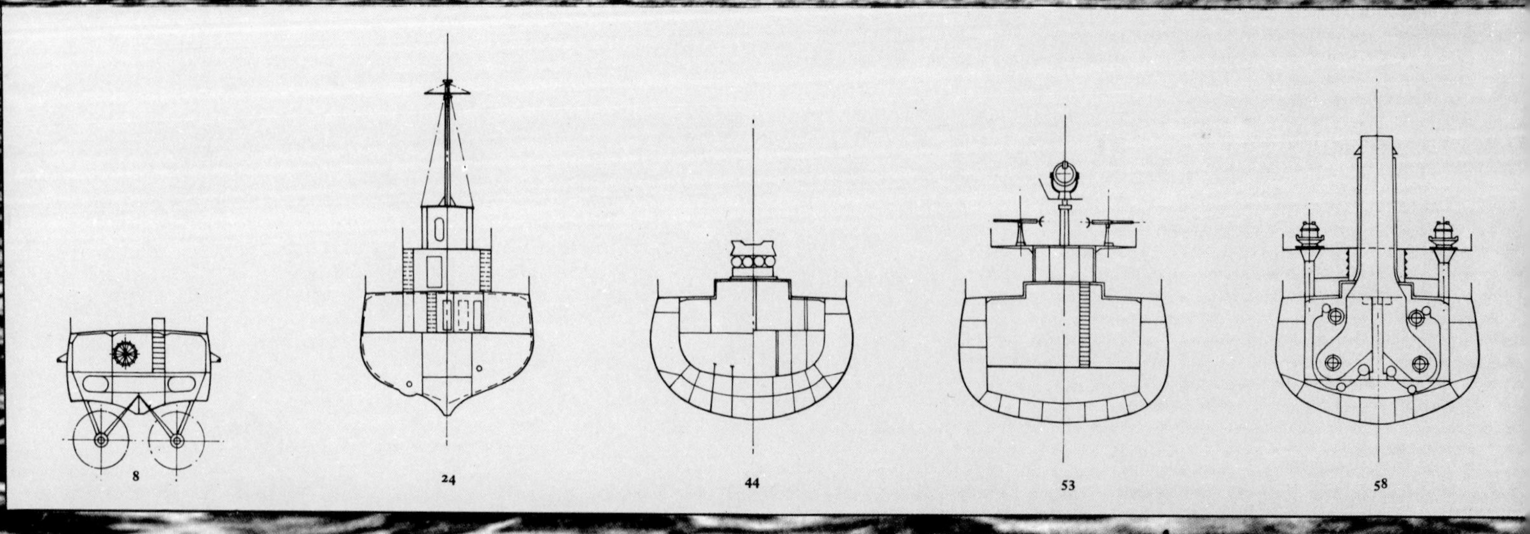

Top and bottom : The shipbuilders view of a destroyer: the layout of the German *Z.38* which became the British *Nonesuch* in 1946. The transverse sections at the bottom of the page show clearly how slender the hull of a destroyer is and how little water she draws. Note also the size of the twin 15cm gun mounting.
Centre : The *Z.37* shows off her typically German profile with a twin 15cm gun mounting forward and three single mountings aft.

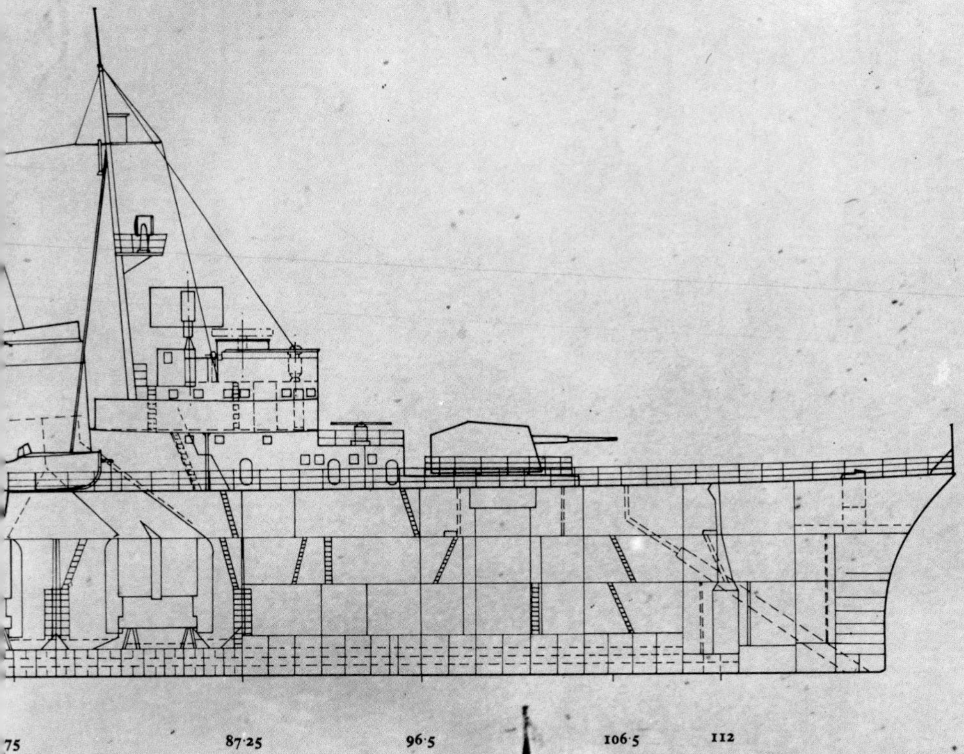

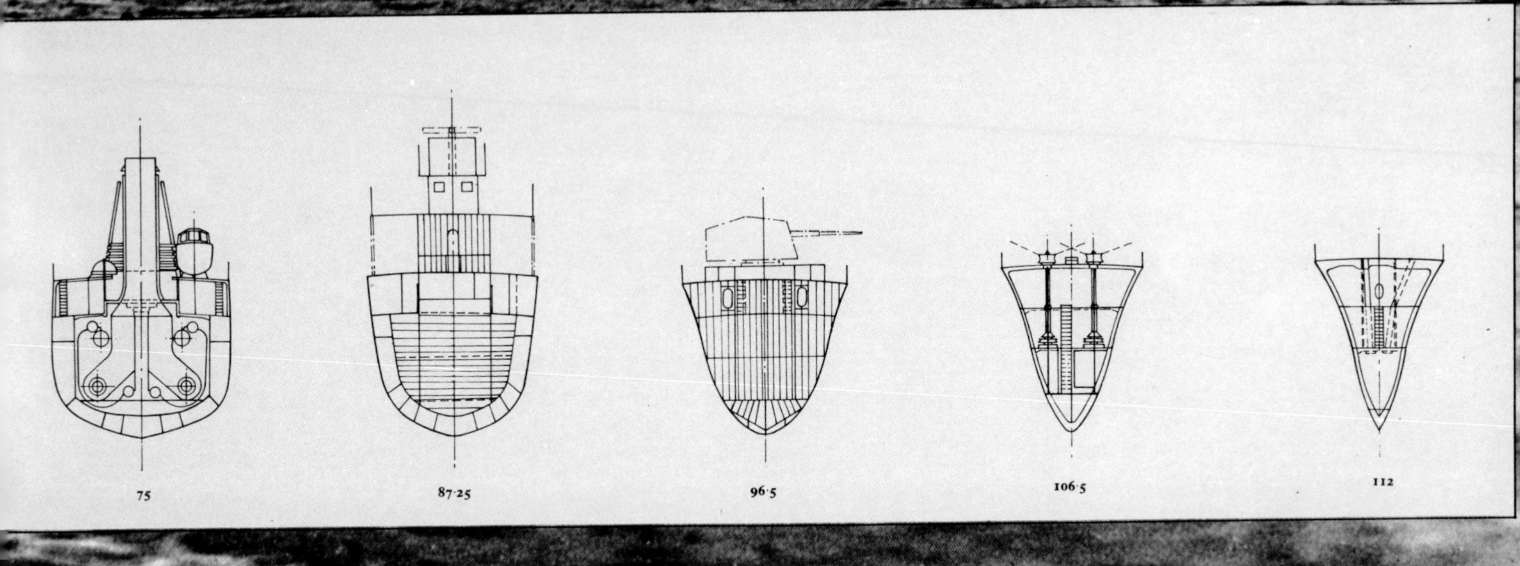

Left : The 2cm light automatic flak gun was the standard close-range defence of German destroyers at the start of World War II.
Right : The destroyer *Z.39* seen in a Baltic port after her surrender in May 1945. The prominent 'girdle' around the hull conceals a 'degaussing' anti-magnetic coil.
Below : Torpedo boat *T.17* had radar aerials on her foremast. Launched in 1940/41, she survived the war and became the Soviet *Porivisty*.

BRITISH DESTROYERS

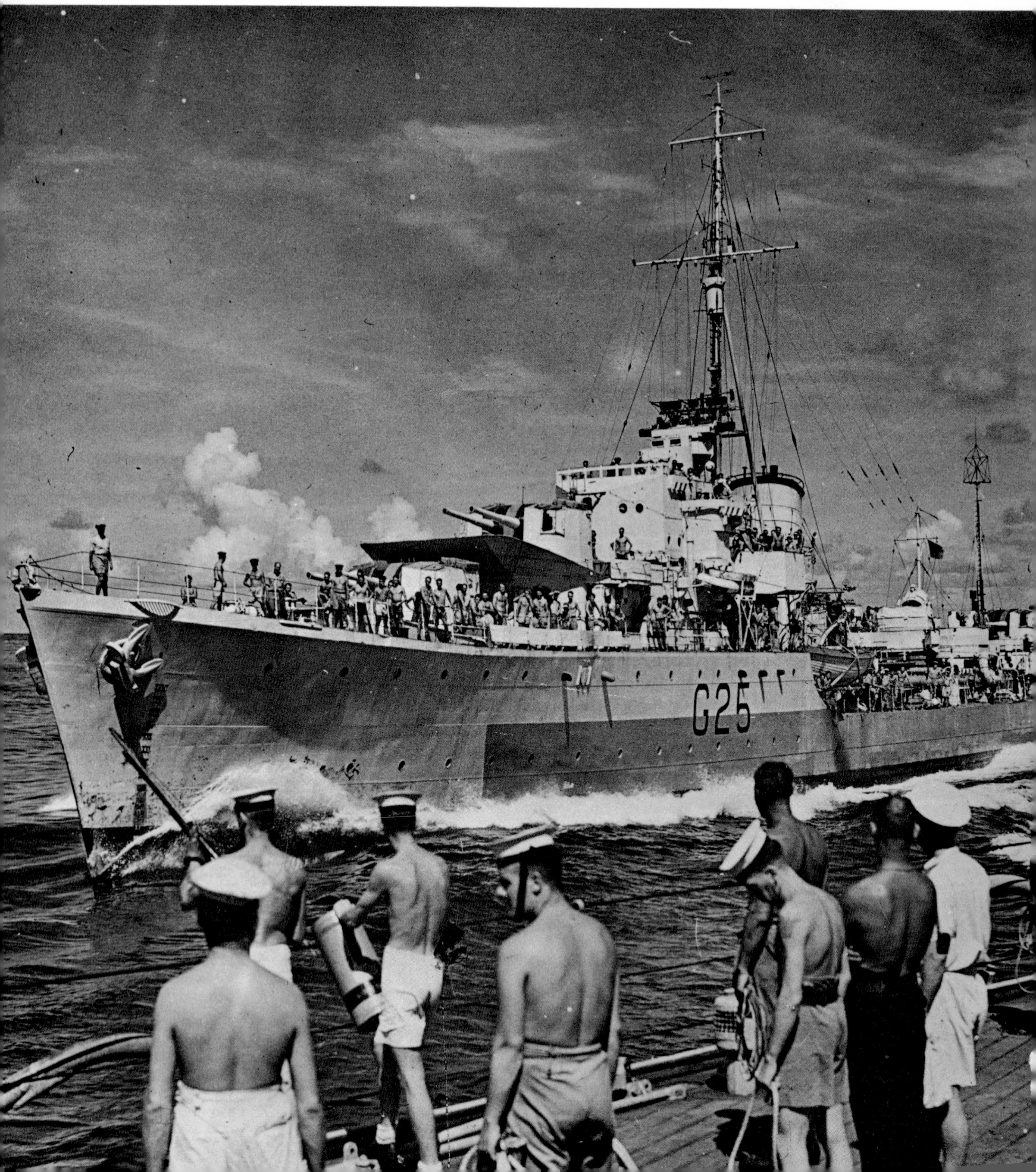

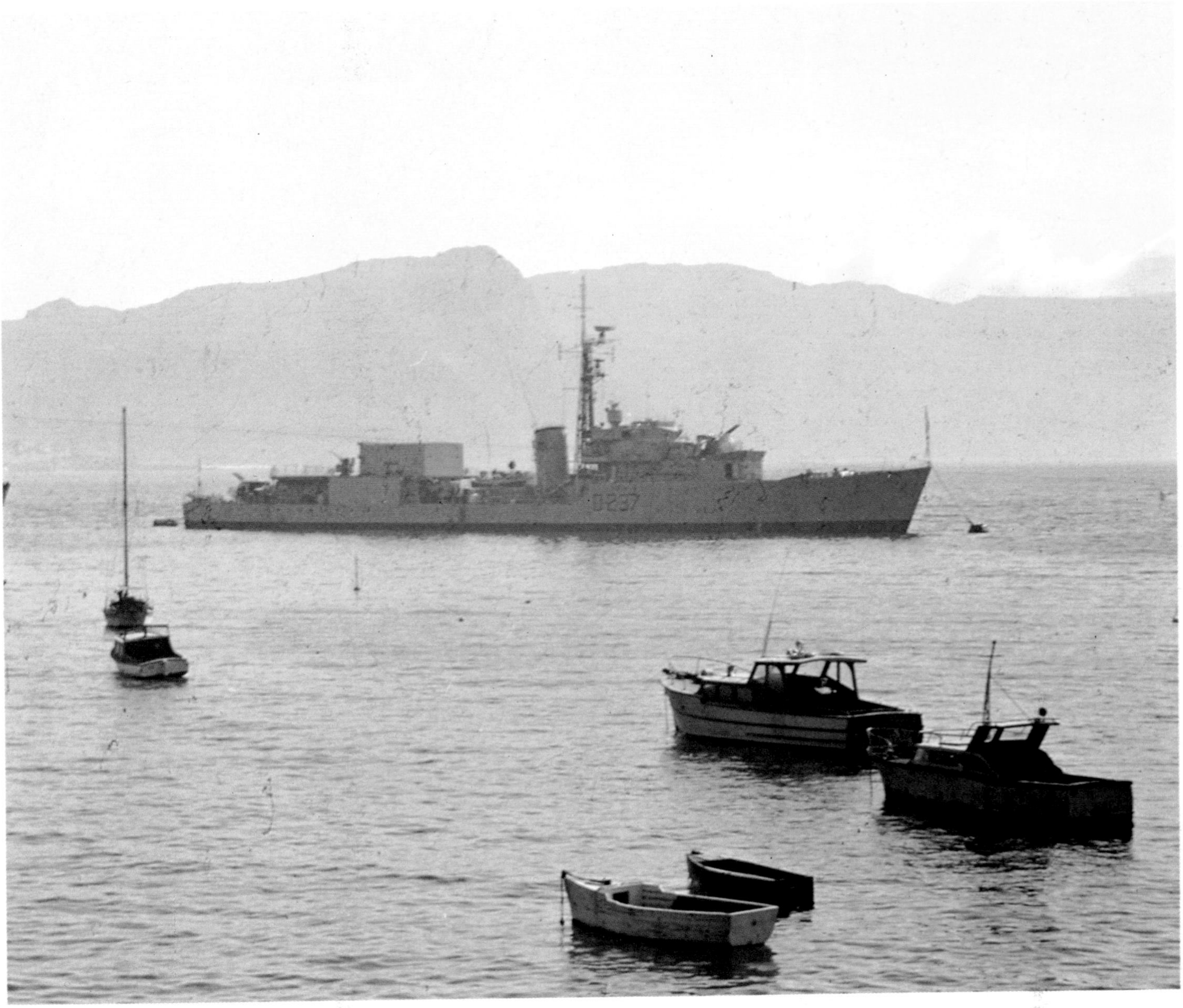

Left: The British destroyer *Norseman* was bombed by German aircraft while building. She was renamed *Nepal* and was the only one of her flotilla to be British manned during the war, her sisters being part of other navies. Here she is seen seen approaching the *Queen Elizabeth* as a seaman prepares to fire a line.

Below: HMS *Onslaught* was one of the first British war-built destroyers to enter service. She is wearing a Western Approaches camouflage scheme but she would normally have the pendant number G04 painted on her side. The single-funnel layout became the trademark of British destroyers and 176 ships were built to the same basic design.

Above: The South African Navy destroyer *Simon van der Stel* is seen at Simonstown. She was converted for anti-submarine work with new four-inch AA guns and a double helicopter hanger aft. This type was not dissimilar to the *Onslaught* and other British destroyers used in the early part of the war.

JAPANESE DESTROYERS

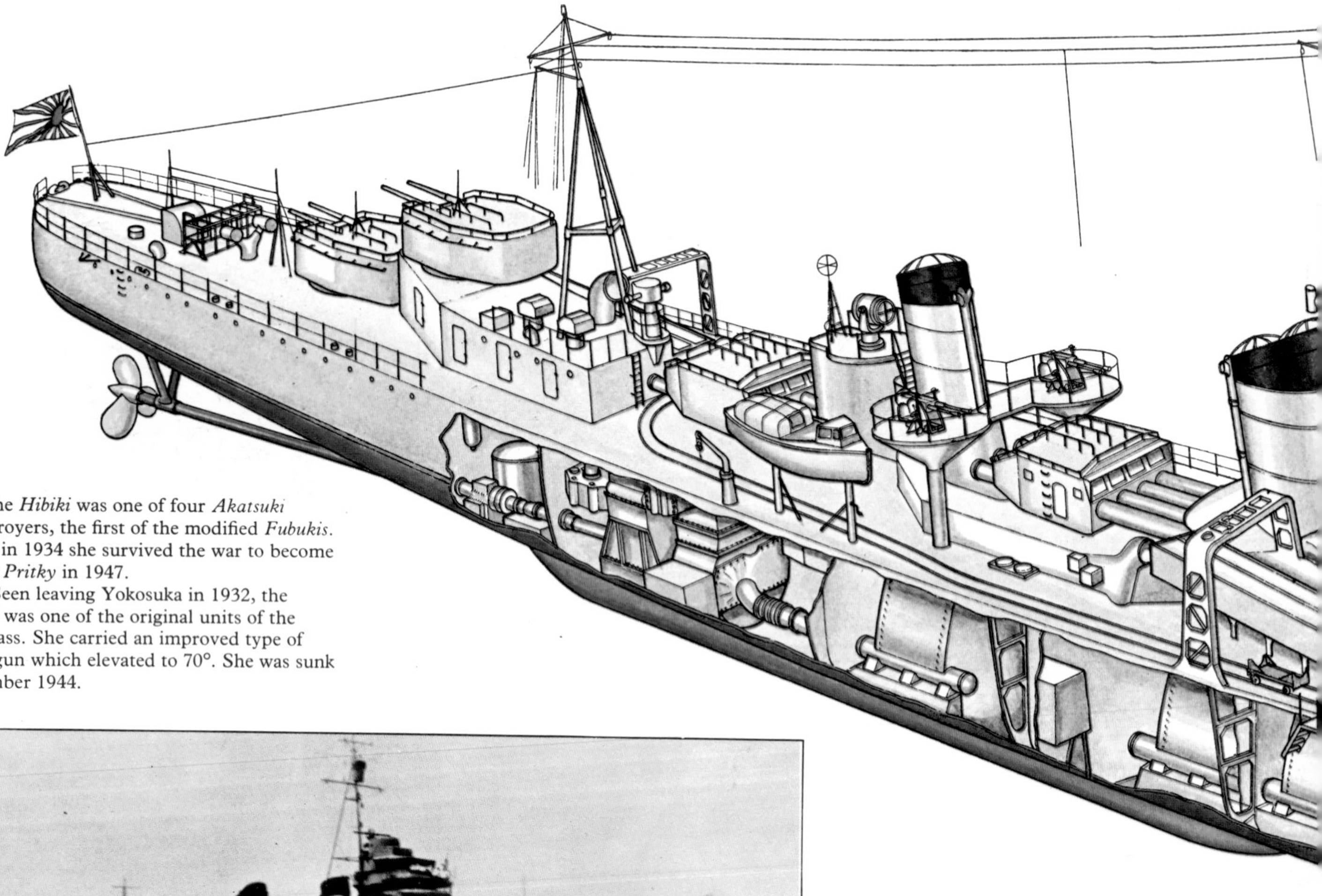

Below: The *Hibiki* was one of four *Akatsuki* Class destroyers, the first of the modified *Fubukis*. Seen here in 1934 she survived the war to become the Soviet *Pritky* in 1947.
Bottom: Seen leaving Yokosuka in 1932, the *Shikinami* was one of the original units of the *Fubuki* Class. She carried an improved type of five-inch gun which elevated to 70°. She was sunk 12 September 1944.

Right: The *Yugiri* was one of the intermediate group of *Fubuki* Class destroyers as was the *Shikinami*. Only one of the 20 *Fubukis* survived the war. Seen here in 1932 leaving Yokosuka, she was sunk 25 November 1943.
Centre right: The *Hatsuyuki* was one of the unmodified *Fubuki* Class destroyers. This photograph was taken in 1929 well before the war. She lost her bows in the heavy storms which overwhelmed the Fourth Fleet in 1935.

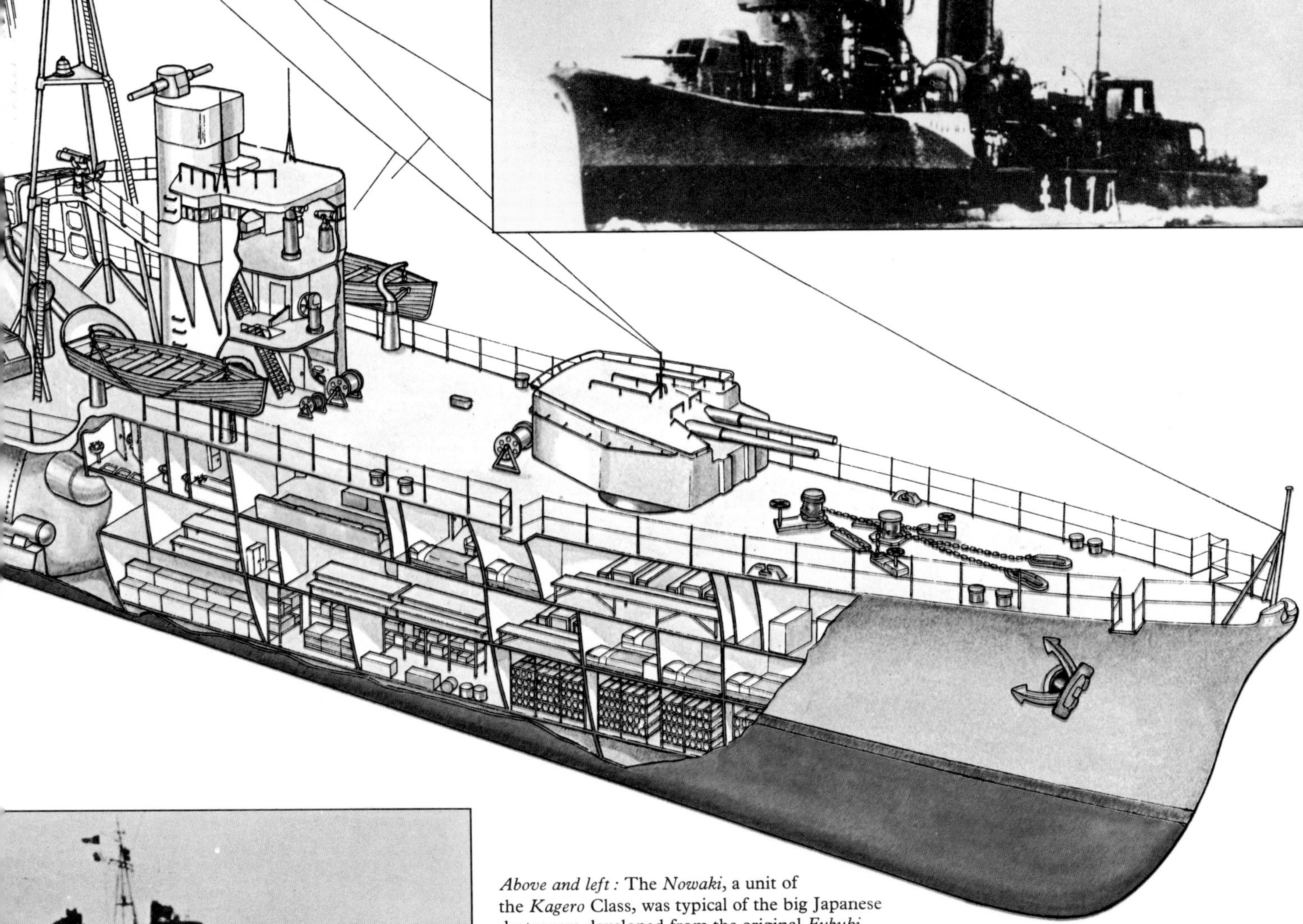

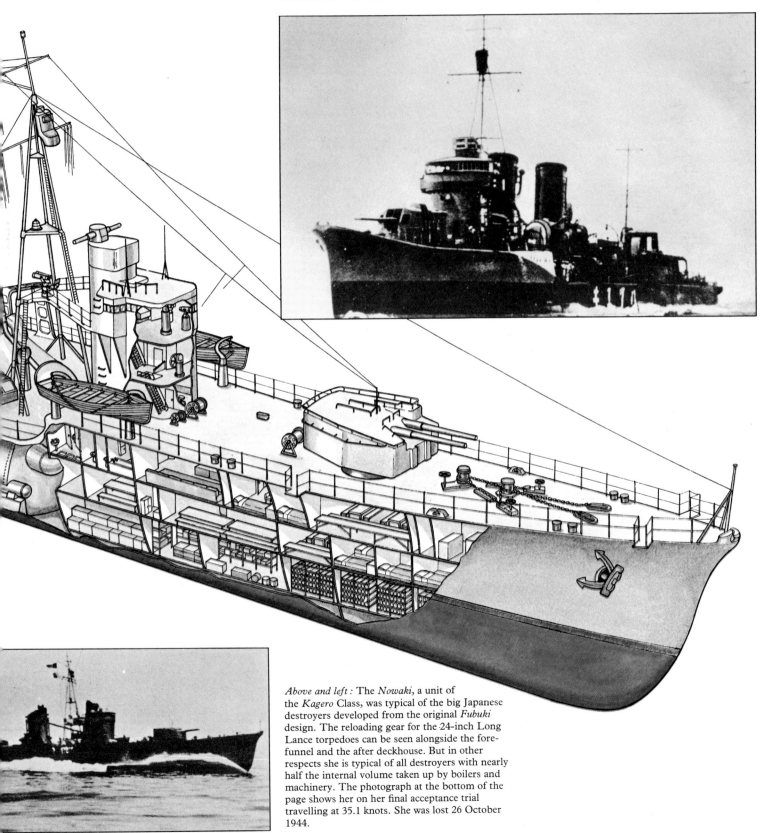

Above and left: The *Nowaki*, a unit of the *Kagero* Class, was typical of the big Japanese destroyers developed from the original *Fubuki* design. The reloading gear for the 24-inch Long Lance torpedoes can be seen alongside the fore-funnel and the after deckhouse. But in other respects she is typical of all destroyers with nearly half the internal volume taken up by boilers and machinery. The photograph at the bottom of the page shows her on her final acceptance trial travelling at 35.1 knots. She was lost 26 October 1944.

AMERICAN DESTROYERS

Left: The USS *O'Bannon* (DD.450) of the *Fletcher* Class was commissioned in March 1942. Looking aft from the forecastle while at sea in 1943, the forward five-inch guns can be seen trained to port. She was not scrapped until 1970.
Right: The USS *Trippe* (DD.403) survived World War II only to be expended as a target at Bikini in 1946 and later scuttled in February 1948. Here she is seen prior to her involvement in World War II, circa 1940.
Below: The destroyer escort *Coates* (DE.685) of the *Rudderow* Class runs her trials in the Caribbean in 1944. Note her triple 21-inch torpedo-tubes abaft the funnel.

Left: *Fletcher* Class destroyers reverted to the flush-decked hull and introduced double reduction geared turbines for greater economy at cruising speeds. This *Fletcher* Class destroyer heads towards the Japanese Home Islands in 1945 in a heavy sea.
Right: A close-up of the *Fletcher* Class, USS *O'Bannon*'s, after-20mm battery on the quarter-deck while at sea in 1943.
Below: The USS *Fletcher* (DD.445) as she was when first commissioned in June 1942. The most noticeable feature is the smooth sheerline and the long deckhouse carrying the capped funnels and torpedo-tubes. As the war progressed the *Fletcher* and her sisters accumulated more 40mm and 20mm AA guns, but otherwise remained unchanged. Even when twin five-inch guns were adopted in the *Allen M Sumner* Class in 1944, the basic *Fletcher* design was retained. The combination of good range, fire power and seaworthiness made the 175 *Fletchers* the best all-round destroyers of World War II.

Bottom left: Authorized in 1940, the *Bristol* Class destroyers followed the design of the *Benson/Livermore* Classes except for armament; the five-inch 38/cal gun at the fore-end of the after shelter deck was omitted so that the light AA armament could be augmented. The USS *Ellyson* was converted to a fast minesweeper (DMS.19) only to become DD.454 once again in 1954. That same year she was sold to the Japanese and renamed the *Asakaze*. In 1970 she became part of the Taiwan Navy. In the background is an escort carrier.

Bottom right: Commissioned DD.737 in 1944, the USS *Shannon* of the *Allen M Sumner* Class was converted in the same year to a fast minelayer (DM.25). Seen here in the centre of the picture, she steams past task forces gathering for the Okinawa operation in April 1945. In the background are USS *Enterprise* (CV.6, far left), *Flint* (CL.97, left) and *Miami* (CL.89, right).

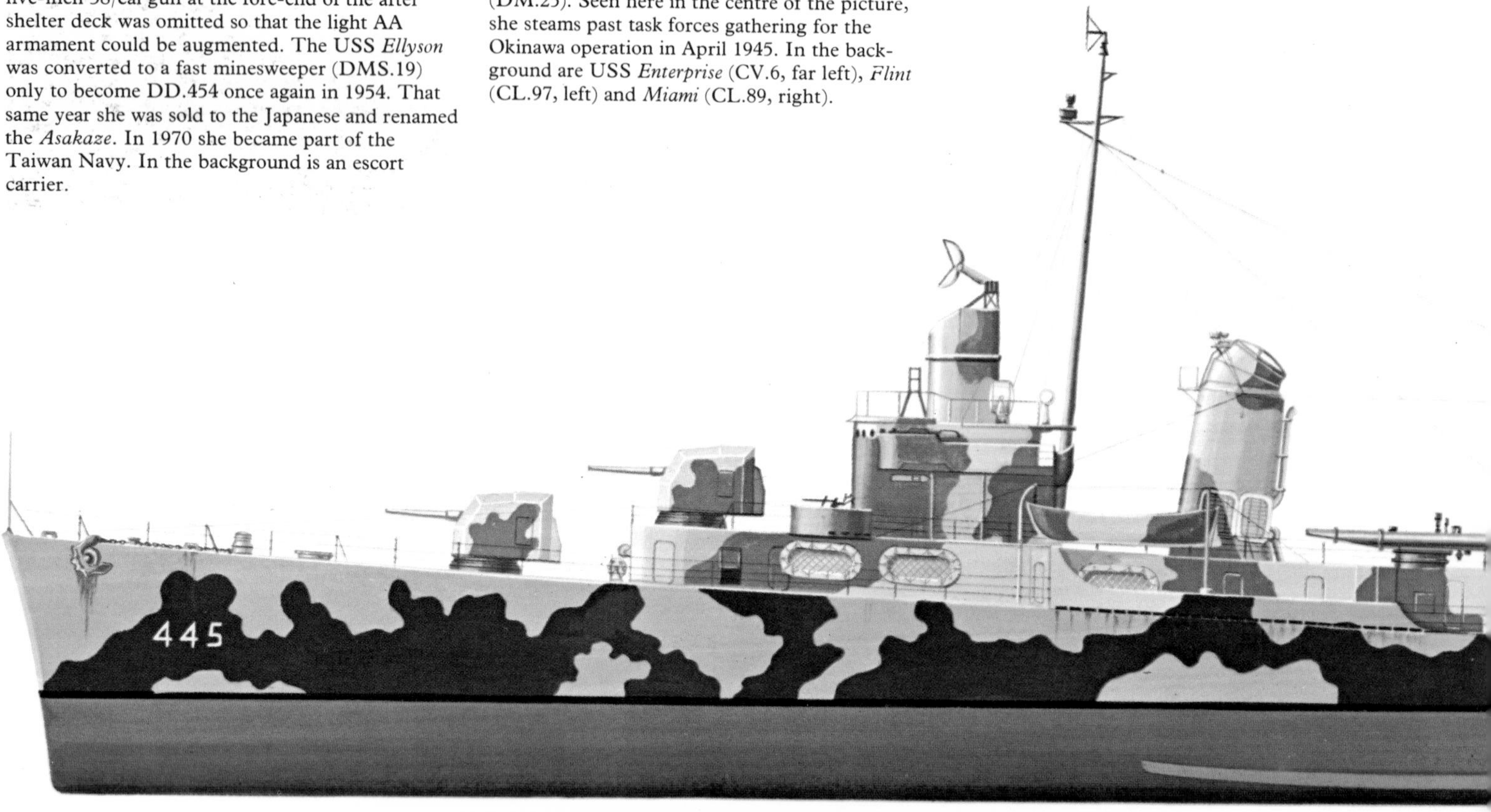

Left: Two LCGs (Landing Craft Gunboat) steam past a *Fletcher* Class destroyer headed for the beach for close-in fire-support for US forces as they stormed Okinawa, 1 April 1945.
Right: Dusk falls over the New York Navy Yard in Brooklyn as a dockside crane swings over a destroyer. For destroyermen in wartime, repairs were often the only chance of leave.
Below: The USS *Buchanan* (DD.484) was launched 22 November 1941. She was photographed in her dappled camouflage scheme from the USS *Wasp* (CV.7) in June 1942. In 1949 she was transferred to the Turkish Navy and was renamed *Gelibolu*.

Above: The crew of the USS *O'Bannon*, a unit of the *Fletcher* Class, takes a dip in the cool waters of Tulagi Harbour, 1943.
Left: Ships of DesRon 23 manoeuvre in the Solomons, 1943/44.
Below: DesRon 3 and DesDiv 6 at San Diego, California in October 1941. Ships are (from inboard) USS *Clark* (DD.361) Squadron Flagship, USS *Case* (DD.370) Division Flagship, USS *Cummings* (DD.365), USS *Shaw* (DD.373) and USS *Tucker* (DD.374).

Above: The USS *Drayton* (DD.366) of the *Mahan* Class was nicknamed 'The Blue Beetle' due to her unusual camouflage. This photo was taken from a Navy Douglas SNJ in 1941 off the West Coast of the USA.

Below: The *Bristol* Class, USS *Edwards* (DD.619), on her shakedown cruise in the Caribbean in 1942. She is wearing a two-tone camouflage scheme.
Bottom left: By the time the US entered World War II, 32 of the *Wickes* Class destroyers had been scrapped and 27 transferred to the Royal Navy in 1940. The USS *Roper* (DD.147), one of five of the Class which were converted into fast transports (APD), is pictured here in 1942 on convoy duty. She was scrapped after the end of the war.
Bottom centre: Chief torpedo-man aboard the USS *O'Bannon* checks her 21-inch quintuple torpedo-tubes before an operation in the Pacific in 1943. Note the personal insignia on the cupola.
Bottom right: Victory markings are applied to the five-inch gun director of a US destroyer. She appears to have conducted a shore-bombardment and destroyed two Japanese fighters and two bombers.

This view of NATO's Standing Naval Force Atlantic (STANAVFORLANT) shows a typical cross-section of modern destroyers and anti-submarine escorts. Front to rear: the Danish frigate *Peder Skram* (F.352), the US guided missile destroyer *Coontz* (DDG.40, ex-DLG.9), the Norwegian frigate or DE *Trondheim* (F.302), the Dutch frigate *Isaac Sweers* (F.814), the Canadian helicopter-destroyer *Huron* (DDH.281), the Portuguese DE *Almirante Magalhaes Correa* (F.474), the British DLG HMS *Norfolk* (D.21) and the German destroyer *Bayern* (D.183).

281
40

Destroyers in the Atlantic 1939-43

The newspapers called it a 'phoney war', but there was nothing artificial about the naval war, which began in earnest only hours after the expiring of the Anglo–French ultimatum to Germany on the morning of 3 September 1939. Two weeks later, on 14 September, the new carrier HMS *Ark Royal* was cruising in the Western Approaches with a hunting group of four destroyers. Suddenly tracks passed close astern of the carrier, as *U.39* fired a salvo of four torpedoes. The destroyers pounced, and their Asdics soon picked up the echo of the U-Boat; after a short hunt the U-Boat was destroyed, the first of many to fall to destroyers. Three days later, however, the carrier *Courageous* was sunk by *U.29* in very similar circumstances, and her destroyers failed to find the attacker.

German destroyers escorted the battle-cruisers *Scharnhorst* and *Gneisenau* on a foray up the Norwegian coast in October, and again in November, but their first big success came in December. On 6 December the *Hans Lody*, *Erich Giese* and *Bernd von Arnim* set out to lay mines off the east coast of England. The *Bernd von Arnim* had to return to base because her boiler-tubes had ruptured, but the other two successfully laid 76 contact and magnetic mines off Cromer. After the lay had been completed the two destroyers headed for home but ran into the British destroyer *Jersey* and hit her with a torpedo. In all, 11 missions were carried out between October 1939 and February 1940, and they accounted for 33 merchant ships sunk, totalling 82,700 tons.

The German destroyers paid a heavy penalty for their advanced steam plant, and in the early months of the war half of them were out of action. Pipe-bursts were common, and the weary stokers got used to donning leather coats, so that they could crawl past the still red-hot fire-bricks to detach the offending pipe. In the *Max Schultz*, steaming hard off the Norwegian coast, the main feed pump became blocked, cutting off steam to the boilers. An alert engineer turned on the emergency pump but as he did so cold sea water caused an explosion in the main turbine. He was scalded so badly that he died later, while a petty officer and two stokers were also injured. In the confusion a bilge-pump valve was left open and the boiler-room began to flood; another engineer braved the steam to close it, but then water short-circuited the electrical switchboard and put the bilge-pumps out of action. The catalogue of disasters was not yet complete, for loss of feedwater was causing the other boilers to lose pressure. Eventually the destroyer lost all power and lay helpless in a Force 9 gale, while two of her sisters tried without

Above: In 1939 half the RN's destroyer strength was made up of ships which should have been scrapped by 1933. HMS *Malcolm* commissioned in 1918 served with distinction until 1945.

success to take her in tow. To complicate matters the flotilla was close to a German minefield, and there was a danger that the crippled destroyer might drift into it.

The *Max Schultz* survived her ordeal, thanks to the exertions of her engine-room complement, who coaxed first one boiler and then a second to produce enough steam to drive the starboard shaft. Other German destroyers reported similar breakdowns, but to be fair, the need for high speed made all destroyers vulnerable to machinery problems. To lie stopped in submarine-infested waters for hours while a major machinery repair was completed must have been worse in some ways than going into battle. One old British destroyer ran a main bearing and had to spend 24 hours hove to in the Bay of Biscay, a notorious haunt of U-Boats.

The German destroyers were involved in a humiliating incident which underlined and exacerbated the poor relations between Navy and Air Force. On 22 February 1940 the 1st Flotilla was steaming in line ahead in the North Sea when it was attacked by aircraft. A bomb hit the *Leberecht Maas* and damaged her, and later a second explosion broke her in two. The rest of the flotilla closed in to rescue survivors but when the *Theodor Riedel* reported a submarine contact on her hydrophones and tried to attack with depth-charges she misjudged her run and the blast damaged her steering. The flotilla was ordered to disperse to start a search for the submarine, and when they returned to the wreck of the *Leberecht Maas* the *Max Schultz* was missing. A prolonged investigation showed that the original attack had been by a 'friendly' Luftwaffe bomber, but the mysterious submarine was never found. The only clue came to light after the war, when British records revealed a large minefield in what the Germans had regarded as a swept channel. The most likely explanation of the disaster is that a German bomb hit the first destroyer, while the subsequent confusion threw out the 1st Flotilla's navigation and allowed it to stray out of the safe area into the British minefield. As the *Max Schultz* was lost with all hands we can only assume that when she blew up her flotilla-mates mistook the explosion for depth-charges. In all 578 officers and men lost their lives in this strange incident.

German ships made frequent use of Norwegian territorial waters, keeping inside the 'Inner Leads' to dodge the British patrols. When it was learned that the oiler *Altmark*, which had been the pocket-battleship *Graf Spee*'s supply-vessel in the South Atlantic, was trying to slip back to Germany with 300 of the *Graf Spee*'s prisoners aboard, the Admiralty decided

Below: HMS *Eskimo* had her bow blown off in the Second Battle of Narvik in April 1940 but she was towed home and repaired.

Above: HMS *Volunteer*, another World War I veteran, served as an escort destroyer in the Battle of the Atlantic.

to stop her. At 2300 on 14 February 1940 HMS *Cossack*, leader of the 4th Destroyer Flotilla, left with two cruisers and four destroyers from Rosyth, bound for Northern Norway. The *Intrepid* was sent in to ask the two old Norwegian torpedo boats escorting the *Altmark* whether she would be permitted to search the German oiler for prisoners. This the senior Norwegian naval officer would not allow, claiming that he had already searched the *Altmark* and had found no prisoners. The *Altmark* slipped into Jössing Fjord, and the Admiralty concluded that the Norwegians had been unable or unwilling to conduct a proper search. A signal to Captain (D) Philip Vian authorized him to board and search the *Altmark*, and so that night the *Cossack* threaded her way up the fjord, a journey which required navigation of the highest order.

When the *Cossack* found her quarry at last, the *Altmark* tried to ram her and the Norwegian torpedo boat *Kjell* tried to intervene. But the *Cossack* dodged them both, and the *Altmark* ran aground. In a stirring echo of the days of Nelson it was 'boarding parties away', and the astonished prisoners battened down in the forward hold were greeted by the shout, 'The Navy's here'. It was only a small incident in what had been up till then a quiet period of the war, but the *Cossack*'s triumphal return to Leith with her decks crowded with liberated prisoners was a well-earned success. To the British it merely confirmed that Norway could do nothing about German infringements of her neutrality, while Hitler saw it as further proof that the British and French intended to invade Norway. One side prepared to lay mines in Norwegian waters while the other prepared a full-scale invasion, and as these measures coincided they ushered in the Norwegian campaign.

Between 5 and 6 April a strong force of British minelaying destroyers and covering forces sailed for Northern Norway. One of the escorting destroyers, HMS *Glowworm*, ran into the German heavy

Below: HMS *Walker*, seen with her convoy in the background, scored a dramatic success in the Spring of 1941 by sinking *U.99* and capturing her commander, K/Lt Otto Kretschmer, the top-scoring U-Boat ace.

Above: The old 'S' Class, like HMS *Scimitar*, were also adapted as Atlantic escorts, with extra depth-charges.

cruiser *Admiral Hipper* off Trondheim, part of the force covering the German invasion. She was sighted by the *Bernd von Arnim*, and being more weatherly she was able to outpace her. But the *Hipper* turned back when she received the sighting report, and she boldly charged through the *Glowworm*'s smoke-screen. Trapped, Commander Roope of HMS *Glowworm* could only do as much damage as possible to his 13,000-ton adversary, and turned at high speed to ram her. She struck the cruiser's starboard bow with a terrible crash and rolled over, crushed by the sheer size and power of the *Hipper* but her forged steel stem ripped open 120 feet of plating. The shattered wreck of the *Glowworm* sank, leaving only 39 dazed survivors in the water, but the *Hipper* had 500 tons of water on board and as soon as her troops were ashore she had to be sent back to Germany for repairs. When the details of the *Glowworm*'s exploit became known in 1945 Roope was awarded a posthumous Victoria Cross.

German destroyers played an important part in the seizure of Narvik on 9 April 1940. With a mixture of treachery and bluff ten of them entered the fjord to land troops, and parleyed with the Norwegian ships defending the harbour. Commodore Bonte's flagship, the *Wilhelm Heidkamp*, broke off negotiations and without warning fired two torpedoes into the old coast defence battleship *Eidsvold*; a few minutes later the *Bernd von Arnim* put seven more into her sister *Norge*. But Bonte's flotilla was not to be allowed long to savour its easy victory, for the British 2nd Destroyer Flotilla was already on its way, four 'H' Class boats led by Captain Bernard Warburton-Lee in the flotilla leader *Hardy*. Warburton-Lee knew that Narvik was in German hands, and had decided to attack the transports, but he only knew of six destroyers, rather than the ten which were there. The weather was atrocious, with continuous snow squalls and poor visibility, but it allowed the five destroyers to reach Narvik at 0400 on 10 April without being spotted.

At 0430 three of the destroyers swept into action, taking the Germans completely by surprise. No sooner had the alarm sounded than a torpedo hit the *Wilhelm Heidkamp*, killing the Commodore and sinking her. Two more torpedoes blew the *Anton Schmidt* in half and shells damaged the *Diether von Roeder* and *Hans Lüdemann*. All five destroyers came in a second time and shot up the transports, but a third attack ran out of luck. Lieutenant-Commander Erich Bey had been given sufficient warning to get his three destroyers out of the neighbouring Herjangs Fjord, while further down the main fjord Lieutenant-Commander Fritz Berger brought out the remaining two to cut off the British retreat. Warburton-Lee's destroyers were now caught between two fires. A five-inch shell wrecked the *Hardy*'s bridge and killed Warburton-Lee, and the ship ran aground out of control. The *Hunter* was also sunk and the *Hotspur* badly damaged, but the *Hostile* and *Havock* turned back to support their flotilla-mates. The Ger-

Above: The Captain and a group of officers and ratings of HMS *Vañoc* in 1943, 25 years after the ship commissioned.

man destroyers were also being hit, and were unable to prevent the crippled *Hotspur* from escaping. Even though two British destroyers had been sunk Warburton-Lee's attack had sealed the fate of the eight German destroyers left at Narvik. On the way down the fjord HMS *Havock* sank an ammunition ship bringing five-inch shells for the flotilla, and as they had fired away nearly all their ammunition and torpedoes in the occupation of the port and the destroyer action they were unable to face further action with any hope of success.

On 13 April the blow fell. Vice-Admiral Whitworth, flying his flag in the battleship *Warspite*, was ordered to recapture Narvik and wipe out the remaining enemy destroyers. Taking nine destroyers with her the battleship thrust up Narvik Fjord, with her floatplane reconnoitring for the destroyers and using her 15-inch guns with terrible effect. The destroyer *Eskimo* had her bows blown off by a torpedo but all eight of the German flotilla were sunk. The two Battles of Narvik did more than finish off the destroyers which had taken Narvik; with ten destroyers sunk, the *Kriegsmarine* destroyer strength was now reduced to nine vessels, and in the precarious months after Dunkirk, when the German Naval Staff was asked to support the Army's Sealion invasion plan, lack of destroyers to screen the big ships was one of the most crucial problems. Three of these were still under repair in August 1940, leaving only six destroyers to face the Royal Navy in the English Channel.

Destroyers at Dunkirk

The evacuation of the British Expeditionary Force from Dunkirk could not have been achieved without destroyers. It is always described as an epic of the 'little ships', but the facts are that destroyers lifted 103,399 men out of the total of 338,226, followed closely by the 'personnel ships', high-capacity cross-Channel ferries. The reason was that destroyers could make a two-way passage between Dunkirk and Dover at high speed, and so reduce the 'turn round' time to a minimum. The destroyers also played an important role in securing the flanks of the beach-head, guarding against attacks by German *schnellboote* (motor torpedo boats) and firing at formations of troops and armour on shore.

On 20 May 1940 the Admiralty warned Vice-Admiral Ramsay at Dover that his command might have to evacuate the BEF, the first hint of disaster. During the following days destroyers carried troops across to Calais and Boulogne to secure these ports for the evacuation. It was nearly too late, and at Boulogne the *Keith* and *Whitshed* had to run the gauntlet of machine-gun fire while embarking stretcher-cases from the dockside. The *Venetia* was hit by an artillery shell, which wiped out a gun crew and wounded everyone on the bridge, and ran aground, but she extricated herself. Then the *Wild Swan*, which had followed her into the harbour, sighted a column of enemy tanks making its way down a side street towards the quay. Here at last was a worthwhile target for a destroyer's high-velocity guns, and a direct hit knocked out the leading tank and blocked the street. An even more rash attack was made by a motor cycle detachment, which fanned out across the quay, apparently in the belief that the destroyer *Venomous* could be attacked with infantry weapons because she was immobile. The two pom-poms were meant to fire at aircraft, but they made lethal anti-personnel weapons. When the *Vimiera* left at 0245 on 24 May she was carrying 1400 Belgian, British and French troops, the last defenders to escape from Boulogne.

Although Ramsay hoped to be able to rescue the defenders of Calais, the Brigade of Guards had been told to fight to the end. This left only Dunkirk in Allied hands, and on Saturday 26 May at 1857 Ramsay ordered the start of Operation Dynamo. At first destroyers were restricted to escorting the personnel ships, Dutch *schuyts* and coasters which had been pressed into service, but next day, when it was learned that Belgium had surrendered, every ship was sent in. On 28 May when Ramsay learned that Dunkirk harbour was still usable, the figures of men being brought out rose sharply. Eleven more destroyers were lent to Ramsay and they provided a welcome boost; by midnight 17,804 men had been lifted, and in some instances destroyers had carried as many as 900 men at a time.

Next day the Germans realized what was happening, and the scale of attacks increased. The *Wakeful* and *Grafton* were zigzagging at 20 knots, on their way to Dover with their decks crowded with soldiers, when a torpedo hit the *Wakeful* amidships. She broke in two and sank in 15 seconds, trapping hundreds of soldiers between decks, and while the *Grafton*, two fishing vessels and a minesweeper tried to pick up survivors two more torpedoes hit the *Grafton*. One of the rescuers, the trawler *Comfort*, had circled out of sight in the darkness, and when she loomed out of the darkness the gun-crews of the dying *Grafton* and the minesweeper *Lydd* mistook her for the *schnellboot* which had fired the torpedoes. A hail of fire wiped out most of her crew and the soldiers on board, and then the *Lydd* rammed her at full speed. The tragedy cost the lives of a thousand or more sailors and soldiers, but in view of the opportunities presented for attacks by enemy torpedo craft it is only remarkable that other disasters did not occur. In all six British and eight French destroyers were lost in the fall of France, and scores were damaged. The evacuation of other troops from the Biscay ports continued until 23 June, and destroyers played an equally important part – a final total of 338,226 men reached England.

Destroyers-for-Bases

The Royal Navy had 162 destroyers left after the evacuation from France but only 74 of these were undamaged. The British Prime Minister had already asked the United States' President to consider lending 50 of the old flush-deckers to tide the RN over until its big building programme began to produce new destroyers in 1941, but now destroyers were desperately needed to fight off the threatened invasion of the British Isles. On 5 September the two governments agreed to the exchange: 50 old destroyers in return for a 99-year lease on British bases abroad. Captain Taprell Dorling ('Taffrail') is credited with the happy idea of naming the ships after towns common to the USA and the United Kingdom, but to the RN they were always known as the 'four-pipers'. They were delivered to the Canadian base at Halifax, Nova Scotia, and there they were commissioned into the RN. The RCN took seven, and apart from HMCS *Annapolis*, they took the

Below: HMS *Havant*, one of six destroyers building for Brazil, is seen on 3 May 1940 a month before she was sunk by German bombs off the Dunkirk beaches.

Far left: The four distinctive funnels of an ex-US flush-decked destroyer in the Atlantic in the winter of 1940.
Right: Four-inch gun crew stands by, ready to load the forecastle gun in a flush-decker.
Below: HMS *Churchill*, originally the US Navy's *Herndon*, was launched 31 May 1919. She became the Soviet Navy's *Deiatelnyi* in 1944/45 and was credited with torpedoing the German submarine *U.956* in the Arctic in January 1945.

names of common rivers rather than towns.

The Admiralty was not over-impressed by the flush-deckers' stability, and as they were in any case intended for escort work they were soon taken in hand for re-armament. Out came half the 12 torpedo-tubes and two of the four four-inch guns. This automatically provided a reserve of ammunition and torpedoes and made room for a big increase in depth-charges and throwers aft. They were a puzzle to British destroyermen, for the crew's quarters were divided between forward and aft, and the officers and Chief Petty Officers messed forward. This arrangement allowed bridge personnel to be relieved during long periods of bad weather, but the galley was in a deck-house on the upper deck, and it was often too dangerous to approach when waves broke across the decks. One feature was never liked by their British and Canadian crewmen: the bunks proved far more uncomfortable than the traditional ham-

Top left: A flush-decker on patrol in the North Atlantic in the Winter of 1940. The port Hotchkiss machine gun is silhouetted against the setting sun.
Top right: The captain wears a duffle coat as protection against the bitter cold.
Below: Two ships of an Atlantic convoy seen over the port two-pounder anti-aircraft pompom in the destroyer *Vanoc*.

Above: 'Away sea-boat's crew'. Boats were used for rescue work and for boarding other ships.

Above: Torpedoes were stowed in their tubes, but could be partially extracted for routine maintenance.

mocks, and the officers complained so bitterly about their 'soft ride' inner-spring mattresses that the Admiralty had to replace them with thin hair mattresses.

Despite the grumbles the British and Canadians achieved a lot with their flush-deckers. Several accounted for the sinking of U-Boats in the Battle of the Atlantic and on 28 March 1942 the *Campbeltown* (ex-USS *Buchanan*) blew up the giant Normandie dock at St Nazaire to deny it to the battleship *Tirpitz*. Eight were lost, including one lent to the Soviet Navy in 1944. Towards the end of the war they were reduced to humbler duties, often serving as training ships or aircraft targets. One of the last to survive was the *Leamington* (ex-USS *Twiggs*), which lay forgotten in a Welsh harbour until 1951, when she was spotted by a film unit wanting to make a film of the raid on St Nazaire. She re-enacted the role of her sister *Campbeltown*, which had penetrated the river leading to the Normandie dock, with two of her distinctive funnels removed and the remaining two cut down to make her look like a German torpedo boat.

The Battle of the Atlantic was the most gruelling test for destroyers, whether ancient flush-deckers and 'V & Ws' or the latest fleet destroyers. The winter conditions varied from grim to fearful, and tested human endurance to its limits. Although destroyers were effective submarine hunters they were far from ideal for the task. Even in normal weather they were lively, and would 'roll on wet grass'; in foul weather their slim bows tended to plough through waves rather than lift to them, so that they were battered far more than the tubby little corvettes and trawlers. Life under such conditions was endured but nothing more, and the only consolation was that the U-Boats were equally hampered by bad weather.

Maintaining full speed was out of the question, for the destroyer would begin to pitch heavily, flinging her bows out of the water and then plunging down again. Green seas would break over the forecastle and drench the bridge with spray, soaking charts and stinging faces like hail. Even the most experienced sailors were liable to seasickness, and as often as not there would be someone heaving over a bucket in a corner. Down below, life would be even nastier, with trickles of water finding their way into cabins and mess-decks, and anything movable such as books working their way onto the deck, to lie in the water sloshing to and fro. Convoys to Northern Russia were the worst, for in the Arctic winter temperatures were so low that spray quickly froze and formed tons of topweight on the upperworks. Destroyers drew compara-

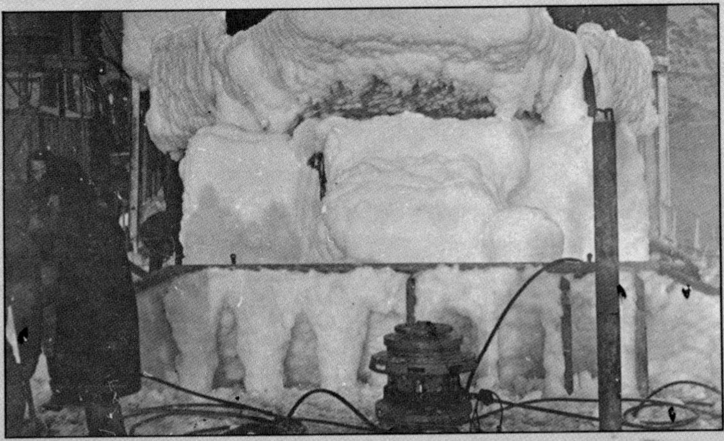

Left: The forecastle party ensures that the anchor is correctly hoisted and stowed.
Below left: Convoys in the Arctic were even more hazardous for destroyers than those in the North Atlantic as icing added tons of top-weight.
Below: HMS *Vimiera* was one of several old 'V & W' destroyers converted with anti-aircraft guns for escort work. Known as 'Wairs', most of them served on the East coast of England and Scotland.

tively little water, and as they ran low on fuel the excess topweight made them tender, and there was always the risk of being 'pooped' by a following sea. Added to this was the knowledge that a man would last no more than two minutes in the water, with the temperature in the Arctic often below freezing point.

Living conditions in the older destroyers were particularly bad, for the increase in anti-aircraft and anti-submarine weapons and radar meant a big increase in complement, to provide gun-crews and technicians. Twenty of the old 'V & Ws' were earmarked for modernization in 1938, and during their conversion to escorts with anti-aircraft guns the opportunity was taken to provide electric heating, asbestos lagging and lining for the deckheads and bulkheads. Ventilation needed to be improved to cope with the damp, and drying rooms were provided to give men a chance to dry their clothing. But many other destroyers went to war without these refinements and had to wait until a major refit before anything could be done. In 1942 there was an investigation into the tough conditions in RN destroyers, and it was revealed that in some cases complements had risen from the pre-war 134 to as many as 160–170. In the 'V & Ws' the upper mess-deck, designed for 43, now accommodated 60–65 ratings. To compensate for the appalling overcrowding the Admiralty reintroduced the old 'hard-lying money',

Above: Hvalfjord in Iceland was used as a base to allow escorts to accompany convoys further westwards. HMS *Vanoc* is seen in this anchorage.

Below: A cloud of seagulls hovers expectantly over HMS *Vega* as she picks up her moorings.

Above left: A battered HMS *Valorous* passes under the stern of a merchantman in an East coast convoy.
Above: HMS *Georgetown*, formerly USS *Maddox*, shows her slim lines in this overhead view taken in May 1943.

Above: A depth-charge salvo dropped by HMS *Skate*, the oldest British destroyer to serve in World War II.

a small extra pay allowance for ratings serving in 'V & W' and ex-US 'Town' Class destroyers. Hard-lying money was payable between 1 October and 31 March each year, and it remained in force until 1945.

With their powerful turbines destroyers could never achieve high endurance, and as the U-Boats moved westwards into the Atlantic destroyers found it very difficult to stay with a convoy. Replenishment under way from a tanker was done whenever possible but tankers themselves were so precious that few could be spared for this job. A convoy escort used far more fuel than the merchantmen in her convoy, for she had to chase underwater contacts or round up stragglers and then steam at high speed to catch up with her charges. The answer was to build a new type of high-endurance escort known as the frigate, but several of the 'V & W' Class and the flush-deckers were refitted as Long Range Escorts. This involved the removal of the forward boiler (two in the case of the flush-deckers) to allow the installation of an extra fuel tank. The 'V & Ws' looked particularly odd, with the short funnel set well back from the bridge, but the additional 80 tons of oil gave them about 800 miles more endurance. The upper part of the stokehold was also used to extend accommodation, which relieved pressure on space. Despite losing a third of their power these 'long-leggers' could still steam at 25 knots, enough speed for escort work.

The Norwegian Campaign of 1940 showed that destroyers were very vulnerable to air attack, with far too weak an anti-aircraft armament. All British destroyers sacrificed their after bank of torpedo-tubes for a three-inch or four-inch AA gun, but the 'Tribals' were given a twin four-inch AA mounting in place of one of the after 4.7-inch low-angle mountings. The older destroyers also lost the after gun in exchange for more depth-charges and throwers. The older escort destroyers initially sacrificed their remaining torpedo-tubes, but these were put back in 1942 so that they could fire an awesome weapon known as the one-ton depth-charge. This super-charge was designed to attack deep-diving U-Boats,

Below: The old flush-decker HMS *Clare* lost her distinctive silhouette in 1941 when two boilers were replaced by extra fuel tanks, turning her into a Long Range Escort.

Top left: Loading a 4.7-inch gun aboard HMS *Hesperus*.
Top right: Long Range Escort *Watchman* in 1942.
Above: The after four-inch high-angle guns and depth-charge throwers of the 'Wair' HMS *Wolfhound*.

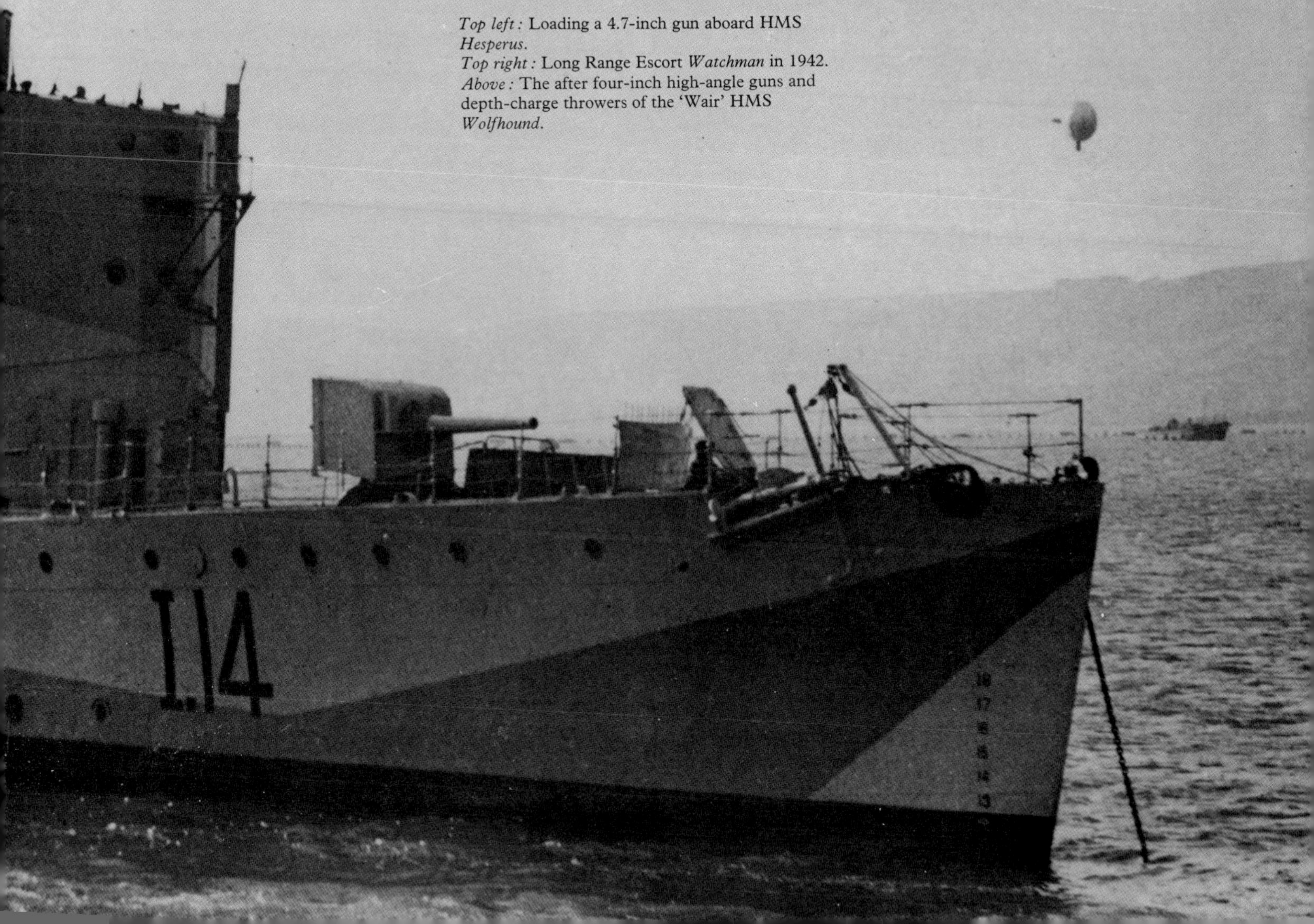

Above: USS *Gleaves* skirts the pack ice on her way to Argentia, the Canadian escort base. American destroyers began escorting North Atlantic convoys in the Summer of 1941.

and was shaped to allow rapid sinking; as long as it was dropped at a speed of 11 knots or more its 2000lbs of high explosive would probably not blow off the destroyer's stern. On occasions it was even used by a stationary destroyer against a U-Boat at 900 feet or more. The foremost gun was often replaced by a 'Hedgehog' multiple spigot mortar capable of throwing 32lb bombs ahead of the ship. The 24 Hedgehog bombs were impact-fuzed and a single hit was sufficient to sink a U-Boat.

US Destroyers in the Atlantic

The transfer of 50 destroyers to the RN in 1940 was only the beginning of the United States' involvement in World War II. In March 1941 the Lend–Lease Bill was enacted to allow more warships to be 'lent' to the RN to ease the shortage of escorts. In April the Defence Zone, in which US freighters could be escorted regardless of whether they were carrying war material to Britain or not, was extended to longitude 26° West. In the middle of the year the US Government took responsibility for guaranteeing the 'neutrality' of Iceland by putting American troops in place of the British and Canadians who had been there for a year. As Iceland was used by British and Canadian warships for refuelling there was now the likelihood of a U-Boat mistaking a USN destroyer for a hostile escort. The flush-decker's distinctive silhouette was common to both Navies, and the latest *Benson* and *Bristol* Classes were similar in general build and layout to the British 'A to I' types.

From the Spring of 1941 three destroyer squadrons were operating in the North Atlantic, DesRons 7, 30 and 31. The first 'hostile' action seems to have been an attack on a sonar contact by the destroyer *Niblack* in April, but the first serious provocation was the '*Greer* Incident' on 4 September 1941. The old flush-decker belonged to DesRon 30 but was proceeding independently, carrying supplies and mail to Reykjavik, when a British maritime patrol aircraft signalled to her to warn her that a U-Boat had been sighted ten miles ahead. The *Greer* slowed down to allow her sonar operator to track the U-Boat, purely as a precaution, but one which was inevitably taken by the U-Boat to mean that the *Greer* was hunting her. For nearly four hours the destroyer tracked the U-Boat, during which time the British patrol plane dropped four depth-charges. Eventually the U-Boat commander, exasperated at what he regarded as highly 'un-neutral' tactics, fired a torpedo. To this the *Greer* replied by dropping depth-charges, but when it was clear that the U-Boat had escaped she continued on her way to Iceland. The outcome was that US warships were given clear instructions to defend shipping in the North Atlantic, the 'shoot on sight' order which permitted USN escorts to attack German or Italian submarines.

The next incident was more serious, for on 17 October the new destroyer *Kearny* (DD.432) was torpedoed by *U.568*. Once again the US destroyers were hopelessly mixed up with British, Canadian and even Free French escorts, all trying to cope with a Canadian convoy which had been heavily attacked by a wolf-pack. It was about 0200 and she had just dropped depth-charges (US destroyers were permitted to drop charges to 'embarrass' or frighten off U-Boats). In the intermittent glare from a burning tanker the U-Boat fired a spread of three torpedoes, and one of these caught the *Kearny* in the forward fire-room. There was a tremendous explosion, which tore up the deck and killed or scalded to death 11 men and wounded 24 more. The ship had been at battle stations, so the flooding could be contained as long as the forward fire-room bulkhead held up under the strain.

The *Benson*s were the first destroyers built with machinery on the 'unit' system, with turbines and boilers alternated to reduce the risk of the entire steam plant being knocked out by one hit, and the *Kearny*'s experience showed how important it was in enabling destroyers to withstand action damage. Certainly the unit system saved the *Kearny*, and she was able to limp to Iceland under her own power, escorted by the *Greer*. There she was secured alongside the repair ship *Vulcan* and patched up for the journey back to a proper repair yard. Longevity in destroyers is largely a matter of luck, but the *Kearny* was one of the last of her class to remain in the Reserve Fleet, and was not stricken until 1971.

The old four-stacker *Reuben James* (DD.245) was not so lucky. Exactly two weeks after the torpedoing of the *Kearny* she was escorting an eastbound convoy near the 'Momp' or Mid-Ocean Meeting Point at which US destroyers handed over convoys to British and Canadian escorts. Just before dawn on 31 October she was torpedoed on the port side, and her entire fore-part disappeared in a massive explosion. Evidently the forward four-inch magazine had detonated, because all that was left of the *Reuben James* was the after-part from the fourth funnel to the stern. The shattered remnants of the hull stayed afloat for about five minutes, and as it sank the depth-charges exploded killing many of the survivors. More than two-thirds of her complement, including her captain, were killed or drowned, but even this was not enough to end isolationism in the United States. President Roosevelt immediately sought approval from Congress to transfer the Coast Guard to the control of the Navy, and within two weeks further amendments to the Neutrality Act were passed, but it was to take Pearl Harbor to convince Americans that World War II had arrived.

Paradoxically, once the United States was at war with Germany the confrontations between US destroyers and U-Boats in the Atlantic diminished. The reason was simply that destroyers were

Right: Members of the crew of the destroyer *Kearny* (DD.432) inspect the hole in her deck caused by a U-Boat's torpedo off Iceland.

desperately needed for the Pacific, and so it was agreed that the main contribution to the Battle of the Atlantic would be maritime aircraft for the RAF and destroyer escorts (DEs) for the Royal Navy. The destroyers earmarked for Atlantic duties were more urgently needed to convoy troopships to the British Isles, but in August 1942 the *Emmons* and *Rodman* escorted the cruiser *Tuscaloosa* to North Russia. In September 1942 a South Atlantic Force of four old light cruisers and eight destroyers was created, to protect Brazilian shipping against U-Boats, and some of the old destroyers operated in the Caribbean to cope with the U-Boats' *Paukenschlag* ('Drumroll') offensive against American shipping.

Destroyers against the *Bismarck* and *Scharnhorst*

In the last week of May 1941 the 4th Flotilla of the Home Fleet, comprising four 'Tribals', the *Cossack*, *Maori*, *Sikh* and *Zulu* and the Polish *Piorun* (ex-HMS *Nerissa*) was escorting a troop convoy when the news came that the German battleship *Bismarck* had broken out through the Denmark Strait, and had sunk the battlecruiser HMS *Hood* and shaken off the battleship *Prince of Wales* and two shadowing cruisers. On 26 May Captain Vian was ordered to join the Home Fleet, but when he intercepted a PBY Catalina's sighting report he altered course for the *Bismarck* on his own initiative, with the intention of slowing her down by torpedo attack.

Taking station on the cruiser *Sheffield*, which was in radar contact with the *Bismarck*, Vian led his destroyers through heavy seas to take up positions for a night attack. So bad were conditions that his own leader, HMS *Cossack*, and her next astern, the *Maori*, were swung right around at a speed of 26 knots. The two destroyers missed one another by a matter of feet, and found that they had changed places in the line, but in the heat of the moment nobody paused to draw breath. At about 2200 the massive bulk of the *Bismarck* was sighted by the *Piorun*, silhouetted by the flash of her own guns. Vian wanted his destroyers to box her in before launching a co-ordinated attack, but the weather was so bad that even when easing down to 18 knots the lookouts were blinded by spray. There was no moon either so Vian decided to allow his

Centre right: The *Kearny* is lashed alongside the repair ship USS *Vulcan* (AR.5) off Reykjavik in October 1941.

Right: The USS *Reuben James* (DD.245) was the first US destroyer to be sunk in World War II. This photo was taken in April 1939.

Left : USS *Bainbridge* (DD.246) returns a rescued Navy pilot to the escort carrier *Santee* in July 1943.
Right : Hunting the *Bismark*.
Bottom right : Lt Charles H Hutchins receives the Navy Cross after his gallant action in command of the USS *Borie*.
Below : The *Alden* (DD.211) lifts to the Atlantic swell while on Atlantic convoy duty in January 1944.

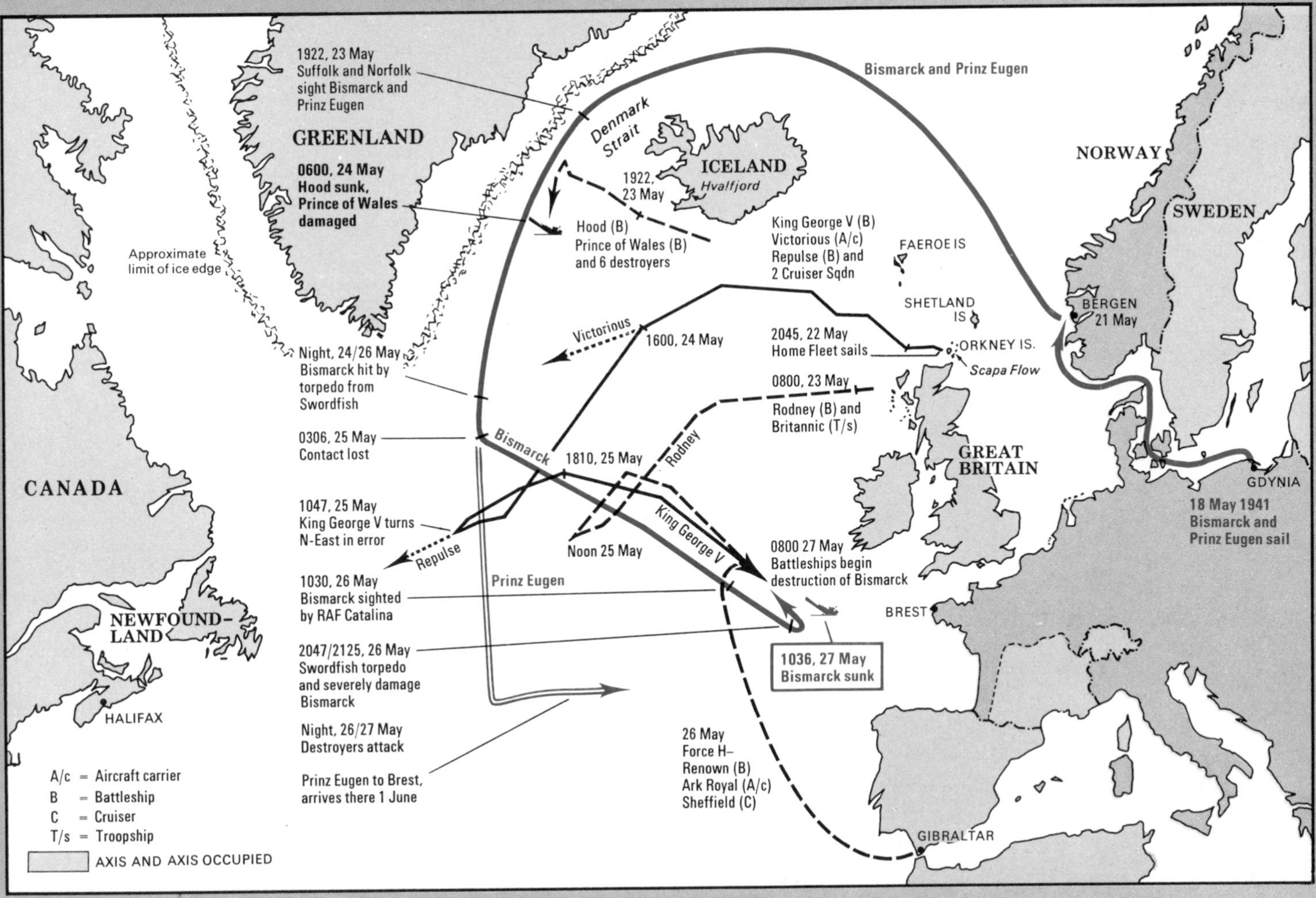
1922, 23 May
Suffolk and Norfolk sight Bismarck and Prinz Eugen
Bismarck and Prinz Eugen
GREENLAND
Denmark Strait
0600, 24 May Hood sunk, Prince of Wales damaged
1922, 23 May
ICELAND
Hvalfjord
Hood (B)
Prince of Wales (B)
and 6 destroyers
King George V (B)
Victorious (A/c)
Repulse (B) and
2 Cruiser Sqdn
NORWAY
SWEDEN
FAEROE IS
Approximate limit of ice edge
SHETLAND IS
BERGEN 21 May
Victorious
1600, 24 May
2045, 22 May
Home Fleet sails
ORKNEY IS.
Scapa Flow
Night, 24/26 May Bismarck hit by torpedo from Swordfish
0800, 23 May
Rodney (B) and
Britannic (T/s)
0306, 25 May
Contact lost
Bismarck
Rodney
GREAT BRITAIN
1810, 25 May
CANADA
GDYNIA
18 May 1941
Bismarck and Prinz Eugen sail
1047, 25 May
King George V turns N-East in error
Repulse
Noon 25 May
King George V
0800 27 May
Battleships begin destruction of Bismarck
Prinz Eugen
1030, 26 May
Bismarck sighted by RAF Catalina
BREST
NEWFOUND-LAND
2047/2125, 26 May
Swordfish torpedo and severely damage Bismarck
1036, 27 May
Bismarck sunk
HALIFAX
Night, 26/27 May
Destroyers attack
Prinz Eugen to Brest, arrives there 1 June
26 May
Force H–
Renown (B)
Ark Royal (A/c)
Sheffield (C)
A/c = Aircraft carrier
B = Battleship
C = Cruiser
T/s = Troopship
AXIS AND AXIS OCCUPIED
GIBRALTAR

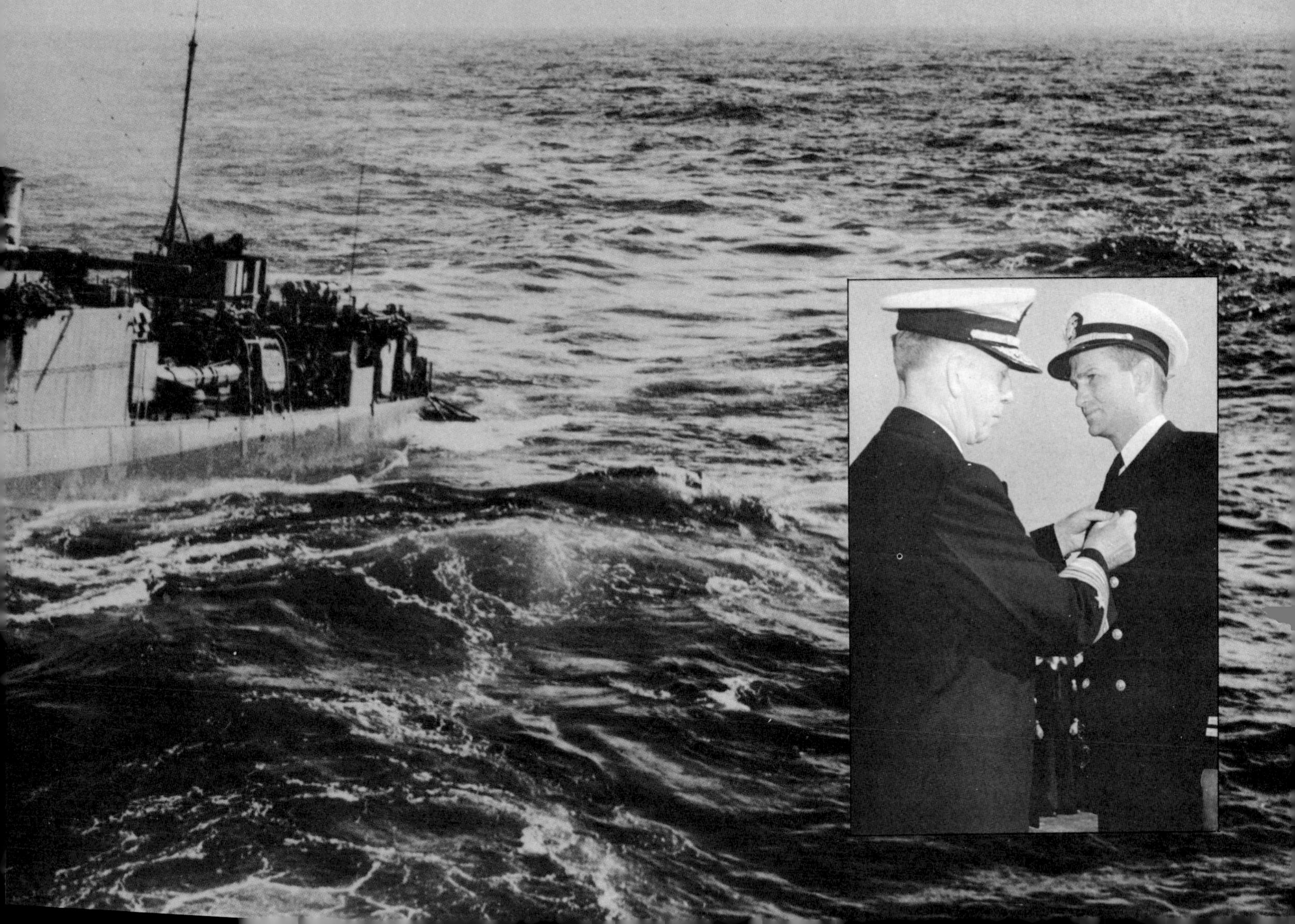

destroyers to attack independently. At ranges which varied from 6000 down to as little as 4000 yards the five destroyers dodged and weaved, while the tired gun-layers aboard the battleship tried to blast them out of the water. It was probably only their wild gyrations which saved the destroyers from being hit by anything bigger than splinters, but for all their efforts they could not hit the *Bismarck*. During the action the worried radar operator aboard the *Cossack* reported a number of shapes on his screen; it was realized that the air-warning radar had picked up the *Bismarck*'s 2000lb shells in mid-flight.

At about 0300 the battered destroyers lost touch with the *Bismarck*, and failed to find her. Although her radio aerials had been shot away the *Cossack* had broadcast a series of bearings to the Commander-in-Chief, Home Fleet. Although a final attempt was made by the *Maori* and *Sikh* to attack at 0700, the battleships *King George V* and *Rodney* were in sight, and so Vian's destroyers hauled off and left it to the big ships to play out the final act of the drama. Although they had not damaged the *Bismarck* they had carried out the destroyer's traditional role of shadowing and harassing an enemy capital ship, and the constant alarms and expenditure of ammunition can have done nothing to improve her chances of surviving the fleet action next morning.

Although nobody envisaged that the old destroyers would ever be called on to carry out a torpedo attack, on one occasion it did happen. On 12 February 1942 six destroyers were lying at Harwich, the leader *Campbell* (Captain Pizey), the *Vivacious* of Pizey's 21st Flotilla and the *Mackay*, *Whitshed*, *Worcester* and *Walpole* of the 16th Flotilla. That morning news came through of the daring Operation Cerberus, the daylight dash by the German battlecruisers *Scharnhorst* and *Gneisenau* through the English Channel. At first it was believed that the concentration of bombers, coastal guns and motor torpedo boats would stop the German ships but as the day wore on and all the piecemeal attacks were repulsed, it became clear that the breakthrough was going to succeed. The Harwich destroyers had been kept there for this eventuality but it had been assumed all along that the Germans would come at night. A daylight attack on capital ships had long been considered suicidal, even for the most modern destroyers, and even more so for 25-year old veterans of the previous war.

The destroyers were at sea on exercise at 1145 when they were told that the 'Cerberus' force was off Boulogne, and that they were to attack it with torpedoes as previously planned. Steering a course which took him over 'friendly' minefields at 28 knots, Captain Pizey took his force by the shortest route to the interception point. The *Walpole* had machinery trouble and had to turn back, leaving only five destroyers to face two capital ships, the heavy cruiser *Prinz Eugen*, six large destroyers and 15 torpedo boats as well as E-Boats and aircraft. An attack by German aircraft was ignored, but when a lone RAF bomber did its best to sink the *Mackay* and *Worcester* the gunners' restraint was tested to its utmost.

The Germans were heavily engaged in dealing with a torpedo attack by Beaufort bombers, and failed to notice the five destroyers deploying for their attack. Suddenly the screening E-Boats were swept aside by the first division, which got within 3300 yards of the *Gneisenau*

Above: The German torpedo boat *T.11* passes below the flak guns of a larger warship.

Right: Torpedo boats *T.1* to *T.2* displaced 844 tons and sacrificed endurance for high speed.
Below: *T.1* was followed by 20 sister ships built between 1937 and 1944. They were useful additions to German destroyer strength, but carried too light a gun armament to be effective.

Above: *T.17* has a full load of 40 mines on her quarterdeck but in addition she is towing a barrage balloon as a defence against low-flying aircraft.

and *Prinz Eugen*. Belatedly they opened fire and hit one destroyer, which they claimed to have sunk. This was the *Worcester*, which ought to have been sunk, for she was hit by several 11-inch and eight-inch shells and had 17 killed and 45 wounded. But the Germans dared not wait to finish her off, and so she was able to put out the fires and raise steam once more. When Pizey returned he was amazed to see her under-way at eight knots. As with the 4th Flotilla's attack on the *Bismarck*, no hits were scored, but the action is an outstanding example of destroyer handling.

The *Gneisenau* never went to sea again, but the destroyers were given a second chance to attack her sister *Scharnhorst*, and this time they took their revenge. This occurred in December 1943, nearly a year after Admiral Raeder had been replaced by Karl Dönitz as Commander-in-Chief of the *Kriegsmarine*. The immediate cause of this reshuffle of the naval command had been Hitler's understandable anger when a force of eight British destroyers had fought off an attempt by the pocket-battleship *Lützow*, the heavy cruiser *Admiral Hipper* and destroyers to attack their convoy. This action, known as the Battle of the Barents Sea, was fought in December 1942, and

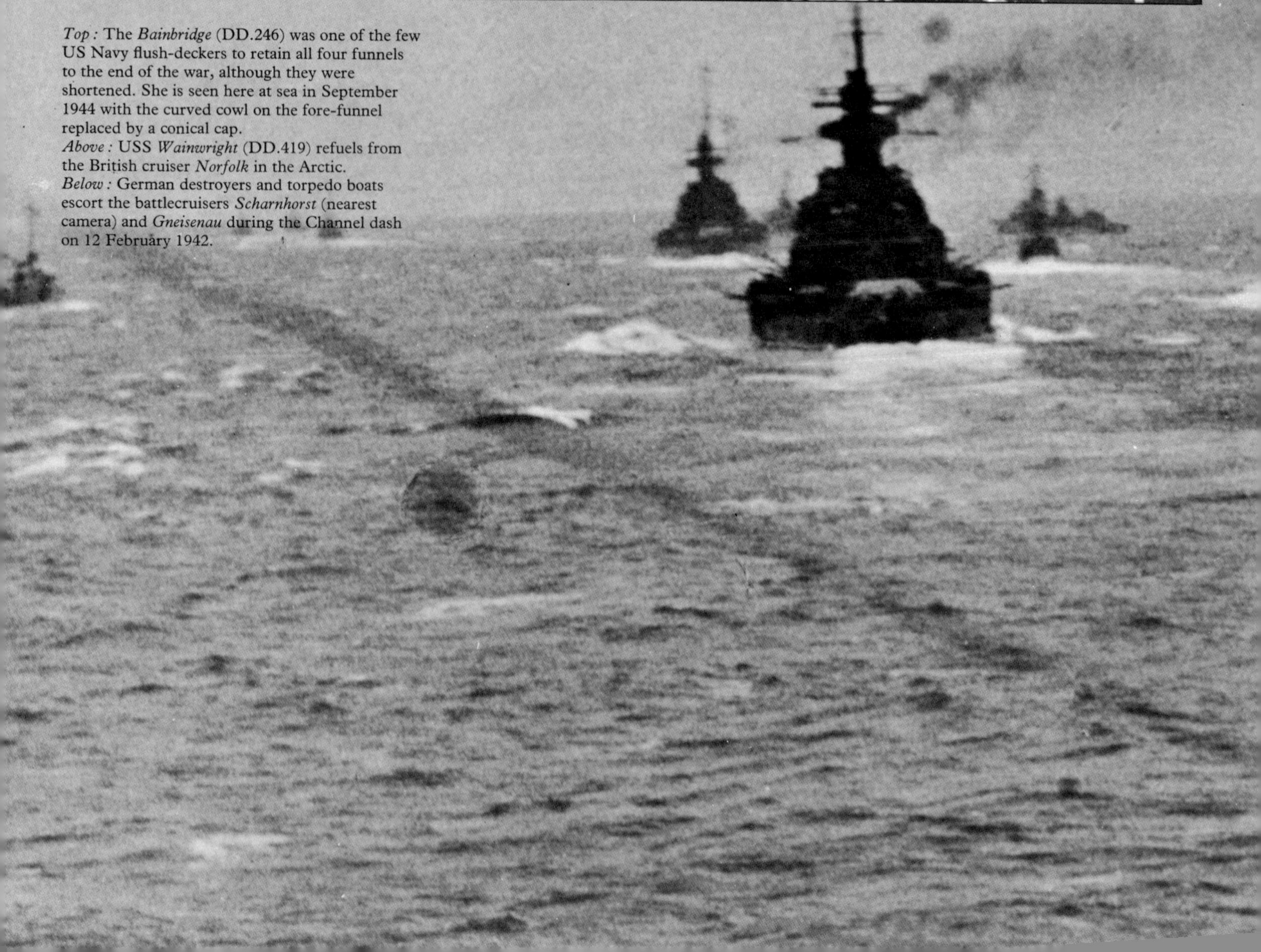

Top: The *Bainbridge* (DD.246) was one of the few US Navy flush-deckers to retain all four funnels to the end of the war, although they were shortened. She is seen here at sea in September 1944 with the curved cowl on the fore-funnel replaced by a conical cap.
Above: USS *Wainwright* (DD.419) refuels from the British cruiser *Norfolk* in the Arctic.
Below: German destroyers and torpedo boats escort the battlecruisers *Scharnhorst* (nearest camera) and *Gneisenau* during the Channel dash on 12 February 1942.

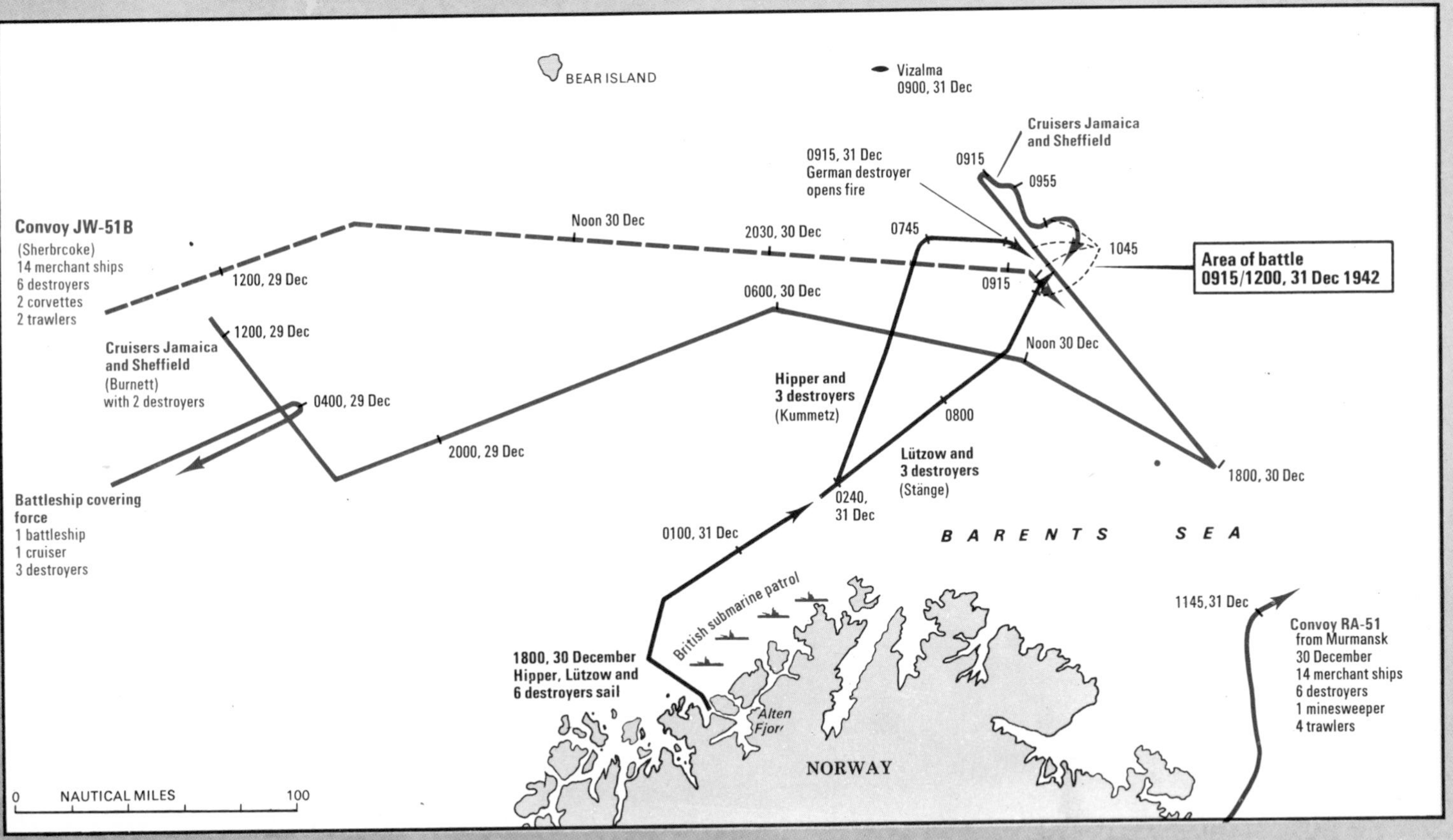

Above: The Battle of the Barents Sea.
Overleaf: The destroyer escort *Amesbury* (DE.66) goes down the ways on 5 June 1943 at the Bethlehem Hingham Shipyard.

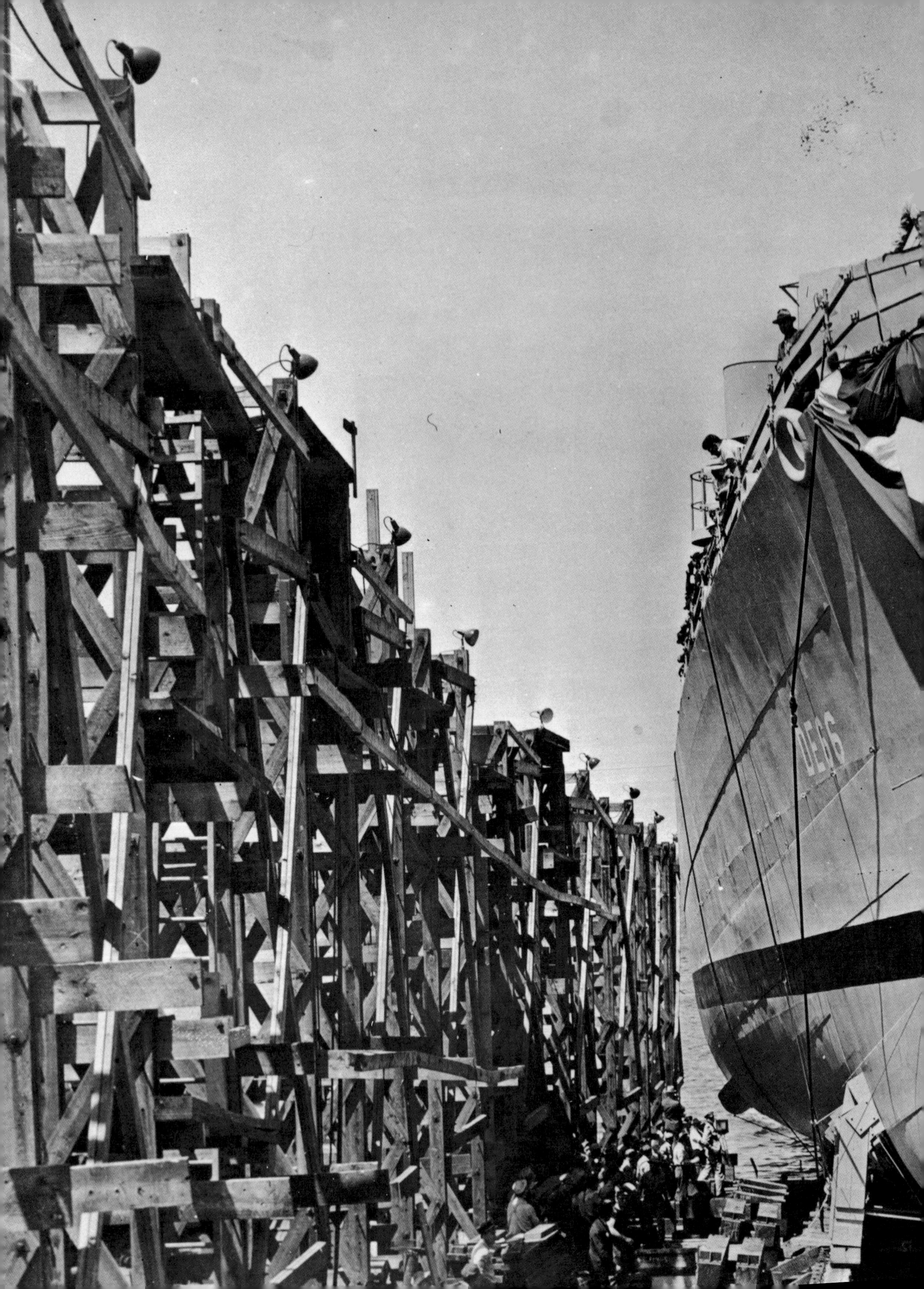
DE66

DE66

although one of the destroyers was sunk the convoy escaped. The British destroyers fought a brilliant delaying action to give time for the distant escort of two cruisers to come up and drive away the *Lützow* and *Hipper*. It was at this point that the luckless destroyer *Friedrich Eckholdt* closed the cruisers *Jamaica* and *Sheffield* under the impression that they were friendly, only to be blasted with six-inch shells.

Raeder, only too well aware that it was Hitler's reluctance to risk any damage to his warships which had led to the debacle, resigned when the Führer threatened to scrap the surface fleet. His successor managed to save the big ships, however, for Hitler was not prepared to allow the Allies to run convoys to North Russia or to deploy their heavy ships in other theatres. Another operation against a convoy was planned in 1943, and this time the *Tirpitz*, *Scharnhorst* and destroyers were to be used. So far so good, but in November two Allied convoys slipped through to Murmansk without loss, and Northern Group was told to organize a convoy raid at the first favourable opportunity. It was not the best moment, for the *Tirpitz* was still under repair and would not be ready until March. A proposal to use the big destroyers alone was amended to include the *Scharnhorst*, but the greatly superior British radar would count against the Germans during the long hours of Arctic night.

Admiral 'Achmed' Bey, the man who had turned the tables on Warburton-Lee's destroyers at the First Battle of Narvik in 1940, commanded Northern Group's destroyers, and he took over as Flag Officer Northern Task Force when

Top left: Crewmen of the *Tirpitz* watch her escorting destroyers make a turn to port.
Above: Capt R Sherbrooke VC DSO RN, hero of the Barents Sea Action.
Top right: German destroyers blanketed in spray as they plough through Northern seas.
Left: *Z.24* was the second of a new class of large German destroyers designed in 1936 with five 15cm (5.9-inch) guns.
Far right: *Z.26* in a Norwegian Fjord.
Right: *Z.25* in dock at Brest shows the massive twin 15cm gun mounting forward. The weight reduced seaworthiness by making these destroyers pitch into a head sea.
Below: Capt Sherbrooke's flotilla leader HMS *Onslow* (nearest camera) and the *Ashanti* in the Arctic.

Admiral Kummetz went on leave in November. When his flagship sailed from Altenfjord at 1900 on Christmas Day he was not to know that all the assumptions made by his staff were wrong. There was not one convoy but two, JW.55B homeward bound for England, and RA.55A bound for Murmansk. Aerial reconnaissance had detected only JW.55B, covered by a close escort force of three cruisers and destroyers, and although the Home Fleet had been detected leaving Iceland, the Luftwaffe report had been vaguely worded. It mentioned the possibility of a battleship being included, but in accordance with the rule that only facts were to be passed on to the Navy, this afterthought was deleted. But there was a battleship, the 38,000-ton *Duke of York*, flagship of the Commander-in-Chief Home Fleet, Admiral Fraser. Fraser was very well-informed about the *Scharnhorst*'s intentions, almost undoubtedly as a result of 'Ultra' cryptanalysis, and had already ordered four destroyers to transfer from the undetected convoy to JW.55B's close escort. Bey was moving into a trap, with a battleship, a cruiser and four destroyers moving up at high speed to cut off his retreat and a total of 14 destroyers actually with the convoy, in company with three modern cruisers.

As a destroyerman himself, Bey must have had misgivings when he allowed his own destroyers to turn back, as they could not keep station with the flagship in the worsening weather. The Luftwaffe reconnaissance aircraft were now grounded as well, and the *Scharnhorst* was without any information apart from what could be seen by her radar and the eyes of her lookouts. U-Boats had given him reasonable estimates of the size, speed and course of the convoy, but they failed to sight the Home Fleet. Fraser's signals to his scattered forces were concise, to minimize the risk of attacks on friendly forces, but the German destroyers lost contact with the *Scharnhorst* early on the morning of 26 December and there was no way to recall them.

At 0840 on 26 December the cruiser flagship *Belfast* picked up a large 'blip' on her radar screen, which indicated that the *Scharnhorst* was only 30 miles away. As the *Duke of York* was still 200 miles away, the cruisers had to fight a holding action which they proceeded to do in masterly fashion. At 0924 starshells from the *Belfast* lit up the *Scharnhorst* in the predawn Arctic gloom, and in only two minutes one of HMS *Norfolk*'s eight-inch shells demolished the forward fire-control

director and its radar antenna. The startled *Scharnhorst* sheered off, and in the heavy seas she soon pulled away from the three cruisers. Admiral Burnett was too wily to allow his cruisers to be drawn away from the convoy, and confidently forecast that the enemy would be back. Within three hours his prediction was proved correct when the *Scharnhorst* was sighted again, coming up from the South. This time she made a more determined effort to push past the cruisers, and the range came down to 11,000 yards as her 11-inch shells bracketed them with accurate salvoes. The *Norfolk* was hit several times, but the delay distracted the Germans' attention, and during the *mêlée* the *Duke of York* was able to approach to within 12,000 yards without being seen.

There were four destroyers with the cruisers, the *Matchless, Musketeer, Opportune* and *Virago,* and they had already launched a torpedo attack to take the pressure off the cruisers. The heavy seas made it very difficult to overhaul the *Scharnhorst*, and although all four destroyers got close enough to fire their puny 4.7-inch and four-inch guns at the battlecruiser the range was too great for an effective torpedo attack.

The British battleship had plenty of time to manoeuvre and bring the maximum number of guns to bear, and at 0450 the first starshell burst overhead, followed immediately by salvoes of 14-inch and six-inch shells. Once again the *Scharnhorst* tried to break away, but this time her opponent was able to keep up, for the heavy seas evened out any nominal differences between the two ships' top speeds. The cruisers were left behind as the big ships traded punches at a range of 17,000–20,000 yards. A 14-inch hit damaged one of the *Scharnhorst*'s propeller shafts, and Admiral Fraser signalled to his four destroyers to attack with torpedoes.

It has already been mentioned that the weather was too rough for the German destroyers, and so bad that 10,000-ton cruisers were unable to maintain full speed. The *Saumarez, Savage, Scorpion* and *Stord* (Norwegian Navy) displaced only 2000 tons fully loaded, and their frail hulls whipped and shuddered as they plunged through the waves and buried themselves in clouds of spray. The *Saumarez* and the *Savage* slowly drew away from the *Duke of York* and crept up on their quarry. The *Scorpion* and *Stord* worked their way on to the starboard quarter, leaving the other pair of destroyers to draw fire on the port side. The *Saumarez* and *Savage* came under heavy fire, but the German shooting was wild, and the *Scorpion* and *Stord* managed to approach to within 3000 yards, virtually point-blank for a torpedo attack. At least one of the *Scorpion*'s torpedoes hit, and the *Scharnhorst* turned away, straight into the arms of the other two destroyers. Once again shuddering underwater explosions told that three torpedoes had hit. The destroyers had done their job, and they eased down thankfully as the *Duke of York* took over the work of finishing the battle. The range was now only 10,400 yards and the cruisers were joining in, firing at the dull smoky glow that was all that anyone could make out in the murk. It was all over by 1945, when the cruisers closed in to find only 36 men out of the 2000 who had been aboard in Altenfjord only a day before.

The Battle of North Cape was the last major action in European waters, and it marked the end of the German Navy's attempt to dominate the Atlantic. Undoubtedly the contribution of the destroyers in the battle was a most important part of the victory, for if they had not slowed the *Scharnhorst* down she could have eluded the Home Fleet and possibly have returned safely to base.

Top centre: The German destroyer *Z.34* leaves Kiel.
Above: HMS *Savage* was unusual in having a twin 4.5-inch enclosed turret forward, and 4.5-inch guns aft in place of the usual 4.7-inch guns.

Below: HMS *Musketeer* and her sisters were specially adapted for Arctic service, with steam heating for all gun mountings and torpedo-tubes and asbestos lagging to bulkheads and the deckhead.

Top right: An aerial view of HMS *Scorpion* showing the typical layout of British war-built 'Emergency' type destroyers.
Above: HMS *Saumarez* was the leader of the group of destroyers which torpedoed the German battlecruiser *Scharnhorst* in the Battle of the North Cape.

The Mediterranean

Destroyers played an important part in Mediterranean naval operations partly because of the shorter distances but above all because the British destroyers were often the only vessels capable of matching the Italian warships' high speeds. If the British and Australian destroyers were handled so well it is possibly because the Commander-in-Chief of the Mediterranean Fleet, Admiral Sir Andrew Cunningham, was the Royal Navy's leading expert on destroyers. Most of his record-breaking seven-year commission in the *Scorpion* from 1911 to 1918 had been spent in the Mediterranean, and it was said of 'ABC' that he handled even the battle fleet as if it were a division of destroyers.

The very first action of the Mediterranean, the action off Calabria on 9 July 1940, set a pattern which was to become familiar in the next three years. The Italian Fleet was sighted by the British cruisers at long range, and although a gunnery duel started, the Italians broke off when the flagship *Giulio Cesare* was hit by HMS *Warspite* at nearly 25,000 yards. Cunningham's destroyers, three flotillas totalling 14 boats, raced after the fleeing Italians but failed to make contact. The Italian destroyers did their work well, laying dense smoke-screens and engaging with gunfire. By the time the British flotillas pushed past and penetrated the smoke-screens the Italian battleships were hull down on the horizon, heading for home. The next action, off Cape Spartivento four months later, was even more disappointing, and the destroyers could not even get into action, but in March 1941 the third of these 'stern-chase' engagements turned into the decisive battle which Cunningham hankered after, the Battle of Cape Matapan. The invasion of Greece had begun and the *Regia Navale* had been ordered to make a 'demonstration' off the Western coast of Greece to try and hamper the flow of British reinforcements from Egypt. If the Italians could achieve this they would dominate the Central Mediterranean basin and bring much-needed support to the Axis armies in North Africa.

As before the cruiser screen sighted the Italians first, when on the morning of 28 March the battleship *Vittorio Veneto* opened fire on them at a range of 16 miles. The Italian fire was uncomfortably accurate, and when the cruiser *Gloucester* reported engine trouble and dropped back, what might have been an awkward moment was averted by the destroyer *Hasty*, which shielded her with a smoke-screen. The British cruisers and their four destroyers retired, knowing that Cunningham was only 80 miles away with three battleships and an aircraft carrier. An attack by HMS *Formidable*'s Albacore torpedo-bombers scored a hit on the *Vittorio Veneto*, and she turned for home. Cunningham was determined to cut her off if he could, and a second strike scored another hit, but the *Vittorio Veneto* was still able to steam at 12–15 knots, and with a powerful escort of cruisers and destroyers there was no chance of launching a destroyer attack.

As it was now nearly dark there seemed little hope of bringing the Italians to action, but as the light faded the *Formidable*'s aircraft scored another success, hitting the heavy cruiser *Pola* with a single torpedo. The anti-aircraft fire was so heavy and the light so bad that the pilots and observers had no idea which ships were which and did not see the torpedo-hit.

In the hope that he might still be able to catch the *Vittorio Veneto*, and knowing that if he waited until daybreak his battleships would be within range of the Stuka dive-bombers based in Sicily and Southern Italy, Cunningham unleashed his beloved destroyers. Away went the eight destroyers of the 2nd and 14th Flotillas under Captain Philip Mack in HMS *Nubian*. What nobody knew was that Admiral Iachino, the Italian Commander-in-Chief, had detached two more cruisers, the *Fiume* and *Zara*, to help the stricken *Pola*. With his instinct for destroyer tactics Cunningham later criticized Mack's decision to stay too far to the North when taking up his attacking position, as it put the destroyers between the British cruisers and the Italian squadron, and also left an avenue of escape open to the South. As it turned out, Cunningham was right, and if the destroyers had been further South they might have run into the *Vittorio Veneto* herself. They did

Below: French and British warships at Alexandria in the early months of the war.

Above: The Italian 'Soldati' Class destroyers *Fuciliere* (left) and *Alpino*.
Right: HMS *Faulknor*, launched in 1934, escorts British reinforcements for the Mediterranean in August 1940.

not, and so a magnificent chance went begging, but the destroyers were still to have their moment of glory.

At 2225 two darkened shapes were seen crossing the bows of the Battle Fleet, at a range of less than 4000 yards. The destroyer *Greyhound* switched on her searchlight revealing the hapless *Fiume* and *Zara* in its glare, their guns trained fore and aft. They were hit by the first salvoes of 15-inch shells from *Warspite*, *Valiant* and *Barham*, all veterans of the gallant action fought by the 5th Battle Squadron at Jutland 25 years before. There was nothing for the destroyers to do but stay out of trouble while the battleships did their work of destruction in a few short minutes. Throughout the action Cunningham was worried about

Above: The old destroyer *Venomous* crosses under the stern of the aircraft carrier *Formidable*.

Above: The *Folgore* was sunk by gunfire from British cruisers and destroyers on 2 December 1942.

his destroyers being sunk by friendly ships and was certain that the *Havock* had been sunk but in fact she was only straddled by a 15-inch salvo.

When some Italian destroyers were sighted Cunningham ordered the *Stuart*, *Havock*, *Greyhound* and *Griffin* to deal with them, and in the ensuing *mêlée* they sank the destroyer *Vittorio Alfieri*. The rest of the destroyers now rejoined after their vain hunt for the *Vittorio Veneto*, which had unwittingly provoked the battle, and stumbled across the crippled *Pola*. The *Jervis* rescued as many of the *Pola*'s crew as she could before the *Nubian* sank her. The *Jervis* then finished off the shattered and burning *Zara* (the *Fiume* had already sunk). The destroyers also sank the Italian destroyer *Carducci* in what Cunningham described as their 'wild night'. He also recorded his relief next morning, when all his destroyers answered the flagship's signals, just as if he was still a flotilla commander.

Matapan showed that the malign influence which had ruined Jutland had been eradicated from the British tactical book. Cunningham himself said of the battle:

'At sea it has always been one of the principal objections to a pursuit at night that the pursuer always laid himself open to what might be a series of highly dangerous attacks by the enemy's light forces. The Italians must have known this quite well. They had some 18 destroyers and a considerable number of cruisers with which they might have launched a night attack upon us. They didn't do so, their argument being that it was so highly dangerous for a Fleet to pursue at night that the British wouldn't attempt it. Therefore what was the good of sending their light forces to attack something that wouldn't be there!'

The fortunes of war change very rapidly, and the triumph of Matapan was quickly followed by the Royal Navy's most gruelling test of the entire war, the Battle of Crete. Following the rough handling of the Italian invaders by the Greek Army and its British allies, Hitler decided to retrieve Mussolini's fortunes by sending German troops into Yugoslavia on 6 April 1941. Within two weeks the British and Greek ground-forces had been overwhelmed and had withdrawn to Crete. They were virtually devoid of air cover as the RAF had been pulled back to Egypt, and so the defence of the island was left to the Mediterranean Fleet. The Royal Navy had two tasks: first to prevent a seaborne invasion, and second, to

Top: The *Nicolo Zeno* of the 'Navigatori' Class at sea in 1941–42. She was scuttled in Trieste in September 1943.
Above: The *Monzambano* was a torpedo boat completed in 1924 seen here in July 1942 camouflaged.
Below: The Yugoslav flotilla leader *Dubrovnik* was captured by the Italians and renamed *Premuda* but before completion she was captured by the Germans and renamed *TA.32*.

Far left: The 'Soldati' Class *Corazziere* under repair at Genoa in 1943. She fell into German hands and was sunk by Allied bombs in 1944. *Below:* The torpedo boats *General Antonino Cascino* (right) and *Giacomo Medici* at anchor.

cover the evacuation of as many of the garrison as possible. It succeeded in both these aims, but at a terrible cost in lives and ships.

On 20 May 1941 the *Luftwaffe* began to attack the ships patrolling North of Crete in conjunction with landings of gliders and paratroops on the island. Next day the destroyer *Juno* was sunk South East of Crete when a bomb from an Italian high-level bomber detonated her magazine; she sank in two minutes. That night Rear-Admiral Glennie, with the cruisers *Dido*, *Orion* and *Ajax* and the destroyers *Janus*, *Kimberley*, *Hasty* and *Hereward* found a convoy of light craft, including *caïques* or commandeered Greek fishing boats, crowded with German invasion troops. Here at last was a tangible enemy, and the cruisers and destroyers ran amok, firing indiscriminately at anything they could see. When they had finished two-and-a-half hours later the invasion convoy had ceased to exist, and an estimated 4000 German troops had been killed or drowned. A seaborne invasion of Crete was not possible so long as the sea passage was disputed.

Next day the air attacks began again with renewed ferocity. The destroyers were particularly vulnerable when unsupported by larger ships for their anti-aircraft armament was painfully weak. First to go was the *Greyhound*, and although the cruisers *Gloucester* and *Fiji* tried to protect her, they were very low on anti-aircraft ammunition; as soon as their defensive fire slackened the Stukas closed in and sank them as well. The destroyers patrolled north of the island on the lookout for invasion forces, but in fact the Germans and Italians had given

Above: One of the most famous destroyers, Lord Louis Mountbatten's flotilla leader *Kelly*. After being badly damaged twice, she was sunk in the Battle of Crete.

up trying to run another convoy. Under cover of darkness destroyers found time to evacuate the King of Greece and the British envoy to Greece, another of the responsibilities which tended to be given to destroyers. On the morning of 23 May the already famous 5th Flotilla under Captain Lord Louis Mountbatten found itself without heavy support as the big ships had been prematurely withdrawn because it was feared that they were low on ammunition.

It was about 0800, and the *Kelly* was leading the *Kashmir*, *Kipling*, *Kelvin* and *Jackal* back to Alexandria after attacking a force of troop-carrying *caïques*. Suddenly the drone of aero-engines heralded the arrival of the dreaded Stukas, two dozen of them. The *Kashmir* was hit and sank very quickly, for the flimsy hull of a destroyer was easily ruptured by the explosion of a heavy bomb. Then the *Kelly*, making 30 knots and belching smoke, was hit as she put her helm hard over. She lurched to port, and still moving fast, slid over and lay bottom up for half an hour before disappearing. The dazed survivors, covered in oil fuel, had to endure machine-gunning until the Stukas ran low on fuel and returned to base. The *Kelvin* and *Jackal* were ordered to make their escape to avoid further losses, but the *Kipling* bravely stayed behind for three hours, and managed to rescue 279 survivors. The risks she ran were terrible, but abandoning flotilla-mates was not part of the destroyer tradition. On the way back to Alexandria the *Kipling* had another 80 bombs dropped on her, and when still 70 miles from home she suffered the ultimate indignity; she ran out of fuel and had to be towed into Alexandria.

Once the German paratroops gained a sizeable bridgehead in Crete the island was doomed, and the call went out to the Navy to make an even greater effort than it had already, by evacuating the 32,000 men of the garrison. It was another Dunkirk but under much greater difficulties, for the nearest friendly port was in Egypt.

Above: The *Aviere* was one of the 'Soldati' Class of large destroyers, which reached 39 knots on trials. She was torpedoed by a British submarine in December 1942.

Destroyers and the fast minelayer *Abdiel* had already been running in with urgently needed ammunition and stores as even the fastest merchantmen found the trip suicidal. The problem with Crete was that the only good port for offloading stores or embarking was on the North side, the side most exposed to German air attack. On the night of 28–29 May Rear-Admiral Rawlings took the cruisers *Orion*, *Ajax* and *Dido* and six destroyers into Heraklion in an attempt to evacuate all the defenders.

At first everything went well, and by 0320 the 4000 troops were safely embarked. Then the *Imperial*'s steering gear jammed, probably as a result of near-misses during the daylight passage to Crete. Admiral Rawlings dared not allow his force to be caught so close to the *Luftwaffe*'s airfields at daybreak and so he ordered the *Hotspur* to take off her troops and sink her. With 900 men aboard the *Hotspur* rejoined an hour later, but it was too late, and the sun was up when the eight warships headed southwards through the Kaso Strait at the Eastern end of Crete. Soon they were picked up by Axis reconnaissance aircraft, and the bombing began at 0600. The *Hereward* was hit, but there was no question of turning back to help her; she drifted inshore before sinking, so fortunately the larger part of her crew and the soldiers she had embarked survived to become prisoners-of-war. The *Decoy* was also hit, but managed to limp along at reduced speed. The *Dido* and *Orion* were hit by bombs, and a second attack two hours later killed or wounded over 500 troops packed in the *Orion*'s forward mess-decks.

While this was going on another four

Right: Three generations of Italian torpedo craft, (left to right) *Tilfone* (1942), *Antonio Mosto* (1915), and *Augusto Riboty* (1917).

Below: The *Camicia Nera* and a sister at sea in 1940.

Above: The *Calatafimi* was captured by the Germans in September 1943 and became *TA.19*. She was torpedoed in 1944 by a Greek submarine.

destroyers had managed to get 700 troops out of the tiny harbour of Sphakia on the South East coast virtually without loss. The reason was that, unlike Admiral Rawlings' force, the air cover planned had been in the right place at the right time. Encouraged, Cunningham decided to continue the evacuation, and the following night the cruisers *Phoebe*, *Perth* and *Calcutta*, the fast transport *Glengyle* and three destroyers rescued a further 6000 men from Sphakia without losing a ship. The destroyers made one last effort on the night of 31 May–1 June and saved 4000 men, bringing the total to over 18,000 landed safely in Egypt.

The fall of Crete left the British in a precarious position with all the gains since July 1940 wiped out. Their only forward base, the island of Malta, was cut off and liable to be bombed or starved into submission. The defeat of the 8th Army in Libya meant that the Italian Navy could run supply convoys into Benghazi and Tripoli out of reach of the surface and air forces. Malta was now unusable by surface forces and its airfields were only barely usable by its defending fighters. To add to the Navy's burdens, the fortress of Tobruk and the 8th Army's advance bases on the Libyan frontier had to be supplied by sending ships along 'Bomb Alley', a route dotted with wrecks.

The supply run to Tobruk will always

Below: The *Maestrale* limped into Genoa in January 1943 minus her stern. She fell into German hands but was scuttled in April 1945.

Left: The *Antonio Pigafetta*, scuttled at Fiume in 1943, was refloated by the Germans and became *TA.44* in October 1944 but was sunk by British bombs in 1945.

be associated with the Australian 'Scrap-Iron Flotilla', otherwise the 10th Flotilla (19th Division). Under Captain 'Hec' Waller, the old leader *Stuart* and four 'V & W' Class, the *Vampire*, *Vendetta*, *Voyager* and *Waterhen*, all transferred to the Royal Australian Navy from the RN in 1933, had been attached to the Mediterranean Fleet since 1940. The *Stuart* had, despite her age, played her part in the Battle of Cape Matapan, and all five were in the evacuation of Greece and Crete. The *Vampire* returned to Australia the same month but the other four remained in the Mediterranean. The *Waterhen*, known to her officers and men and the Australian defenders of Tobruk as 'The Chook', finally sank on 29 June 1941 after receiving heavy damage from Italian and German bombers the day before. She and the *Stuart* and *Vendetta* had been running what amounted to a nightly ferry-run from Alexandria taking in ammunition and supplies. Normally two destroyers made the trip down 'Bomb Alley' each night, berthing in the wreck-infested harbour in total darkness; the cargo was discharged inside an hour and they were on the way back to Alexandria. Once a week the larger fast minelayers *Abdiel* and *Latona* took in fresh troops and brought out sections of the garrison for rest and recuperation. During the months of August–October 1941 19,568 men were taken into Tobruk this way and another 18,865 brought out. The siege lasted 242 days in all, and 34,000 tons of stores were ferried during that time. In July 1941 another destroyer, HMS *Defender*, was sunk as was the *Latona* in October, both by bombing, but in December the 8th Army's Operation Crusader achieved the reoccupation of Cyrenaica and Tobruk was relieved.

The need to keep Malta supplied required far greater exertions. As early as May 1941 the Admiralty had increased the number of submarines in the Mediterranean, first by ordering a flotilla based on Gibraltar to operate against Italian shipping in the Tyrrhenian Sea and then by allocating some of the newly constructed submarines to the flotilla based on Malta. Throughout the summer of 1941 these submarines played havoc with the Italian supply convoys, backed up by air attacks. In September two aircraft carriers, the *Ark Royal* and *Furious* ferried 49 Hurricane fighters as a prelude to flying in twin-engined bombers to re-establish a strike force on the island. The success of these moves led to the re-establishment of a surface strike force at Malta in October 1941. Known as Force

Left: The torpedo boat *Impavido* became the German *TA.23* and was sunk by mines in 1944.
Below left: The Yugoslav *Beograd* and her sister *Ljubljana* were captured in 1941 to become the Italian *Sebenico* and *Lubiana*.
Right: HMS *Loyal* was badly damaged by a mine off the coast of Italy and was never repaired.
repaired.

K, it comprised the light cruisers *Aurora* and *Penelope* and the destroyers *Lance* and *Lively*, under the command of Captain W G Agnew RN.

Force K had only one brief, to deny the Axis forces the sea-route between Italy and North Africa, and it quickly showed how vulnerable that route was. On 8 November a reconnaissance aircraft reported a convoy 40 miles East of Cape Spartivento, seven merchant ships escorted by six destroyers, with a support force of two heavy cruisers and four destroyers. Ignoring these odds Agnew took his two cruisers and two destroyers in at first light next day and annihilated the convoy. All the merchant ships were sunk as well as the destroyer *Fulmine*, without loss, and the *Libeccio* was later torpedoed by HM Submarine *Upholder* while trying to rescue survivors; the support force apparently took no action to avoid the catastrophe.

A week later the same four ships achieved another 100 per cent success by wiping out a special convoy of two ships, the *Maritza* and *Procida*, carrying aviation gasoline urgently needed by the *Luftwaffe* in North Africa. The convoy was sighted 100 miles West of Crete, and despite a valiant defence by the two escorting torpedo boats, Force K sank the gasoline carriers with ease. On 29 November a further reinforcement arrived at Malta, Force B under Rear-Admiral Rawlings, comprising the cruisers *Ajax* and *Neptune* and two more destroyers. Malta was an ulcer which threatened to drain the Axis strength in the Mediterranean, and for the first time the German command in North Africa began to talk of the possibility of defeat if Malta was not subdued. As if to underline this gloom, on 1 December Force K attacked and sank a supply ship and a tanker bound for Libya, as well as its escorting destroyer, the *Alvise da Mosto*.

On 13 December another action occurred, one of the most brilliant destroyer actions of World War II. This time there was no premeditation for the *Sikh*, *Legion* and *Maori* and the Netherlands Navy's *Isaac Sweers* were en route from Gibraltar to Alexandria as reinforcements for Cunningham's 14th Flotilla. So desperate had the fuel situation become in North Africa that the light cruisers *Alberico da Barbiano* and *Alberto di Guissano* had taken on a deck cargo of cased gasoline at Palermo, destined for Tripoli. When the first sighting was made by a Wellington bomber from Malta it was intended that land-based torpedo-bombers and Force K would intercept, and the *Sikh* and her division were only meant to act in support, but at the last moment Force K was ordered to remain in Malta. Commander Stokes in HMS *Sikh* received fresh orders too late to reach the interception point, and to his chagrin he saw the two cruisers disappearing behind the high cliffs of Cape Bon. Stokes maintained course with little hope of catching the Italians, but suddenly he realized that the two cruisers had reversed their course and that he had

an opportunity denied to most destroyer-commanders, a set-piece attack against major warships.

What had happened was that the Italian squadron had been attacked by the RAF bombers without success, but Admiral Toscano expected to be attacked in much greater strength at daylight, and had decided to turn back. Stokes led his destroyers close inshore so that they were hidden by the land behind them with the Italians silhouetted against the skyline. At 0225 the *Sikh* fired a salvo of four torpedoes and saw the leading cruiser, the *Alberico da Barbiano* burst into flame as three of her 'fish' hit amidships. The *Legion* hit the *Alberto di Guissano* with only one torpedo, but she too burst into flame as gasoline drums on her decks burst and scattered flaming fuel everywhere. The *Maori* and *Isaac Sweers* pumped shells into the two hapless cruisers as they raced past. Only the second cruiser had time to fire three wild salvoes with her six-inch guns, and seeing that their victims were beyond hope the four destroyers disappeared as quickly as they had arrived. The torpedo boat *Circe* picked up survivors, but a large number of lives were lost including the unlucky Admiral Toscano. His superiors at *Supermarina*, the Italian Naval HQ, had warned him of the presence of the four enemy destroyers but had considered that four destroyers would not dare to tackle two cruisers; he would have done better to take his chances with the RAF at daybreak, for British land-based bombers had a dismal record of failure against Axis warships.

Despite the brilliant success of the Malta-based destroyers and cruisers, they were about to be eclipsed. On 18 December the cruiser *Neptune* and two destroyers met Admiral Vian (the same man who had liberated the *Altmark*'s prisoners in 1940) who was escorting the fast supply ship *Breconshire* carrying a vital cargo of gasoline and supplies for Malta with three cruisers and 14 destroyers. The entire force escorted the *Breconshire* safely to Malta and then left immediately to intercept yet another Italian convoy bound for Tripoli. At 0100 the next morning, about 20 miles off Tripoli the *Neptune* was rocked by the explosion of two mines, one of which wrecked her steering. Although the rest of the squadron immediately steered clear, the *Aurora* and *Penelope* also struck mines. The *Aurora* struggled clear and limped back to Malta with two destroyers escorting her, and as the *Penelope* was not badly damaged she stayed to try and tow the *Neptune* home. The stricken ship drifted onto a third mine and was soon listing heavily to port, and when the destroyer *Kandahar* tried to come alongside a massive explosion destroyed her stern.

The captain of the doomed flagship of Force K, Captain Rory O'Conor, acted to minimize further risk to his ships, and a lamp flashed the order 'Keep away' to them. The wisdom of this was clear when the *Neptune* touched off a fourth mine shortly afterwards. Even so the destroyer *Lively* tried to go alongside the sinking *Kandahar*, and had to be peremptorily ordered back by the *Neptune*. The decision was a cruel one but O'Conor and Commander Robson of the *Kandahar*

Above: HMS *Nerissa* became the Polish *Piorun* in 1940.
Below: The *Lookout* was the only one of eight British 'L' Class destroyers to survive the war. She is seen here at Greenock in January 1942.

knew that any further attempts to save life would merely endanger others. Robson signalled to the *Penelope*, 'Suggest you go', to which Captain Nicholl sadly replied, 'I clearly cannot help. God be with you'. A last despairing plea from the *Lively* to be allowed to go back was overruled, and the two sinking ships were left to their fate.

At daybreak the *Kandahar* was still afloat, although the entire after-part was submerged and water was lapping around the base of the funnel. Commander Robson kept his ship's company busy preparing for the destruction of confidential books and for scuttling, much as Barry Bingham had done on board the *Nestor* at Jutland, to pass the time and to distract people's minds. All day and most of the following night the *Kandahar* wallowed in the swell, but the rising wind carried her clear of the minefield. Then at 0400 her sister *Jaguar* arrived on the scene, sent from Malta to find her. A heavy sea was now running, but Lieutenant-Commander Tyrwhitt's seamanship was well above average, and he managed to rescue 165 men. Sadly, only one survivor from HMS *Neptune* was found alive by an Italian torpedo boat four days later.

The close of 1941 saw the British on the defensive in the Mediterranean, for the destruction of Force K was only one of several disasters to follow closely one upon another. The torpedoing of the battleship *Barham* and the carrier *Ark Royal* and the 'human torpedo' attack on the battleships *Queen Elizabeth* and *Valiant* in Alexandria knocked out the last major units, and prevented Admiral Cunningham from putting pressure on the Axis. Conversely the Axis land, sea and air forces prospered with the relaxation of the attacks on their supply routes. Another factor was the withdrawal of ships to fight in the Far East for Japan had shown her hand at last by launching attacks on Pearl Harbor and the British and Dutch possessions in the East Indies. The heavy losses in ships had been merely the fortunes of war, but they could not have come at a worse time.

The need to replenish Malta was growing more and more urgent. Throughout 1941 there had been many efforts to keep the island supplied, and each one had been a major operation. Any force approaching Malta from the Western or Gibraltar end of the Mediterranean had to run the gauntlet of attacks from the air, from submarines and from surface craft of all sizes. In the beginning, the large number of Axis sympathizers and agents in Spain made it easy to know the size, composition and moment of departure of any convoy leaving Gibraltar. Airfields in Southern Sardinia and Tunisia made aerial reconnaissance over the Central Mediterranean easy, and as soon as any force entered the Sicilian Narrows it was within range of every form of attack. The main Italian naval bases at Naples and Taranto were close, and motor torpedo boats were based on the island fortress of Pantelleria in the middle of the Channel. Given the large numbers of warships available to *Supermarina* it is surprising what poor use was made of the surface fleet in attempting to interrupt the passage of convoys, but the *Regia Navale* had never really recovered from the blows at Taranto and Matapan, and although individual units acquitted themselves bravely the high command frequently dithered and issued a stream of conflicting orders to its forces.

In 1941 many battles had been fought with Italian surface units, and in all of them destroyers had played their part. The losses were heavy, and included the *Airedale, Bedouin, Eridge, Fearless, Foresight, Gallant, Grove, Gurkha, Hasty, Heythrop, Hostile, Hyperion, Jackal, Kingston, Kipling, Kujawiak* (Polish), *Lance, Legion, Lively, Maori, Mohawk, Nestor* (Australian), *Quentin* and *Southwold*.

In January 1942 the 8th Army's fortunes improved, and with the airfields in Cyrenaica back in British hands Admiral Cunningham felt more optimistic about the Navy's chances of running a convoy through to Malta. In March he asked Admiral Vian to escort a small convoy of fast merchantmen from Alexandria to Malta. It was a desperate mission, for Malta was nearly on its knees, but Cunningham pointed out to Vian that the Italians had never yet attacked through a smoke-screen.

The Second Battle of Sirte (the first had been a brief engagement with the Italian Fleet just before the loss of the *Neptune* and *Kandahar* in December 1941, and Vian had also been in command) was one of the most dashing exploits in Vian's career. It showed that even without a battle-fleet behind them the Royal Navy's light forces were able to force the Italians to treat them with respect. The 'Fighting Fifteenth', otherwise known as Vian's 15th Cruiser Squadron, left Alexandria early on the morning of 20 March 1942 with 15 destroyers, escorting the fast transports *Breconshire, Clan Campbell, Pampas* and *Talabot*. Two days later Vian was told the unwelcome news that Italian heavy units had left Taranto. Later the cruiser *Penelope* and the destroyer *Legion* joined the convoy bringing the total number of cruisers up to five, including the elderly anti-aircraft cruiser *Carlisle* which was not equipped for surface action. Throughout the morning Italian bombers made desultory attacks with torpedoes and bombs, but with no result. The midday meal was being eaten at Action Stations, sandwiches and mugs of tea, when a floatplane suddenly dropped a string of red flares ahead of the convoy. A floatplane could only have come from a cruiser or a battleship and the markers were intended to guide an enemy squadron during its attack.

Below: HMS *Kipling* and her sister *Kimberley* of the 5th Flotilla. The 'J' and 'K' Classes bore the brunt of fighting in the Mediterranean. Eleven out of 16 were lost.

At 1410 the cruiser *Euryalus* reported smoke on the horizon and seven minutes later the masts and funnels of three big ships came into view. Vian signalled to the *Carlisle* and the six small 'Hunt' Class destroyers (which had no torpedo-tubes) to stay with the convoy and steer South towards Sirte to keep clear, while his flagship the *Cleopatra*, the *Dido*, *Euryalus* and *Penelope* and the fleet destroyers prepared to fight a surface action. 'Make smoke' was the order, and soon clouds of black funnel smoke and choking white clouds from the chlor-sulphonic acid chemical smoke-floats mixed to form a screen between the Italian Fleet and the convoy. At 1436 the heavy cruisers and a light cruiser, afterwards identified as the *Gorizia*, *Trento* and *Giovanni delle Bande Nere*, opened fire on the 15th Cruiser Squadron at a range of 27,000 yards, but their shells fell short. The British cruisers were also out-ranged, but at a combined approach speed of 50 knots it was only a matter of minutes before the 5.25-inch guns of the *Cleopatra*, *Dido* and *Euryalus* were firing back. The rising wind made shell-spotting almost impossible for both sides and no hits were scored. After an hour the Italian cruisers sheered off to the North but no sooner had Vian's cruisers regained contact with the convoy than the alarm bells sounded again. The destroyer *Zulu* had sighted the enemy again, this time in two groups, the cruisers in one and the battleship *Littorio* 15 miles away with four destroyers.

For two hours the British cruisers and the destroyers played a lethal game with the Italians, daring them to come through the smoke-screen to face a torpedo attack When the Italians tried to work their way around the westward end of the smoke-screen Vian used his destroyers to push them back. Hits were scored on both sides, but no serious damage was done as the ships weaved in and out of the smoke-screen in clouds of spray. Captain Poland and the 14th Flotilla in a determined torpedo attack on the enemy forced him to withdraw. All this time sporadic bombing was taking place, an added distraction. It was 1820 before the Italians finally gave up and withdrew for the last time, leaving the British to cope with what was now a mounting storm. In fact both sides suffered considerably more damage from the storm than from gunfire; the *Littorio* returned to harbour with thousands of tons of water aboard and the destroyers *Lanciere* and *Scirocco* foundered that night. Vian's cruisers had to reduce speed to 18 knots and later to 15 knots; even then the destroyers fell behind and the *Zulu* had her forecastle stove in by a heavy sea.

Above: The French *contre-torpilleur Le Fantasque* in 1940. The lack of endurance of this type of destroyer prevented their employment in the Atlantic.

After such an heroic action the aftermath was all the more tragic. In spite of fighter protection from Malta next day the convoy was attacked by numerous waves of hostile aircraft. The *Clan Campbell* was hit and sank, and the destroyer *Legion* was also hit while coming up in support and sank later. With only eight miles to go the *Breconshire* was stopped dead in the water by a bomb; although eventually towed into Marsaxlokk harbour she was again hit and sank at her moorings. The destroyer *Southwold*

L 61

Left: The Greek destroyer *Pindos* escorts a convoy in the Mediterranean.
Below: The badly damaged tanker *Ohio* limps into Malta, kept afloat by two destroyers lashed alongside,the *Ledbury* to port and the *Penn* to starboard.

struck a mine and sank, but the two surviving merchantmen, the *Pampas* and *Talabot* entered Grand Harbour safely and began to discharge their cargoes immediately. However, they too were sunk before they had been completely unloaded, and in the end only 5000 tons out of the 25,900 tons of stores which had left Alexandria actually reached the people of Malta.

The last great Malta convoy was Operation Pedestal in August 1942 which called for the support of two battleships, three fleet carriers, seven cruisers and 20 destroyers to get only 14 fast cargo ships through. In a four-day battle nine merchantmen, a carrier and two cruisers were sunk, and a carrier and two cruisers were badly damaged. But Malta was saved, particularly by the tanker *Ohio*, whose cargo of aviation gasoline was the most vital of all, for it was needed to keep the Spitfires and Hurricanes flying. The *Ohio* was crippled and had been on fire, but the destroyers *Penn* and *Ledbury* lashed themselves alongside to keep her afloat long enough to crawl into Bighi Bay. Although she sank at her moorings her cargo was intact, and it enabled Malta's aircraft to begin strikes against Rommel's supply convoys once more.

Operation Torch

With Malta secure the Allies were able to go ahead with their long-awaited plans to occupy North Africa. It was a most ambitious plan, with an Anglo-American force landing in Algeria and an American force landing on the Atlantic coast of Morocco. The role played by destroyers was important, both in the initial assault and in protecting shipping against attack from U-Boats and any French warships which chose to resist. To this end the British Force H had 17 destroyers, three cruisers, three carriers and three battleships; the Centre and Eastern Task Forces (British) each had another 13 destroyers as well as larger warships; and the Western Task Force (American) had 38 destroyers, seven cruisers, five carriers and three battleships.

At Algiers two old flotilla leaders, HMS *Malcolm* and HMS *Broke* were to carry assault parties of US Rangers into the harbour with the object of preventing the French from scuttling ships and sabotaging the port installations. A similar role at Casablanca was allotted to the old 'four-stackers', USS *Bernadou* and

Top left: HMS *Broke* of the 'Shakespeare' Class seen off Algiers 7 November 1942, the day before her attempt to break the boom.
Below: The *Malcolm* with US Rangers aboard ready to accompany the *Broke* in her gallant attempt to force Algiers Harbour.

Left: The *Fionda* was typical of the torpedo boats or small escort destroyers built for the Italian Navy between 1934 and 1943. Many fell into German hands.

USS *Cole*, but these two had been specially converted to assault transports with one funnel removed. The attack on Algiers on the morning of 8 November 1942 went badly. The two destroyers failed to find the harbour entrance in the dark and were sighted by the shore gunners. The *Malcolm* was hit several times and had to withdraw with heavy damage, but the *Broke*, living up to the reputation of her namesake of 1917, would not give up. At her fourth attempt she broke through the boom and landed her Rangers successfully, but then came under very heavy fire from French shore-batteries and was forced to leave. She was very badly damaged and sank in tow next day. The *Bernadou* and *Cole* also ran into stiff opposition at Casablanca, but fortunately neither destroyer was hit. Two days later the *Dallas* emulated the *Broke* by breaking the boom at Port Lyautey to allow her complement of Rangers to seize the airfield.

The destroyers screening the Western Task Force Covering Group became involved in a duel with French warships in Casablanca, one of the rare occasions when French destroyers fought their opposite numbers. The Covering Group, which included the battleship *Massachusetts* and the heavy cruisers *Tuscaloosa* and *Wichita*, came under fire from the battleship *Jean Bart* at a range of ten miles. There was nothing the destroyers could do but dodge the French shells, but suddenly at 0815 the *contre-torpilleurs Milan* and *Albatros* and the destroyers *Boulonnais*, *Brestois*, *Fougeux* and *Fron-*

Right: The destroyers *Penn* (left) launched in 1941 and *Lookout* launched in 1940 with the battleship *Rodney* in Mers-El-Kebir after Operation Torch.

deur steamed out at high speed, heading straight for the US task force. In the gunnery duel which followed, the USS *Ludlow* was disabled by a hit but the French destroyers broke off after about ten minutes of firing and retired. This time they were hammered by gunfire from the cruisers and battleships and by aircraft from the US carrier *Ranger*. The *Milan* was set on fire by shells from the *Wilkes* and was driven ashore; the 16-inch guns of the *Massachusetts* registered on the *Boulonnais* and *Fougeux* and sank them, with the *Tuscaloosa* joining in. Two hours later the light cruiser *Primauguet* and seven more destroyers came out, but once again the American fire was too much for them; the *Albatros* had to be beached and the *Brestois* and *Frondeur* were knocked out.

U-Boats were a constant threat, and the Allied destroyers had several encounters. Between 7 November and 15 December they sank four out of the 15 Italian and German U-Boats off Casablanca and Algiers, but HMS *Martin* and the famous Dutch *Isaac Sweers* were sunk. The USS *Hambleton* was badly damaged but was docked in Casablanca for emergency repairs while HMS *Marne* lost her stern. The British *Ithuriel* had to be written off as a total loss from bomb damage in Bone Harbour, while the

Right: Tracer shells illuminate the night sky as the Allied Fleet drives off another air attack.
Below: A shell from a French shore battery explodes off the starboard bow of the USS *Mayrant* (DD.402) during the preliminary bombardment before the Torch landings.

'Hunt' Class *Avon Vale* had her bow blown off by an aerial torpedo. But these losses were comparatively light, and had no effect on the objectives of Torch, which were to clear the Axis forces out of North Africa.

The next step in the Allied offensive was the occupation of Sicily. Destroyers were present in larger numbers, 71 British, 48 American, six Greek and three Polish, but this time they were restricted to screening the amphibious forces and bombarding shore positions. The opposition was less than expected but heavy air attacks were mounted by the *Luftwaffe*; on D-Day, 10 July, the *Maddox* was hit by a single bomb off Gela and sank in two minutes with the loss of 210 of her complement. American and British destroyers sank four U-Boats during the invasion and earned the praise of General Mark Clark for the accuracy of their gunfire support.

The invasion of the Italian mainland in the Gulf of Salerno two months later was

Left: An unusually happy scene between the victors and the vanquished as officers of the USS *Buck* (DD.420) interrogate several U-boat survivors.

Below: The wrecks of French *contre-torpilleurs* litter the harbour of Toulon after the scuttling of the fleet in November 1942.

Right: A destroyer takes it green as her bow plunges into a Mediterranean swell.

a much harder task. There was a strong possibility of the landing being cancelled if the Italians negotiated an armistice with the Allies, but at the last minute the German forces forestalled such moves, and it was clear that the invasion would be opposed. D-Day was 9 September 1943, and from the start the assault forces were heavily engaged. On Green Beach, on the left flank of the British landing zone, German forces even broke through to the beach. Destroyers were standing by about a mile offshore, and were able to take a direct hand by firing at enemy tanks and infantry. Destroyer guns proved to be very effective as tank-busters; the high muzzle velocity and heavy shells put them in a class way beyond any tank or anti-tank gun's performance, and in addition destroyer-gunners were trained to shoot at mobile targets. Not since the evacuation from France in 1940 had destroyers faced tanks and infantry in this way, and once more ground troops learned to treat warships with respect.

The experience was similar on the beaches in the American sector at Paestum. Mark VI Tiger tanks advanced

Below : An American destroyer lays a smoke-screen to protect a cruiser during one of the many Red Alerts off Salerno.
Bottom left : Chemical smoke pours from the fantail of a US destroyer off Salerno. Note the aircraft identification silhouettes painted on the inside of the bridge screen.

to within 200 yards of some infantry positions, and had the cruisers and destroyers of Fire-Support Group not arrived in time the Allied invasion could have been a bloody fiasco. Two US destroyers were lost, the *Buck* and *Rowan*, as well as HMS *Puckeridge*, but the contribution to the success of the Salerno landings was beyond doubt. The shallow draught of destroyers allowed them to lie much closer inshore than any other type of warship, apart from small gunboats and landing craft, and so they could intervene quickly to silence artillery. As long as they were kept in touch with their shore fire-control (SFC) parties they could bring gun-fire to bear rapidly wherever it was needed. Battleships and cruisers could fire a heavier weight of metal but the sight of a destroyer close at hand was a more reassuring sight, just as it had been to the hard-pressed ANZAC infantry 28 years before at Gallipoli.

The Germans remained in control of the Northern part of Italy for much longer than had been expected and operations against their surface forces continued through 1944 and into the first

months of 1945. Many Italian destroyers and torpedo boats fell into German hands at the time of the armistice in September 1943 and these were used to support operations in Elba, Sardinia and Corsica, and in the Adriatic and Aegean. While much bigger events were taking place in other theatres, a series of clashes took place as the Allies extended their control and pushed the German forces back. Inevitably destroyers played an important part in what were officially only 'mopping-up' operations, but the fights were frequently fierce and bloody. The small British 'Hunt' Class, originally intended for escort duties, proved suitable, but the most spectacular results were achieved in the Adriatic by the French *contre-torpilleurs* of the *Fantasque* type. In the restricted waters of the Adriatic they came into their own, for their lack of range did not matter. Running at speeds of 37–40 knots, they carried out offensive sweeps against German shipping and caused havoc. Only four of these magnificent craft had survived the disasters of 1940–1942, but when the Germans had tried to seize the Toulon Fleet they had come over to the Allied cause and had been refitted in the United States. It was ironic that these super-destroyers should have had to wait four years for a chance to show their capabilities.

Left: The Italian *Turbine* and her sisters were built in 1925–28. All eight became war casualties. Five out of the eight were sunk by British Forces.
Right: The lifeless body of a crewman of the USS *Menges* (DE.320) slumped over the edge of a gun tub. The ship was torpedoed by *U.371* in the Western Mediterranean in May 1944 but reached port safely.
Below: The USS *Swanson* (DD.443) seen from the carrier *Ranger* during the Torch landings in November 1942. Sixteen such general-purpose *Livermore* Class destroyers were built.

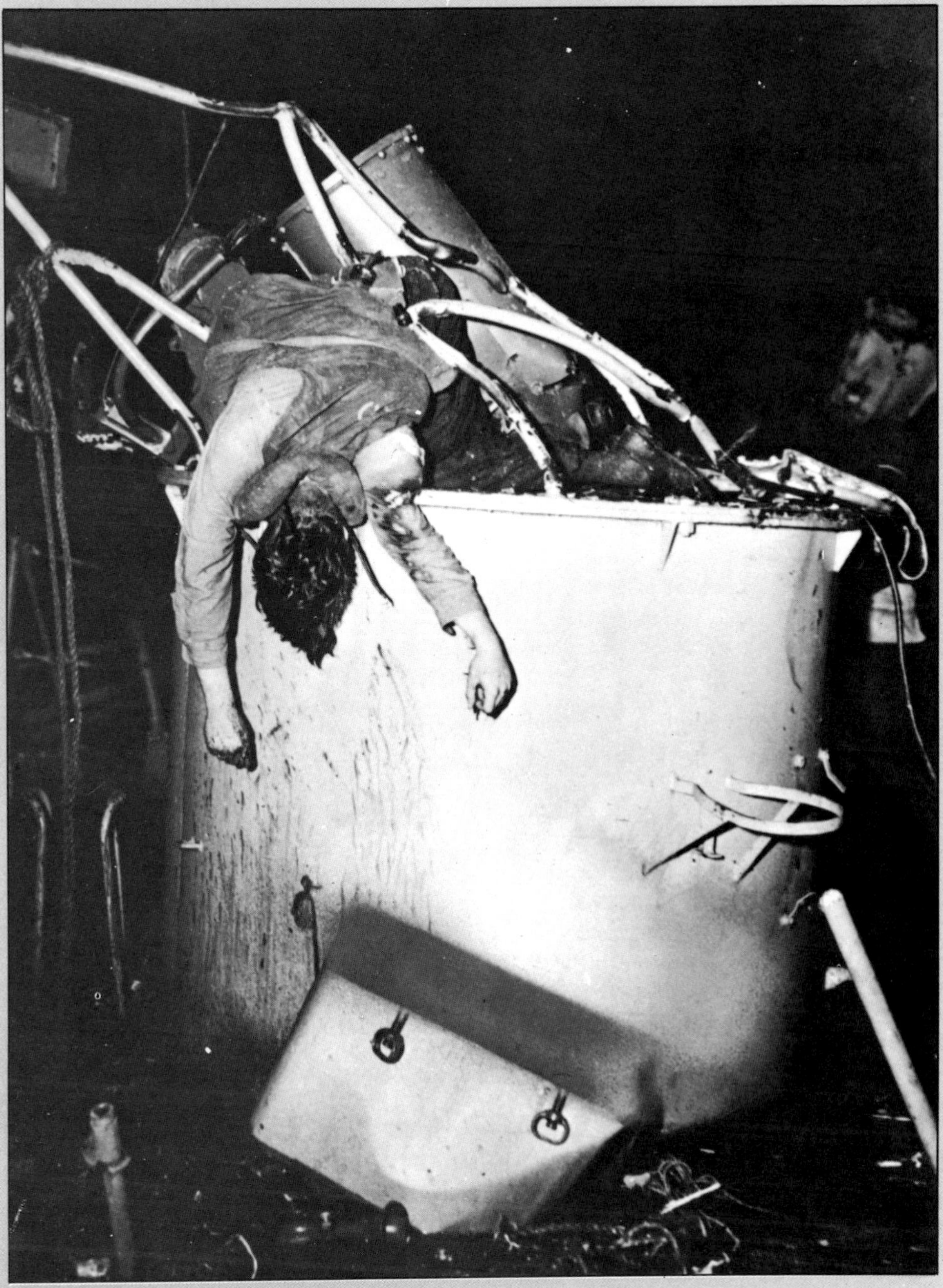

Destroyers on the Defensive

It was a destroyer of the US Pacific Fleet which had the first brush with the Japanese in World War II. The 'four-stacker' *Ward* had been on routine patrol off Pearl Harbor and in the early morning of 7 December she was heading for home after an uneventful two days. At 0357 she was warned by a minesweeper that something resembling the periscope of a submarine had been sighted. A sonar search revealed nothing, but about two-and-a-half hours after the report the *Ward*'s lookouts spotted a small submarine trailing the target ship *Antares* on her way to the main entrance.

The old destroyer's crew was efficient, and the second four-inch shell was seen to hit at a distance of less than a hundred yards. A pattern of depth-charges completed the destruction of the mystery submarine, which was in fact one of a force of midgets which had been launched from Japanese fleet submarines some distance away. The idea was that the attack was to coincide with the air strike which was already winging its way from Admiral Nagumo's carriers, and to profit by the resulting confusion in the anchorage. The subsequent failure to take note of the *Ward*'s timely action was just one more of the oversights and miscalculations which contributed to the disaster of Pearl Harbor.

Pearl Harbor

The Pacific Fleet's battleships were the main target of the Japanese torpedo- and dive-bombers, but they also attacked a floating drydock in which the destroyer *Shaw* was being refitted. Three bombs hit the destroyer and set fire to her oil fuel, and after about 20 minutes the forward five-inch magazine exploded. The dock had already been flooded to put out the fire, and destroyer and dock slowly capsized. A similar disaster befell the *Cassin* and *Downes* which were in Drydock No 1 ahead of the battleship *Pennsylvania*. There was little that the two destroyers could do for they were stripped for overhaul, and even the .50 calibre machine guns of the *Downes* had to be reassembled before they could open fire. They survived the attacks of the first wave of aircraft, thanks to the protecting fire from the *Pennsylvania*, but the second wave scored a hit on the *Downes*. Incendiary bombs set her oil fuel alight and both destroyers were burnt out, despite attempts to extinguish the fires by flooding the dock.

Many of the other destroyers managed to get underway, and so, although they were attacked by Japanese aircraft they avoided casualties. The *Blue* paused on her way out of the harbour to attack what was believed to be another midget submarine; so did the *Helm*. The *Monaghan* spotted a submarine alarm signal flying from the seaplane tender *Curtiss*' halyards and attacked with depth-charges sinking the second of five Japanese midget submarines lost in the Pearl Harbor operation. The spirited handling of the Pacific Fleet destroyers was one of the few *credit* entries in the ledger at the end of that 'day of infamy'.

Top right: The forward five-inch guns of the USS *Downes* (DD.375) after the fires had been put out. *Right:* The wrecks of the destroyers *Downes* (left) and *Cassin* (DD.372) rest in Drydock Number 1 ahead of the battleship *Pennsylvania*. The guns and machinery were salvaged, shipped back to the US and installed in new hulls with the same names.

Below: The detonation of the USS *Shaw*'s magazines provided a most impressive pyrotechnic display at Pearl Harbor.

Destroyers in the East Indies

The Asiatic Fleet had only 13 flush-deckers, all well past their prime, to defend the Philippines. When their base at Cavite was put out of action by Japanese bombers three days after Pearl Harbor, the Commander-in-Chief, Admiral Thomas C Hart had even less chance of protecting such an enormous area. Hart was ordered to get his destroyers to the Dutch East Indies, where in conjunction with Australian, British and Dutch warships, there might be some hope of defending the so-called 'Malay Barrier'. The *Pillsbury* and *Peary* which were undergoing repairs after a collision were among the last ships to leave Manila Bay on 27 December. The *Pillsbury* reached Surabaya safely but the *Peary* was bombed in error by Australian Air Force Hudsons while traversing the Molucca Passage. The Allied naval forces were now united under a new command called ABDA (American–British–Dutch–Australian), but it was too late to stop the victorious Japanese. The US battlefleet had been knocked out and three days later the British capital ships *Prince of Wales* and *Repulse* had been sunk off Malaya leaving ABDA's nine cruisers and 22 destroyers as the only organized opposition.

On 20 January 1942 Admiral Hart ordered the cruisers *Boise* and *Marblehead* and six destroyers of DesDiv 59 to attack a Japanese force of transports heading for Balikpapan in Eastern Borneo. The cruiser *Boise* damaged herself by hitting a pinnacle of rock and had to return to base escorted by a destroyer. Then the *Marblehead* developed machinery trouble and returned taking another destroyer as escort. This left only the elderly *John D Ford*, *Parrott*, *Paul Jones* and *Pope* to deal with an amphibious force escorted by the light cruiser *Naka* and 12 destroyers. But fortune favours the bold, and Commander Talbot's tiny force reached Balikpapan undetected; the Dutch had set the oil refinery on fire and huge clouds of smoke shrouded the anchorage. It was ideal for a destroyer attack with the transports at anchor in the harbour silhouetted against the glow of fires ashore.

The destroyers raced in aiming their first torpedoes at a line of transports outside the harbour. The *Parrott* fired three torpedoes but obtained no hit, and then launched another salvo of fire, but it also missed. Two more torpedoes fired by the *John D Ford* and the *Paul Jones* also missed, although the range was down to 1000 yards. The real culprit was probably the faulty design of exploder fitted to USN torpedoes, and the feelings of the men of DesDiv 59 who had taken so many risks can be imagined. The Japanese were now alert to the fact that an attack was in progress and the anchorage soon bustled with activity as alarm bells sounded and guns fired. Fortunately for the Americans the Japanese destroyers seem to have been ordered to start a submarine hunt, and the ships remained undetected for a while longer. During a second attack three of the *Parrott*'s 'fish' behaved properly, and this time a transport blew up. The column of destroyers left a trail of destruction as they ran southwards sinking another transport and a patrol craft totalling 23,000 tons of shipping. When they had no torpedoes left they used their four-inch guns to sink another transport before leaving the scene. The confusion and destruction they had caused was out of all proportion to their relative strength, for all four were 'four-stackers' built in World War I, and officially regarded as unfit for front-line service.

Below: The USS *Stewart* fell into Japanese hands at Surabaya in March 1942 and became Petrol Vessel No 102. She was extensively altered to give her a more Japanese look and she is seen here after her return to the USN in 1945.

It was the only success scored by ABDA. The Japanese continued their inexorable drive on the East Indies, investing Singapore in the West and reaching as far as Rabaul in the East. With the flanks in enemy hands the centre was soon untenable; Surabaya on the North side of Java was threatened, and Tjilatjap on the South side was the only other suitable base. A holding action was needed, and so the Dutch Admiral Karel Doorman was given command of a Combined Allied Striking Force, comprising the US cruisers *Houston* and *Marblehead*, the Dutch cruisers *de Ruyter* (flagship) and *Tromp*, the US destroyers *Barker*, *Bulmer*, *John D Edwards* and *Stewart* and the Dutch destroyers *Banckert*, *Piet Hein* and *Van Ghent*. To avoid the risk of air attack Doorman proposed a night attack on the Japanese invasion forces in the Makassar Strait but, to be in position by nightfall the task force had to cross the Java Sea in daylight.

Inevitably the Combined Striking Force was sighted by Japanese aircraft and a force of bombers attacked on the morning of 4 February. The cruisers were the main target and when both the *Houston* and *Marblehead* were badly hit Admiral Doorman ordered a return to Tjilatjap. With reinforcements from Surabaya, the British cruiser *Exeter*, the Australian *Hobart*, the Dutch *Java* and three more Dutch and US destroyers, Doorman was ordered to launch another strike to protect Palembang, the capital of Sumatra. This raid on 15 February suffered six hours of bombing, and again Doorman had to order his ships to retire; as the British had learned in the Mediterranean, naval operations could not be mounted without air cover. The surrender of Singapore, announced the same day, marked the beginning of the end. Admiral Hart was recalled to the United States. His successor was the Dutch Admiral Conrad Helfrich.

Attrition was taking its toll of ABDA's destroyers; the Dutch *Van Ghent* and *Kortenaer* both ran aground, while the USS *Peary* was sunk in the devastating Japanese bombing raid on Darwin in North Australia. The *Edsall* was damaged by a premature explosion of one of her depth-charges and the *Whipple* collided with the cruiser *de Ruyter*. The third attempt to halt the Japanese, a raid in the Badoeng Strait on 19 February, at last produced some results. Some damage was caused to Japanese destroyers but in return the Dutch destroyer *Piet Hein* was destroyed and the USS *Stewart* and the cruiser *Tromp* were disabled. The US destroyers were beginning to suffer from wear and tear as well as battle damage; operating so far from a main base meant that their tender, the *Black Hawk*, was running out of spares. Even under ideal conditions a squadron of 'cans' needed constant nursing, and these destroyers had been afloat for a quarter of a century.

Above: The superstructure and funnels of the Japanese destroyer *Hatsushimo* are seen here in March 1939 at the entrance to Shibushi Bay. Note the massive enclosed torpedo-tube mounting between the funnels.

The Battle of the Java Sea

By 20 February the ABDA force was reduced to five cruisers and nine destroyers, including three British, which had escaped from Singapore.

On 27 February Doorman's weary forces finally ran into the heavy ships which had been supporting the Japanese invasion, and the last round began. They were part of Admiral Kondo's Southern Striking Force, the heavy cruisers *Haguro* and *Nachi* and two groups of seven destroyers each, led by two outstanding Japanese destroyer-captains, Rear-Admirals Tanaka and Nishimura. Although on paper they did not have a big margin of strength over the ABDA Striking Force the Japanese had the priceless advantage of air cover, and their modern destroyers had the deadly 'Long Lance' 24-inch torpedo.

When the Japanese ships were sighted just after 1600 hours the Allied force was steaming North, with the three British destroyers spread out in line abreast as a screen ahead of the line of cruisers, and the Dutch and American destroyers steaming in line ahead, parallel and on the port quarter. As the Japanese were steaming roughly South-West across their bows, this disposition meant that the bulk of Doorman's destroyers were on the disengaged side. It was the worst place to be, too far away to fire torpedoes, and as inter-Allied communications at this early stage of the war were poor, the destroyers were relying on garbled orders. At 1616 the Japanese opened fire from about 28,000 yards, bracketing the main column with accurate salvoes, and the cruiser *Jintsu* closed in to 18,000 yards to fire at the three destroyers leading the line. Doorman ordered his line to wheel to the West to avoid having his 'T' crossed, and as a result the destroyers were now level with the flagship *de Ruyter*.

The first casualty was the heavy cruiser HMS *Exeter*, which suffered a severe explosion on board. While the line was weaving to avoid her as she slowed down, a torpedo hit the *Kortenaer*. As a column of steam and smoke billowed up she seemed to pause for a moment, then turned turtle and broke in two. There was no time to look for survivors and the other destroyers hurried on, jockeying desperately for a position from which they could attack with torpedoes. The British destroyers tried to drive off the *Jintsu* but *Electra* was hit by a salvo of shells which left her sinking. The other two fell back to give assistance to the crippled *Exeter*, but the American destroyers were now in a position to attack, and in spite of a last-minute cancellation of the order, they carried out an attack. Unfortunately the range was 10,000 yards, for anything closer would have been suicidal, and all the torpedoes missed.

The cruisers had now disappeared, and the four destroyers tried to catch up. They eventually returned to Surabaya to refuel leaving Doorman and his cruisers to sail on to a further disastrous night action. Harassed by torpedo attacks in the light of flares dropped by Japanese floatplanes, the cruisers steamed on. At 2125 the *Jupiter* was suddenly blown up, and as no Japanese ships could be seen it was assumed that she had been mined, but it was just an example of the staggering range of the 'Long Lance' torpedo. By midnight the ABDA force was all but annihilated, with the *de Ruyter* and *Java* sunk and the *Houston* and *Exeter* badly damaged. The three surviving cruisers and two destroyers made their way back to Surabaya with nothing to show for their sacrifice. There was now nothing to stop the Japanese from capturing the entire East Indies. The following evening the cruisers *Houston* and *Perth* were sunk while trying to escape southwards through the Sunda Strait. On the morning of 1 March the *Exeter* and the destroyers HMS *Encounter* and USS *Pope* were trapped by the *Haguro* and *Nachi* in the Java Sea supported by two heavy cruisers.

The *Exeter* went down fighting, and when it was hopeless she ordered the two destroyers to make their escape while there was still time. The *Encounter* was hit by shellfire just after a destroyer torpedo finished off the *Exeter*, but the *Pope* managed to dodge behind a rain squall

Cruisers	Destroyers	
HMS *Exeter* (British)	*Jupiter* (British)	*Alden* (American)
Perth (Australian)	*Electra* (British)	*John D Ford* (American)
de Ruyter (Dutch)	*Encounter* (British)	*John D Edwards* (American)
Java (Dutch)	*Kortenaer* (Dutch)	*Paul Jones* (American)
Houston (American)	*Witte de With* (Dutch)	

Above: The *Hayanami* steams at full power over Kyogasaki measured mile on 24 July 1943. She is making 35.15 knots with 52,200 SHP at a displacement of 2561 tonnes.

which hid her from the Japanese ships. With a faint chance of survival the old destroyer hurried away, making for the coast of Borneo, but suddenly the rain squall blew over, leaving her exposed once again. There were no ships in sight but a floatplane from one of the cruisers spotted her and within half an hour six dive-bombers from the carrier *Ryujo* were on the scene. Incredibly, the *Pope* survived 13 attacks, and the carrier had to send a second group of bombers to finish her off. Another remarkable feature of the *Pope*'s last stand was that she suffered only one casualty, a crewman killed by one of her own scuttling charges. Commander Welford C Blinn was awarded the Navy Cross and other members of her crew were decorated but, unfortunately for the crew, 27 died in Japanese hands.

Above: The *Nowaki* of the *Kagero* Class makes 34.76 knots over the Kyogasaki mile near Maizuro. Note the absence of smoke and the unusual stern wave.
Below: The US destroyer *Peary* and the heavy cruiser *Houston* in Darwin Harbour before the Battle of Java Sea.

(1)

Above: Crewmen of the USS *O'Bannon* (DD.450) in August 1943 during the Solomons Campaign.
Left: The five-inch 38/cal guns and bridgework of the *Fletcher* Class destroyer *Bullard* (DD.660) in NY Navy Yard, March 1943. The figure (1) indicates the support for the BK radar antenna.

Coral Sea and Midway

For the US Pacific Fleet there was no time to dwell on the mistakes which had led to Pearl Harbor. While salvage teams worked on the sunken battleships the carrier task forces mounted a series of hit-and-run raids in the Central and South Pacific. Screening these highly mobile forces was a particularly arduous task for the hard-working 'cans' of the Pacific Fleet. There was the traditional task of 'planeguard', trailing a carrier while she launched or recovered her aircraft, ready to pick up the crew of any aircraft which 'ditched' in the sea. To this was added the need to reinforce the carrier's anti-aircraft defences. There were convoys to reinforce all the scattered outposts from Australia to the Aleutians, and all these required escorts against submarine and surface attack. As every group of warships needed its screen of destroyers, the demands rapidly outstripped supply.

Fortunately the US Navy had used its breathing space from 1940 to the end of 1941 wisely, and a large number of destroyers were under construction. A superb new type of destroyer had been ordered in 1940, the *Fletcher* Class. These were probably the best all-round destroyers produced in World War II with good endurance and a good margin of stability to cope with all the wartime additions such as radar and AA guns. To give greater longitudinal strength to the hull the flush deck was revived for the first time in 20 years, but with much greater beam to avoid the rolling which had characterized the old destroyers. The armament of five five-inch 28 calibre guns was disposed in the same way as the previous *Benson*s, two singles forward and three aft, with two quintuple sets of torpedo-tubes. The four boilers were divided into two fire-rooms, separated by the forward engine-room on the 'unit' system. The anti-aircraft armament, although it had to be strengthened later, was as good as any other destroyer designed without war-experience: three twin 40mm Bofors mountings, two ahead of the bridge and one crowning the after superstructure. The quadruple 1.1-inch in older destroyers had proved unreliable, and the Bofors proved far superior in all respects. Similarly the *Fletcher*s received the first 20mm Oerlikon automatic guns, rather than the existing .50 calibre machine gun.

The 376-foot hull of a *Fletcher* was cut in half by the machinery, gearing and boilers, which occupied nearly half the length. To allow communication between the two halves there was a deckhouse running from the bridge nearly as far back as No 3 five-inch gun, carrying the two sets of torpedo-tubes. In the fore-part of the hull there were three deck levels num-

bered 2, 3 and 4, with an additional 'half-deck' for storage. On No 2 Deck was the Chief Petty Officers' (CPOs) mess, the handling arrangements for No 1 five-inch gun a deck above, showers and the 'heads' or WCs, and the plotting room, in which the fire-control solutions were computed. The deck below (No 3) had the crew's mess, the forward casualty dressing station and the Combat Information Center (CIC), the fighting heart of a warship. The use of a central co-ordinating organization was a product of World War II (its equivalent in British destroyers was the Operations Room), and it functioned as a clearing house in which all information from radar and sonar, radio and even visual sighting, could be evaluated. The information was then passed back to the captain, who was normally on the bridge. It functioned in much the same way as the plotting room (British equivalent was Transmitting Station) processed 'raw' data about the ship's course, speed etc and the ballistics of the guns, to enable the fire-control system to aim the guns accurately. On No 4 Deck was the Sound Room, in which the sonar gear was housed; the sonar dome itself was housed in a dome directly underneath or lowered below the keel when in use. The five-inch magazines were also on this deck.

Above: The USS *Fletcher* (DD.445) was the first of a new class of powerful destroyers designed for Pacific operations.

Left: The after-superstructure of the USS *Nicholas* (DD.449). Note the 'pillbox' on the after-bank of torpedo-tubes in the immediate foreground and the elevated barrel of the five-inch 38/cal gun.
Below: The *O'Bannon*, *Chevalier*, and *Taylor* of DesRon 21 on 15 August 1943 on route to the Vella Lavella landings.

The taper of the hull towards the stern meant that there were only two deck-levels in the after-part. No 2 Deck was mainly accommodation, but the steering gear was in a large compartment right aft. The deck below had only stores and the after five-inch magazines. Although bigger destroyers followed the *Fletcher*s, very little change was made to this basic layout. The *Allen M Sumner* and *Gearing* Classes of 1944–45 were *Fletcher*s enlarged to give higher endurance and to accommodate the bulkier armament of three twin five-inch gun mountings. Many experienced destroyermen swore

507

Left: A destroyer-minesweeper (DMS) off Tulagi on 8 August 1942. Eighteen old destroyers were converted to fast minesweepers, with one funnel and boiler removed to allow for extra fuel.
Right: 7 May 1942: survivors from the oiler *Neosho* are picked up by the USS *Helm*'s whaleboat during the Battle of Coral Sea.

that the *Fletcher*s were better because they had only one gun fewer and the gun they had was in a handier mounting than the twin five-inch; another objection was the heavier loading of the big destroyers, which made them more likely to bury their noses in green seas. The first of the *Fletcher* Class did not commission until June 1942, and to increase the number of destroyers a further batch of the older *Benson* type were ordered, known as the *Bristol* Class. But in the first year of the war it was on the older destroyers that the main burden was laid and they saw the hardest fighting.

The first clash between the Japanese and American Fleets was the Battle of the Coral Sea, fought on 7 May 1942. It marked the beginning of a new type of warfare in which carrier planes decided the issue without the opposing warships catching sight of one another. Rear-Admiral Frank Fletcher had 13 destroyers to guard his two carriers, and although they had no opportunity to fulfil their proper role they worked as hard as any of the big ships to decide the battle.

The first casualty in the battle was the destroyer *Sims*, which was escorting the oiler *Neosho* well clear of the two carrier groups. Unfortunately the Japanese mistook the oiler for a carrier and so the two ships were attacked by a large number of carrier aircraft. Three bombs blasted the

Left: The *Conway* (DD.507) tucks her stern down as she works up to full speed.
Below: Two *Sims* Class destroyers alongside the burning carrier *Lexington* during the Battle of the Coral Sea 8 May 1942.

Sims in half with the loss of nearly all hands and the *Neosho* was soon set on fire. Not until the following day could a destroyer be spared to search for survivors, but of one group of 68 who were adrift for ten days only four were found alive.

When the carrier *Lexington*'s bomb damage brought her to a dead stop with fires raging deep in her hull, her captain asked Admiral Fitch to send destroyers to help fight the fires. The *Morris* came alongside, and her crew manhandled two hoses across to the blazing carrier while the injured were taken aboard. For nearly two hours the *Morris* stayed with the *Lexington*, while the giant hull reverberated from explosions of aviation gasoline, bombs, shells and torpedoes. The fire was completely out of control and there was grave danger of the ship blowing up and even rolling over on top of the destroyer. At 1707, when it was decided to abandon the *Lexington*, three more destroyers were sent to help the *Morris* take off the survivors. Despite the appalling risks nearly 2800 men were rescued

from the *Lexington*, and not one of the 216 killed was lost by drowning. The final act in the drama was the order to the destroyer *Phelps* to torpedo the smoke-blackened hulk, and at 1853 four of her torpedoes exploded against the carrier's side. Even so it was another hour before the *Lexington* finally rolled over and disappeared.

Less than four weeks later the US Navy was faced by the much bigger threat of an all-out assault by the Japanese Combined Fleet against the island of Midway. The American Fleet was composed of the ships which had survived the Coral Sea battle as they were the only ships that the USN had in the Central Pacific. Fortunately the *Yorktown* had not been as badly damaged as first thought, and so Rear-Admiral Spruance had three carriers instead of the two which the Japanese were expecting. Nevertheless, 17 destroyers and six cruisers were facing a fleet which included four carriers, eight battleships, 11 cruisers and 56 destroyers. The only way for Spruance to fight the battle would be to make sure that his forces were in the right place so as to attack in local superiority if possible.

The battle started on 4 June and at first the US carrier-planes were unable to penetrate the Japanese combat air patrol of Zeroes. The *Yorktown* was hit by two bombs despite all that her escorts' and her own AA fire could do. Her damage control parties fought to bring the fires under control, but as soon as speed picked up to 20 knots another Japanese strike hit her. This time two torpedoes hit and the carrier began to list alarmingly. In the afternoon the destroyers *Gwin* and *Monaghan* arrived to help her, and they put salvage parties on board. The carrier had been abandoned and there was little that anybody could do until nightfall, when her captain led a team with knowledge of the ship's layout back on board. All through the morning of 6 June the firefighting and damage control parties worked to save the *Yorktown*, with the destroyer *Hammann* alongside providing power for the pumps. But it was all in vain, for at 1535 four torpedo tracks were seen heading for her starboard side. Two hit the *Yorktown* and one hit the *Hammann*. Both ships were mortally wounded; the *Hammann* sank very quickly and the *Yorktown* had to be abandoned for the third time, to be sunk later by Japanese destroyers.

Top left: During the Battle of Midway the destroyer *Phelps* ran out of fuel and had to be assisted by the AA cruiser *Atlanta*.
Above: The stern of the USS *Hammann* (DD.412) slides under after a torpedo-hit from the Japanese submarine *I.168*. She was providing power for the *Yorktown* when she was hit by the fourth torpedo of the salvo which sank the *Yorktown*.
Below: A *Porter* Class destroyer stands by the crippled carrier *Yorktown* on 4 June 1942 during the Battle of Midway.

Guadalcanal

On 7 August 1942 the US Marines landed on Guadalcanal in the Solomon Islands and seized an airstrip which had just been completed. They were not to know, as they triumphantly christened it Henderson Field, that they were witnessing the start of the most bitterly contested naval action of the entire Pacific war. Operation Watchtower had been launched to forestall the Japanese attempt to establish a foothold in the Solomons as a prelude to an attack on Australia. The Battle of the Coral Sea had checkmated an attempt to do it by seapower alone, but this time the Japanese intended to use all three services. The Americans were equally determined to stop them, for whoever possessed the Solomons chain held the key to the South-Eastern Pacific.

The first day of the landings went reasonably well, with no opposition from the Japanese Navy, although heavy air attacks were mounted the next day. Not until the night of 8 August was it apparent what sort of nightmare was unfolding. USAAF bombers and a submarine reported seeing a force of Japanese warships leaving Rabaul. A series of delays prevented the reports from being dealt with, and the results were tragic; the force comprised five heavy and two light cruisers under Admiral Mikawa, and it was steaming at high speed towards the 'Slot', otherwise known as Savo Sound, between Guadalcanal and the northern islands of the Solomons chain. Mikawa's cruisers were going to drive their way through the American and Australian warships to clear a path for six transports carrying reinforcements for the defenders of Guadalcanal.

The first mistake occurred on the morning of 9 August when Australian aircraft twice sighted Mikawa off Bougainville but delayed reporting it until late in the afternoon. The message had to go via Brisbane before it reached Admiral Victor Crutchley RN, whose three cruisers and two destroyers were on patrol in Savo Sound, and via Pearl Harbor before it reached Admiral Turner USN, in command at Guadalcanal. It was over eight hours before either flag-officer received the report of the first sighting. The report included an erroneous sighting of 'seaplane tenders', which led Admiral Turner to assume that an air-attack rather than a gun and torpedo attack was most likely and once this idea had taken hold, other incorrect assumptions followed. Aerial reconnaissance might have cleared up the misunderstanding, but the US carriers had been withdrawn the night before to refuel, and bad weather had grounded the land-based search aircraft. At midnight the old submarine *S.38*, the same one which had first seen Mikawa's departure from Rabaul, torpedoed one of the six transports following the Japanese cruiser force. The remaining five turned back to Rabaul, but Mikawa's ships were now only 35 miles from Savo Island, still unsuspected.

The destroyer *Ralph Talbot* raised the alarm when one of the Japanese cruisers' floatplanes flew overhead, but bad radio-reception prevented the call from getting through; her sister *Blue* picked it up and also made radar contact, but she also failed to make contact with Admiral Turner's flagship. In the sultry night, with changing visibility and rain squalls, the Japanese cruisers even managed to pass the *Blue* and *Ralph Talbot* without being detected. Both 'cans' were steaming away from the Japanese cruisers, and the lookouts were gazing ahead only, relying on the SC radar to give all-round cover surveillance. They were not to know that the mass of Savo Island nearby was producing a false echo which masked the echoes from the ships slipping past little more than 500 yards from the *Blue*. The next destroyer was the *Jarvis*, which had been torpedoed by a wave of torpedo bombers the day before; even if she had sighted the line of cruisers steaming at 25 knots her radio had been put out of action and there was no way in which to pass on a warning.

At 0143 the destroyer *Patterson* radioed an alarm, but it was too late. The floatplanes overhead dropped parachute flares to illuminate the Allied ships and a hail of gunfire and torpedoes was unleashed. The Australian cruiser *Canberra* was hit by eight-inch shells and then two torpedoes hit her on the starboard side. She was soon on fire and completely disabled, but the *Patterson* was able to make some sort of reply. The *Bagley*, on the *Canberra*'s starboard bow, managed to get off a salvo of torpedoes, but too late. At 0147 a torpedo blew off the heavy cruiser *Chicago*'s bow, and she sheered off to the

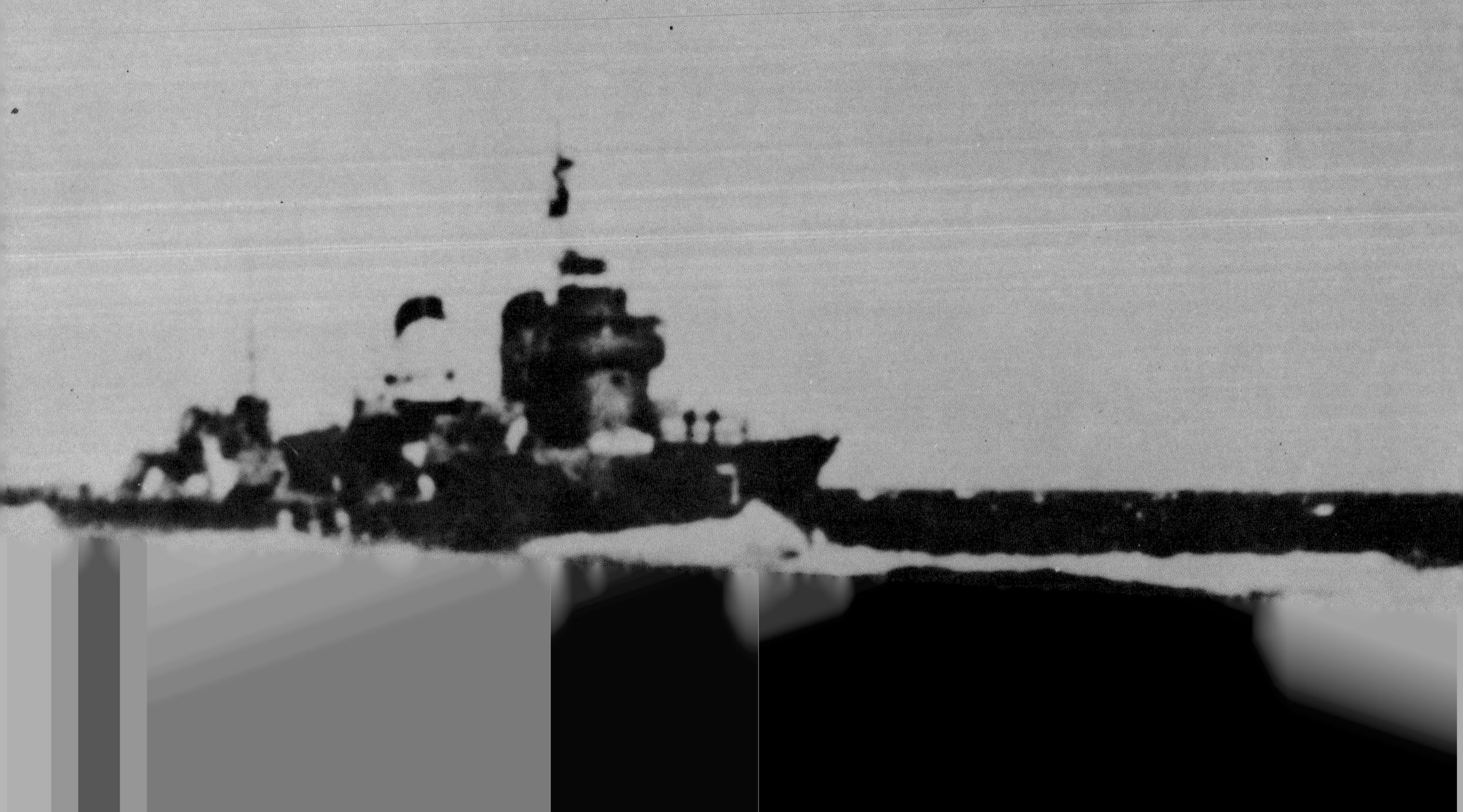

West, away from the battle. The Japanese cruisers now moved North, splitting into two groups, and between Savo and Florida Island they fell in with the Northern Force, the heavy cruisers *Astoria*, *Quincy* and *Vincennes* with two destroyers. Like the Southern Force, which no longer existed, Captain Riefkohl's ships had been at action stations for up to 36 hours, and they had been allowed to stand down to the second state of readiness', with half the crew on watch and the other half turned in. The gun flashes to the South had been mistaken for the *Chicago* firing at aircraft, understandable in the light of the general assumption that an

Above: The USS *Trippe* (DD.403) after her 1943 refit with half her torpedo-tubes removed to reduce top-weight.
Below: The destroyers *Akebono* (right) and *Ushio* of the 7th Destroyer Flotilla manoeuvre in line ahead.

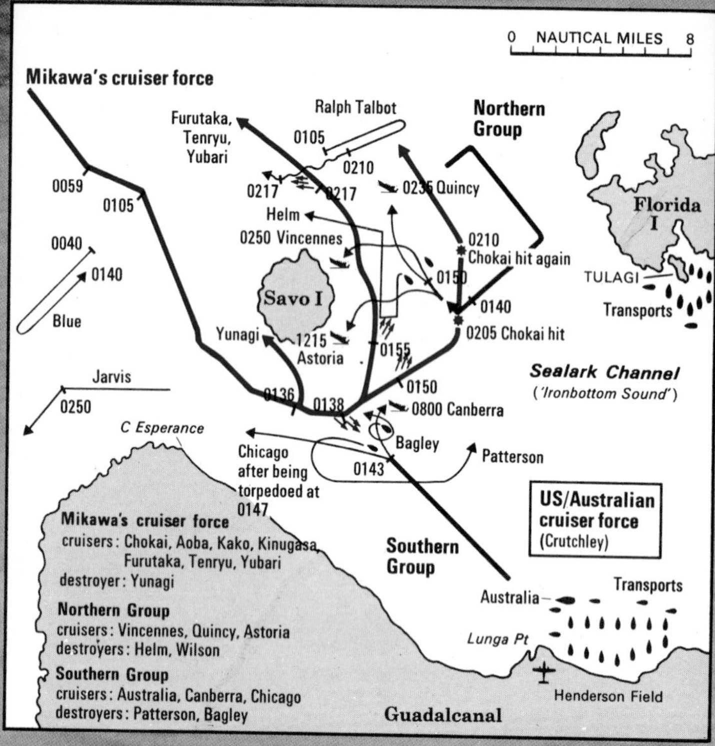
0 NAUTICAL MILES 8
Mikawa's cruiser force
Furutaka, Tenryu, Yubari
Ralph Talbot
Northern Group
0105
0210
0059
0105
0217
0217
Quincy
Helm
0250 Vincennes
0210
Chokai hit again
Florida I
0040
0140
TULAGI
Blue
Savo I
0150
0140
Transports
Yunagi
1215
Astoria
0155
0205 Chokai hit
Jarvis
0250
0136
0138
0150
0800 Canberra
Sealark Channel
('Ironbottom Sound')
C Esperance
Chicago after being torpedoed at 0147
Bagley
0143
Patterson
US/Australian cruiser force
(Crutchley)
Mikawa's cruiser force
cruisers: Chokai, Aoba, Kako, Kinugasa, Furutaka, Tenryu, Yubari
destroyer: Yunagi
Northern Group
cruisers: Vincennes, Quincy, Astoria
destroyers: Helm, Wilson
Southern Group
cruisers: Australia, Canberra, Chicago
destroyers: Patterson, Bagley
Southern Group
Australia
Transports
Lunga Pt
Henderson Field
Guadalcanal

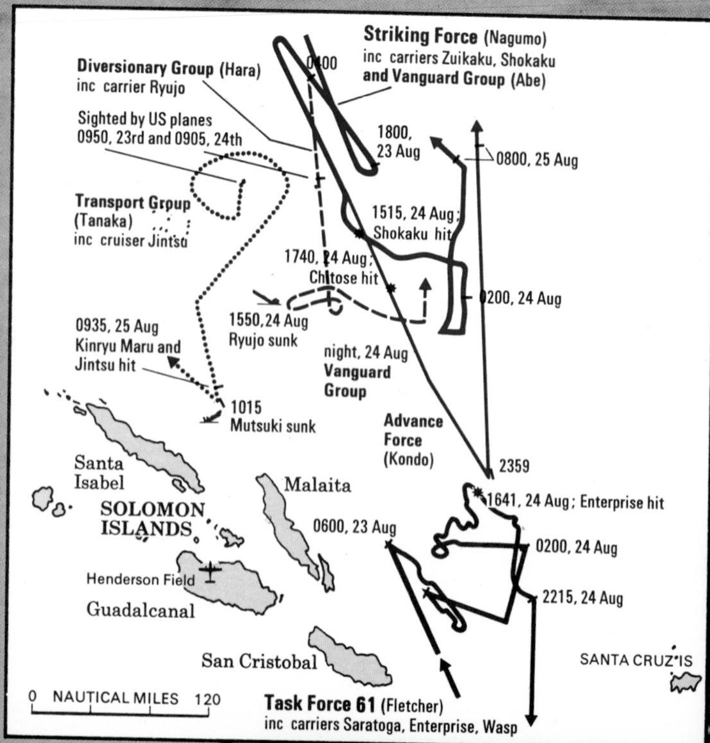
Striking Force (Nagumo)
inc carriers Zuikaku, Shokaku
and Vanguard Group (Abe)
Diversionary Group (Hara)
inc carrier Ryujo
0400
Sighted by US planes
0950, 23rd and 0905, 24th
1800, 23 Aug
0800, 25 Aug
Transport Group
(Tanaka)
inc cruiser Jintsu
1515, 24 Aug; Shokaku hit
1740, 24 Aug; Chitose hit
0200, 24 Aug
0935, 25 Aug
Kinryu Maru and Jintsu hit
1550, 24 Aug
Ryujo sunk
night, 24 Aug
Vanguard Group
1015
Mutsuki sunk
Advance Force
(Kondo)
2359
Santa Isabel
Malaita
SOLOMON ISLANDS
1641, 24 Aug; Enterprise hit
0600, 23 Aug
0200, 24 Aug
Henderson Field
Guadalcanal
2215, 24 Aug
San Cristobal
SANTA CRUZ IS
0 NAUTICAL MILES 120
Task Force 61 (Fletcher)
inc carriers Saratoga, Enterprise, Wasp

air attack was likely as the *Chicago* had not sent any warning about surface ships. The three cruisers were in line ahead on a 'box patrol' at 10 knots, and were just turning on the North-West leg of the 'box' when they were sighted by Mikawa's flagship *Chokai*. The five American ships were in the worst possible position, caught between the two Japanese columns.

The cruisers *Chokai* and *Aoba* opened fire quickly and scored hits on the *Quincy* before turning to the *Astoria* and *Vincennes*. The two destroyers were ignored, for the cruisers were after their own kind. In any case the *Helm* and *Wilson* were so confused that they achieved nothing apart from firing a few five-inch shells. The *Ralph Talbot*, whose sighting of the floatplane three hours earlier had failed to get through, was now punished by the light cruiser *Yubari* on the way out again. None of her torpedoes hit, and in return she was hit by several 140mm shells. All power was lost, but before she could be sunk she was hidden by a rain squall, and managed to extinguish her fires and limp into Tulagi.

It was left to the destroyers to pick up the pieces. First there was the blazing hulk of the *Canberra*, and the *Patterson* risked exploding ammunition to go alongside and fight the fires. The *Blue* also came alongside and took off nearly 700 Australian survivors, and at 0800 the smouldering wreck was torpedoed by the *Ellett*. The *Bagley* and *Helm* had already performed the same melancholy duty for the *Quincy* and *Vincennes* which had capsized about an hour after the action. The *Bagley* also rescued survivors of the *Astoria* and put a large firefighting party back on board to try to save her. With the *Wilson* she stood by all night until relieved by the *Buchanan*, but the efforts of all three destroyers were not enough and the crippled cruiser sank at midday. With four cruisers sunk and over 2000 men dead and injured, the Battle of Savo Island was a disaster for the Allies, and it showed that the lesson of Jutland had not been learned; one side had practiced night-fighting and the other side had not. The only crumbs of comfort were that Admiral Mikawa had failed to sink the transports lying off Lunga Point, and that on the way home the heavy cruiser *Kako* was torpedoed and sunk by the US submarine *S.44*. The men who lived through that night of destruction gave Savo Sound a new name to commemorate the ships which sank, Ironbottom Sound.

The Japanese Commander-in-Chief, Admiral Isoroku Yamamoto, was disappointed at the result of the Savo Island battle, for the brilliant success of Mikawa in rolling up the Allied patrol line had not been followed by the destruction of the invasion force. During the inevitable lull which followed, the Japanese at Rabaul had been able to reinforce their garrisons on Guadalcanal and Tulagi. The ships which covered these supply runs also bombarded the Marines' positions ashore and threatened their supply lines. The chance was taken to build up a strong force for the task of expelling the Americans from the Solomons, with reinforcements from Truk and elsewhere. An Occupation Force of four transports with a close escort of four old destroyers and a cruiser was supported by a Mobile Force composed of the carriers *Ryujo*, *Shokaku* and *Zuikaku*, the seaplane carrier *Chitose*, three battleships, 11 cruisers and 23 destroyers. Against this the Allies had three carriers, the *Saratoga*, *Enterprise* and *Wasp*, with one battleship, seven cruisers and 18 destroyers, split into three task forces.

The Battle of the Eastern Solomons on 24 August was another carrier battle in which the destroyers had little to do but act as handmaidens to the carriers. It was indecisive, as the American carriers' planes sank the carrier *Ryujo* in exchange for serious damage to the *Enterprise*. An interesting feature of the Japanese side of the operation was the use of four old destroyers of the *Mutsuki* Class, built in 1923–27, as fast transports. Their top sea speed was about 30 knots, and so they could keep up with a naval force unlike any ex-mercantile transport, and this made them useful for the high-speed runs from Rabaul to the Solomons. These runs were made with such monotony from August 1942 onwards that they were known to the Allies as the 'Tokyo Express'. On the morning of 25 August the *Mutsuki* was standing by the damaged transport *Kinryu Maru* when Army B-17s from Espiritu Santo scored a hit on her with bombs, which sank her. She was the first victim of USAAF medium-level bombs, and when Commander Hatano of the *Mutsuki* was rescued by the destroyer *Yayoi* it was reported that he said with a wry smile that it only proved that even the B-17s made a hit once in a while (in this case many).

Japanese submarines were also present in the Solomons in growing numbers, and in the weeks after the Battle of the Eastern Solomons they showed how they could influence the campaign. On 31 August the carrier *Saratoga* was hit twice by torpedoes from *I.26*; although she was in the care of seven destroyers the force was zigzagging at only 13 knots to conserve the 'cans'' fuel. The 'Sara' had been hazarded in a misguided attempt to provide cover for the fast convoys bringing supplies to Guadalcanal and Tulagi, and it was the same misuse of a fleet

Left: Destroyer exercises look deceptively simple but there is little margin for error.
Far left centre: Battle of Savo Island, 8 August.
Far left bottom: Battle of the Eastern Solomons. 24 August.

Above: Destroyers again go to the rescue of a crippled carrier – this time the *Hornet* in the Battle of Santa Cruz.
Bottom: Battle of Cape Esperance.

carrier which had caused the loss of HMS *Courageous* in September 1939. The American carrier was luckier, for she survived, but two weeks later on 14 September, three torpedoes from *I.19* ripped into the starboard side of the *Wasp*. This time the carrier was fatally damaged, and as her aviation gasoline burnt it set off explosions of torpedoes and bombs, which made the job of the damage-control parties almost impossible. The sister of the *I.19*, the *I.15*, was on station seven miles away, and she fired a spread of six torpedoes, one of which hit the battleship *North Carolina* abreast of 'A' 16-inch gun turret, while a second ran on much further and hit the destroyer *O'Brien*. She had one of the most remarkable escapes of any destroyer in history for the 21-inch torpedo hit her right on the bow and blew it off in a tremendous explosion, but without sinking her or causing any casualties. The *I.15* nearly got the carrier *Hornet* as well, and the lookouts on the bridge of the escorting destroyer *Mustin* were horrified to see a torpedo track passing *under* their own keel. Fortunately it was this torpedo which hit the *North Carolina*, as a hit on the carrier could have been the knockout blow for the Solomons campaign.

By mid-afternoon the *Wasp* was beyond hope and the fire-fighting parties were forced to abandon ship; when a violent explosion blew out the midships elevator 20 minutes later Rear-Admiral Scott ordered everybody off. The carrier lay burning for another two hours, with continuing explosions tearing her hull apart. Admiral Scott hoped to get fire-fighting parties aboard later, but at 1745 Rear-Admiral Noyes ordered the scuttling of his former flagship. The destroyer *Lansdowne* had the melancholy job of sinking the *Wasp* with four torpedoes. The *O'Brien* managed to limp to Noumea for emergency repairs, but an estimate of her seaworthiness by repair staff of the destroyer tender based there proved to be over-optimistic, and on 19 October her badly strained hull broke up off Samoa, one of the rare examples of structural failure in destroyers.

The 'Tokyo Express' was still running, and it became one of the outstanding achievements of the Imperial Japanese Navy. Without the benefit of radar, the Japanese had still achieved a proficiency in night-fighting shown to overwhelming advantage off Savo Island. After the first battle Admiral Mikawa sent Rear-Admiral Raizo Tanaka and his 2nd Destroyer Flotilla to run 900 troops to Guadalcanal, and the success of this operation led to further attempts. On most evenings, just before nightfall, a force of destroyers or other small warships would leave Rabaul and dash down

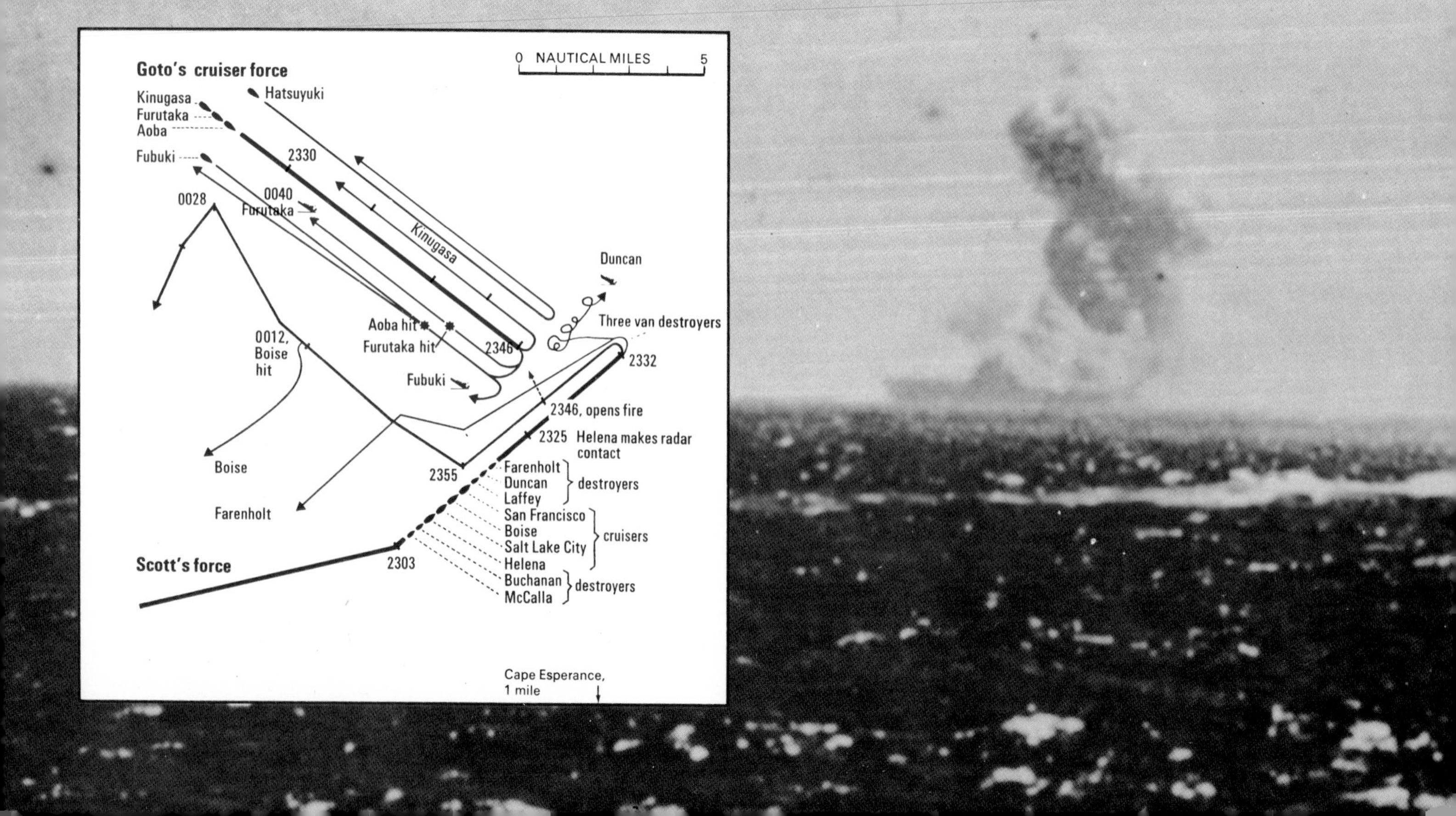

the 'Slot' between New Georgia and Santa Isabel, arriving off Guadalcanal about midnight. The troops and supplies were landed at Cape Esperance or Tassafaronga, and then the 'Tokyo Express' headed South-East to bombard Henderson Field, and then, about an hour-and-a-half after arrival, they were homeward bound. At daybreak the sweating and cursing Marine Corps would fill in the holes in the airstrip to allow the defending fighters to take off, but once night fell the Japanese Navy was once again in command.

It was the 'Tenacious Tanaka' (his nickname was bestowed by his reluctant Marine Corps admirers) who was leading the transports in the light cruiser *Jintsu* in the Battle of the Eastern Solomons on 24 August. When his flagship was damaged by a bomb he transferred to the destroyer *Kagero*. On the night of 4–5 September Tanaka's destroyers sank the flush-deckers *Gregory* and *Little* off Lunga Point with gunfire before escaping. The Japanese did not have it all their own way, and on the night of 11–12 October an attempt to repeat the success of Savo Island by bringing heavier forces down the 'slot' brought on the disastrous Battle of Cape Esperance. This time the Americans were waiting; Admiral Scott's Task Force 64 was plotting Admiral Aritomo Goto's path down the 'Slot' on radar.

The Americans had learned by their mistakes, and although their estimate of Goto's force underestimated its strength the sighting reports were passed rapidly to Admiral Scott's Task Force 'Sugar' guarding the approach to Ironbottom Sound.

The battle which followed was confused to say the least. Admiral Scott had the tactical advantage over Goto's cruisers, and managed to cross his 'T'. The four cruisers went into action as planned but three of their four destroyers got out of station and found themselves between the two opposing battle-lines. As a result Admiral Scott ordered a ceasefire to avoid what he thought was an attack on his own forces, but Admiral Goto was equally confused, and thought that he too was being fired on by his own side. But it was American gunfire which hit the flagship *Aoba* and mortally wounded it. As he lay dying Goto croaked '*Bakayaro*' (stupid bastards), a sentiment close to the hearts of all naval officers involved in a night action. The destroyer *Duncan* had been hit, possibly by an American shell, but Lieutenant-Commander Taylor continued the attack which he was making on the heavy cruiser *Furutaka*. Just as she fired two torpedoes she was hit by another American salvo which crippled her, and she sheered off in flames, nearly out of control. The USS *Farenholt* was also hit by her own side, but she survived a shell in the forward fire-room and crawled out of range.

The Japanese destroyer *Fubuki* came within a mile of the heavy cruiser *San Francisco*, a range at which the eight-inch shells sank her in minutes. The cause of her loss was a turn by the heavy cruiser *Furutaka*, and she too ran into the American cruisers' concentrated fire. Although soon ablaze from end to end she stayed afloat for about another hour. Next day two more Japanese destroyers, the *Murakumo* and *Natsagumo* were sunk by Henderson Field's dive-bombers, making the Japanese losses for the battle three destroyers and a heavy cruiser sunk, and two more cruisers damaged, at a cost of one US destroyer sunk and one destroyer and two cruisers damaged.

The fate of the *Duncan* was harrowing. She was a shambles, with her gun director, bridge, forward funnel and plotting room hit by shells and the forecastle on fire. Her commanding officer was one of the few bridge personnel still alive, and as he and the other survivors in the forepart of the ship were unable to make their way aft through the flames they launched two life-rafts and abandoned ship. The survivors still aboard stood by their posts, not knowing that their captain was even alive, let alone that he had been left behind

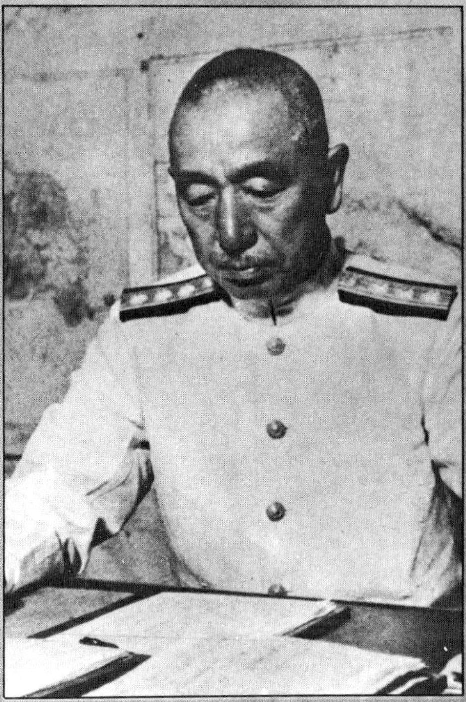

Above: Admiral Mineichi Koga was Commander-in-Chief of the Japanese Combined Fleet from April 1943 to April 1944.
Below: A Japanese torpedo hits the USS *O'Brien* (DD.415) on 14 September 1942 while the carrier *Wasp* blazes on the horizon. Seven miles away another torpedo of the same salvo hit the battleship *North Carolina*.

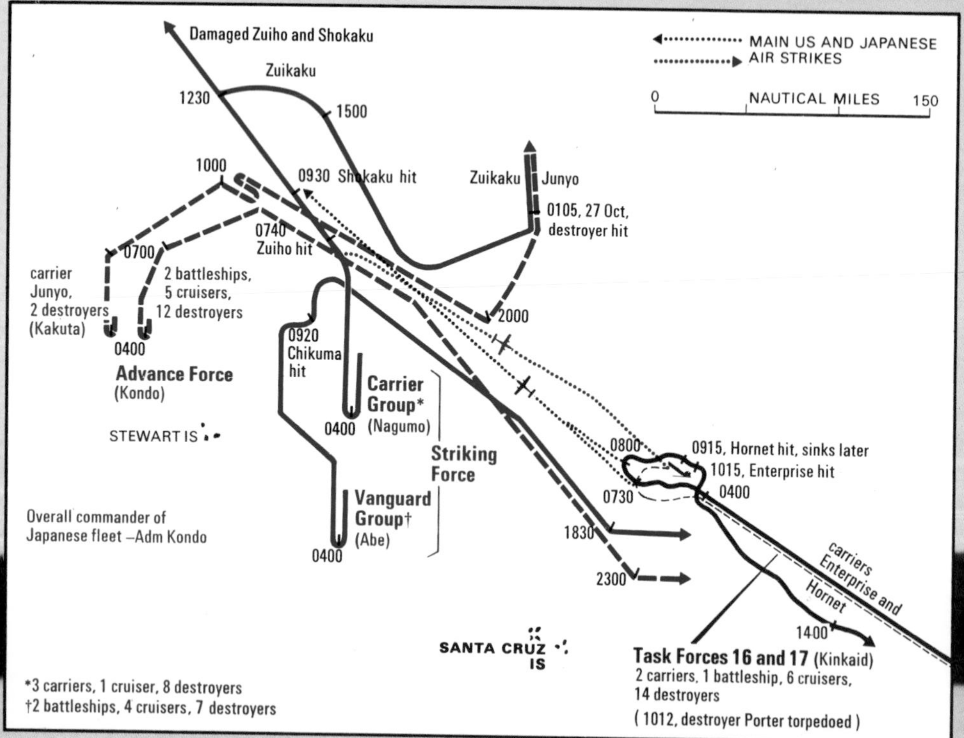

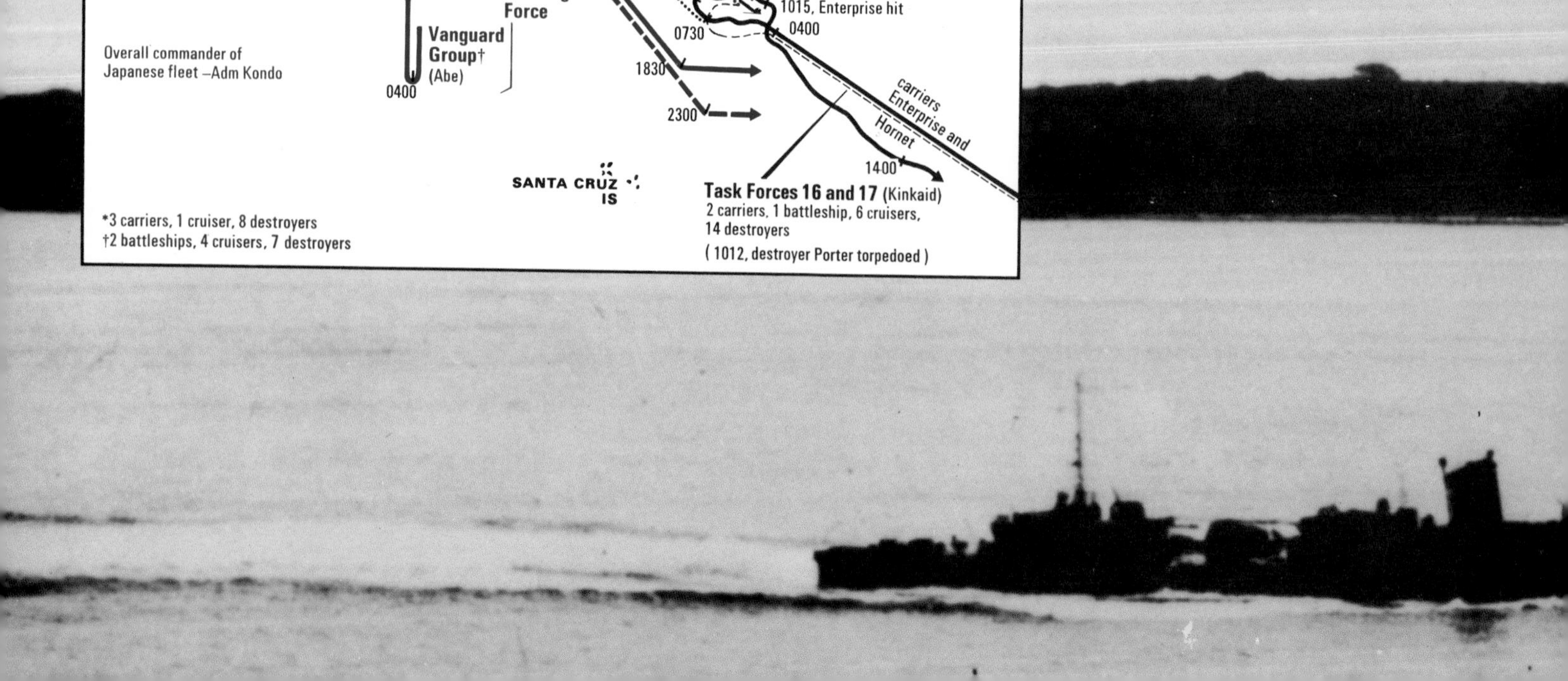

Above: The classic submarine periscope photograph: the destroyer *Yamakaze* was sunk by USS *Nautilus* (SS.168) on 25 June 1942.
Below: One of the older Japanese destroyers, probably the *Fumizuki*, under air attack off Kavieng in January 1944.
Left: Battle of Santa Cruz.

as the *Duncan* continued to steam out of control at 15 knots. Gradually order returned as one of the surviving junior officers made his way to the after-conning position and made contact with the Engineer Officer below. The idea was to beach the *Duncan* on Savo Island but the fires spread to the forward fire-room, and eventually the after-boilers lost pressure from lack of feedwater. At 0200 they abandoned ship, using any flotsam which could keep a man afloat. Savo Island was too far away to swim ashore, but the destroyer *McCalla* had seen the flames and came to investigate. At first she tried to fight the fires but gave up, and then cries were heard some distance away. She had arrived just in time to save the *Duncan*'s survivors from an attack by sharks, and while marksmen kept the sharks at bay with rifles the swimmers were hauled aboard. In all 195 officers and men were saved but another 50 were lost in the initial fires and explosions. The burnt-out hulk of the *Duncan* finally sank at 1130 six miles North of Savo Island.

The Japanese were so galled by the air strikes of the Marine Corps pilots from Henderson Field that only a day later they sent the fast battleships *Haruna* and *Kongo* to shell the airstrip. This caused so much disruption that the following night, 14–15 October, Tanaka's destroyers ran a convoy of five transports into Tassafaronga, bringing 4500 fresh troops and large quantities of ammunition and food for the defenders. The previous night nearly a thousand 14-inch shells had landed on Henderson Field; this time the airstrip was pitted with hits from nearly as many eight-inch shells. The invaders were holding their own against furious attacks, and the vital airfield remained in the Marines' tenacious grip. The strain was almost intolerable, with air attacks by day and bombardments by night. Another attempt to loosen the US Navy's grip resulted in the Battle of the Santa Cruz Islands on 26 October in which the opposing carrier air groups did most of the fighting, and the destroyers could do little but watch. The major casualty was the USS *Hornet* which was set on fire by four bombs early in the battle.

Once again the destroyers had a wounded carrier to look after. The *Morris* and *Russell* were ordered alongside to fight the fires, and within an hour they had checked them. In the afternoon the task of removing the wounded began, and over 800 of the *Hornet*'s crew were taken off by 1540. Twenty minutes later six Japanese torpedo bombers jumped the *Hornet*, and a torpedo hit her on the starboard side. With powerful Japanese forces in the vicinity there was a real danger that the *Hornet* could be captured and towed back to Rabaul, and so the order was given to scuttle her. As darkness fell the *Mustin* stood a mile from the wallowing hulk of the *Hornet* and fired a deliberately aimed spread of eight torpedoes. Two ran 'wild', three more vanished, and the three which ran straight made no impression when they exploded. Then the *Anderson* went closer, and also fired eight torpedoes. Six of them hit, but again nothing happened, visual evidence at last to confirm the awful rumours circulating about the uselessness of the US Navy's torpedoes. In desperation the *Mustin* and *Anderson* took to firing five-inch shells at the carrier's waterline in the hope of increasing the rate of flooding. It was high time to be away, for Japanese floatplanes were illuminating the scene with parachute flares, a sure sign that Admiral Abe's Van Force was nearby. The Japanese did try to take the *Hornet* in tow but they also had to give up, and so the *coup de grâce* was given by the destroyers *Akigumo* and *Makigumo* with two 'Long Lances' apiece.

During the first two weeks of November Tanaka's destroyers continued to run the 'Tokyo Express', with over 60 missions. The Americans were also exerting

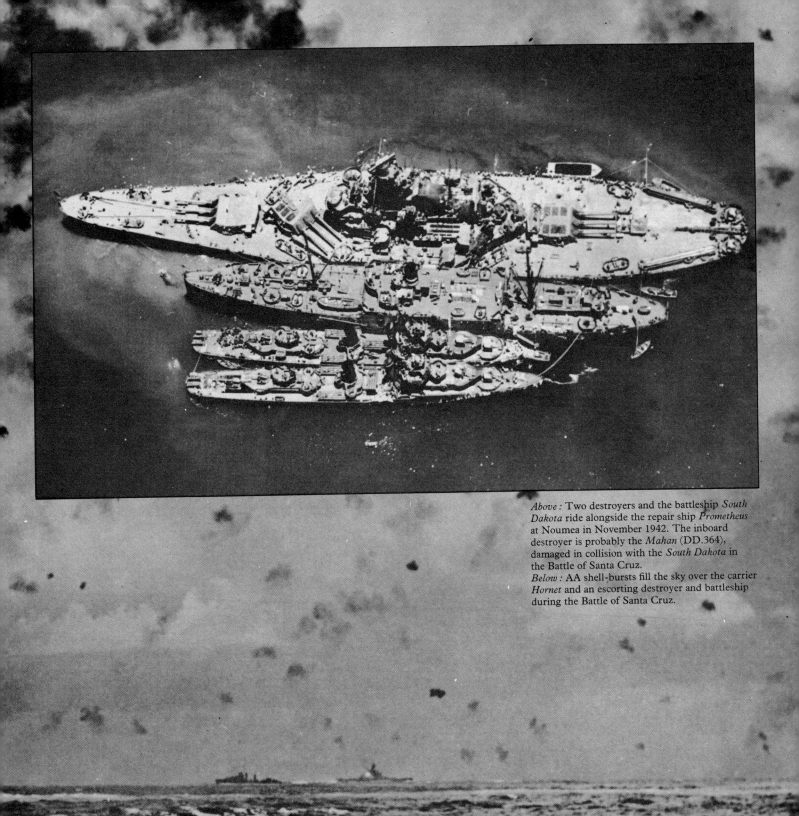

Above: Two destroyers and the battleship *South Dakota* ride alongside the repair ship *Prometheus* at Noumea in November 1942. The inboard destroyer is probably the *Mahan* (DD.364), damaged in collision with the *South Dakota* in the Battle of Santa Cruz.
Below: AA shell-bursts fill the sky over the carrier *Hornet* and an escorting destroyer and battleship during the Battle of Santa Cruz.

every effort to bring in convoys, and the respective covering forces clashed in the action known as the Battle of Guadalcanal. For the superstitious the date, Friday 13 November, was a bad omen, and so it turned out. It was the Japanese who arrived first, Vice-Admiral Hiroaki Abe's Striking Force of two battleships, a cruiser and 16 destroyers, supported by Admiral Mikawa and six cruisers and six destroyers, all to get Tanaka's 12 destroyers and 11,000 men through. Against this the Americans could only put Rear-Admiral Daniel J Callaghan's Task Group 67.4, five cruisers and eight destroyers, although the battleships *South Dakota* and *Washington* and the carrier *Enterprise* were a day's steaming away. It was a savage *mêlée*, and lack of radio-discipline completely cancelled out the American Squadron's advantage of radar. The TBS net was jammed with calls for ranges, bearings, tactical orders, anything which would avert the catastrophe which was fast approaching.

The cruiser *Atlanta* opened fire with her five-inch guns at 1600 yards, but in return a hurricane of fire swept her as the disciplined Japanese gun-crews swung into their night-fighting drill. A shell on the bridge killed Admiral Norman Scott and all but one of his staff, and soon after she was stopped by torpedo-hits. The destroyers were equally bewildered by the sudden loss of cohesion, and found themselves in a welter of ships charging about firing at one another. The *Barton* fired four torpedoes at a target and then had to go hard astern to avoid colliding with her target, but as she did so a brace of torpedoes hit her and broke her in half. The *Cushing*, *Laffey*, *O'Bannon* and *Sterrett* found themselves taking on the battleship *Hiei*, and even fired their five-inch guns at her. The *Cushing* was slowed down by hits from the *Hiei*'s secondary armament and, just when the battleship sheered off into the smoke-haze, Japanese destroyers came up to finish her with gunfire. The *Laffey* fired two torpedoes at the *Hiei* so close that the watchers on the bridge saw the two 'fish' bounce out of the water after hitting the battleship's 'bulge' without exploding. Retribution was swift, and within seconds the *Laffey* was hit by 1400-lb shells and a torpedo,

Above: The sinuous wakes of DesRon 12 in Ironbottom Sound as it returns from the Kavieng bombardment. Savo Island is in the background.
Below: USS *Knight* (DD.633) ploughs into a heavy swell as she comes alongside an escort carrier.

which left her shattered and killed nearly her entire crew. For his determined bravery Lieutenant Commander W E Hank was awarded the Navy Cross posthumously.

The *Sterrett* and *O'Bannon* found themselves on the opposite side of the *Hiei* and probably benefited from the distraction offered by the *Cushing* and *Laffey*'s destruction. At one moment the *O'Bannon* found herself so close to the *Hiei* that, just like the *Spitfire* and the *Nassau* at Jutland, the 14-inch guns could not depress low enough to hit the destroyer. The *Sterrett* was roughly handled by two of the *Hiei*'s escorting destroyers, but she also lived to tell the tale. The *Monssen* also ran into a group of destroyers with the *Hiei*, but she did not escape. She was overwhelmed by gunfire and set ablaze from end to end; some 130 men died in the inferno, although three heroic crewmen reboarded her and rescued some of the wounded. Other destroyers were damaged in the witches' Sabbath that night, but the worst was over for them. Admiral Callaghan, whose confusing and contradictory orders had been a prime cause of the carnage, was killed on the bridge of his flagship, the heavy cruiser *San Francisco*, by gunfire from the *Kirishima*. The *Hiei* was hit by eight-inch shells from the American cruisers, and was seen to make a half-circle turn and stagger North along the East side of Savo Island. At about 1100 next morning the battered cruiser squadron ran into the Japanese submarine *I.26*'s patrol area, and in spite of a depth-charge attack by the *Sterrett* her torpedoes hit the anti-aircraft cruiser *Juneau*. The magazines must have been detonated and the ship blew up with the loss of all but ten out of her 700-strong crew.

The second act of the drama unfolded the following night when the American reinforcements had arrived. Four destroyers, the *Benham*, *Gwin*, *Preston* and *Walke* were escorting the battleships *South Dakota* and *Washington*, which were positioned off Savo Island to intercept Vice-Admiral Kondo's Bombardment Group, the *Kirishima*, four cruisers and nine destroyers. Other targets were the remnants of the latest 'Tokyo Express', which had been badly mauled that day by the aircraft of the carrier *Enterprise*, but Kondo's force was the more important. With the radar coverage provided by his flagship *Washington*, Rear-Admiral Willis A Lee picked up Kondo's ships at a range of 16,000 yards, but once again Japanese eyesight and the superb night-glasses provided to their lookouts gave them the first sighting. The *Preston* was hit just after 2322 and 20 minutes later she was sinking from repeated hits. The *Walke* tried to launch torpedoes but was also hit by shells and then torpedoed. She sank a few minutes after the *Preston* and, almost immediately afterwards, the *Benham* was hit by a torpedo. She was later rescued by the *Gwin*, and the two ships began the long crawl back to Espiritu Santo, but the *Benham*'s bulkheads collapsed under the strain some 12 hours later, and she had to be scuttled.

The two battleships had joined in the firing, but the *South Dakota* was soon in trouble when an electrical failure blacked out the ship, including her radar 'eyes'. She blundered past the burning destroyers and nearly got sunk by approaching too close to the Japanese battle-line. But the *Washington*'s salvoes caused great destruction against the *Kirishima*, and probably helped to distract her attention from the lumbering *South Dakota*. The *Kirishima* sank later, and Admiral Kondo withdrew to avoid further losses. This still left Tanaka's transports, but these were caught just at the moment that they arrived at Tassafaronga and the destroyer *Meade* was able to inflict heavy losses on the four helpless targets.

Guadalcanal was the US Navy destroyer's equivalent of Jutland, a muddled series of actions in which they covered themselves with glory. There was the same blend of muddle and heroism, with faulty communication causing heavy losses, but also a devotion to duty which went a long way to snatch victory out of defeat. There was another parallel with Jutland, for although the Japanese could boast that they had sunk a lot of USN ships they had finally lost the initiative, and were never to regain it.

Tanaka was to have one more success, in the Battle of Tassafaronga on the night of 30 November–1 December 1942. His eight destroyers and fast transports were jumped by Rear-Admiral Carleton H Wright's Task Force 67, but once again Japanese tactics were superior. The US destroyers' torpedoes all missed, whereas four US cruisers were torpedoed, and one later sank. But the 'Tokyo Express' was running out of steam, and the Japanese High Command had come to realize belatedly that they would never expel the Americans from the Solomons. The last runs of the 'Tokyo Express' were made in reverse, evacuating the garrison that had been kept supplied at such a high cost in lives, ships and aircraft. On the night of 1–2 February 1943 a week-long operation started, the lifting of 12,000 soldiers for the loss of only one destroyer. Although Tanaka was no longer in charge it was a fitting tribute to a remarkable destroyerman and the skill of his crews.

Right: The forward torpedo-tubes and 20mm Oerlikon guns of USS *Jouett* (DD.396).
Below: The *O'Bannon* as she appeared when first commissioned in 1942. She still has quadruple 1.1-inch AA guns.

Over to the Offensive

The island-by-island campaign to occupy the rest of the Solomons chain after the Marines' hold on Guadalcanal was established was a land, sea and air campaign, but inevitably the destroyers played an essential role, for their speed and torpedo armament made them tough opponents for the Japanese. The battles could be taken as a destroyer's roll of honour, Kula Gulf, Kolombangara, Vella Gulf, Vella Lavella, Empress Augusta Bay and Cape St George, but in addition there were scores of other actions through 1943 in which destroyers fought hard and often.

The Central Solomons Campaign produced new names to match the magnificent *Fletcher* Class destroyers which were coming out of the shipyards. The *Fletcher* herself commissioned on 30 June 1942 and had the good fortune to come through the Battle of Guadalcanal without a scratch, and another 26 sisters joined her in service by the end of that year. Over a hundred more joined the strength in 1943, as well as a batch of the earlier *Bristol* Class, which had been continued to avoid disruption of production. The policy of building up numbers before making any big changes in design was one of the secrets of the Allies' success against the Axis, and for destroyers it was particularly wise. In all 486 destroyers were authorized for the US Navy after the outbreak of war, and only 69 of these were not completed:

Class	Authorized	Completed	Cancelled
Bristol	72	72	—
Fletcher	124	113	11
Experimental DDs	2	—	2
Improved *Fletcher*	62	62	—
Allen M Sumner	70	70	—
Gearing	156	100	56

The first of the new men to rise to prominence was Rear-Admiral W L 'Pug' Ainsworth, who was appointed Commander Destroyers, Pacific (ComDesPac) in June 1942. He had a distinguished career as a destroyer captain, and had been in command of a destroyer squadron in the Atlantic in 1941. Admiral Halsey appointed him to command Task Force 67 after that force had been roughly handled by Tanaka's destroyers in the Battle of Tassafaronga. He showed his mettle by leading a destroyer-raid on Munda, at the North-West end of New Georgia, on the night of 4–5 January 1943. For the first time the Americans got the better of the exchange, and it showed that a new spirit of confidence had been generated. In his report Ainsworth said,

Below: The Solomons Campaign.

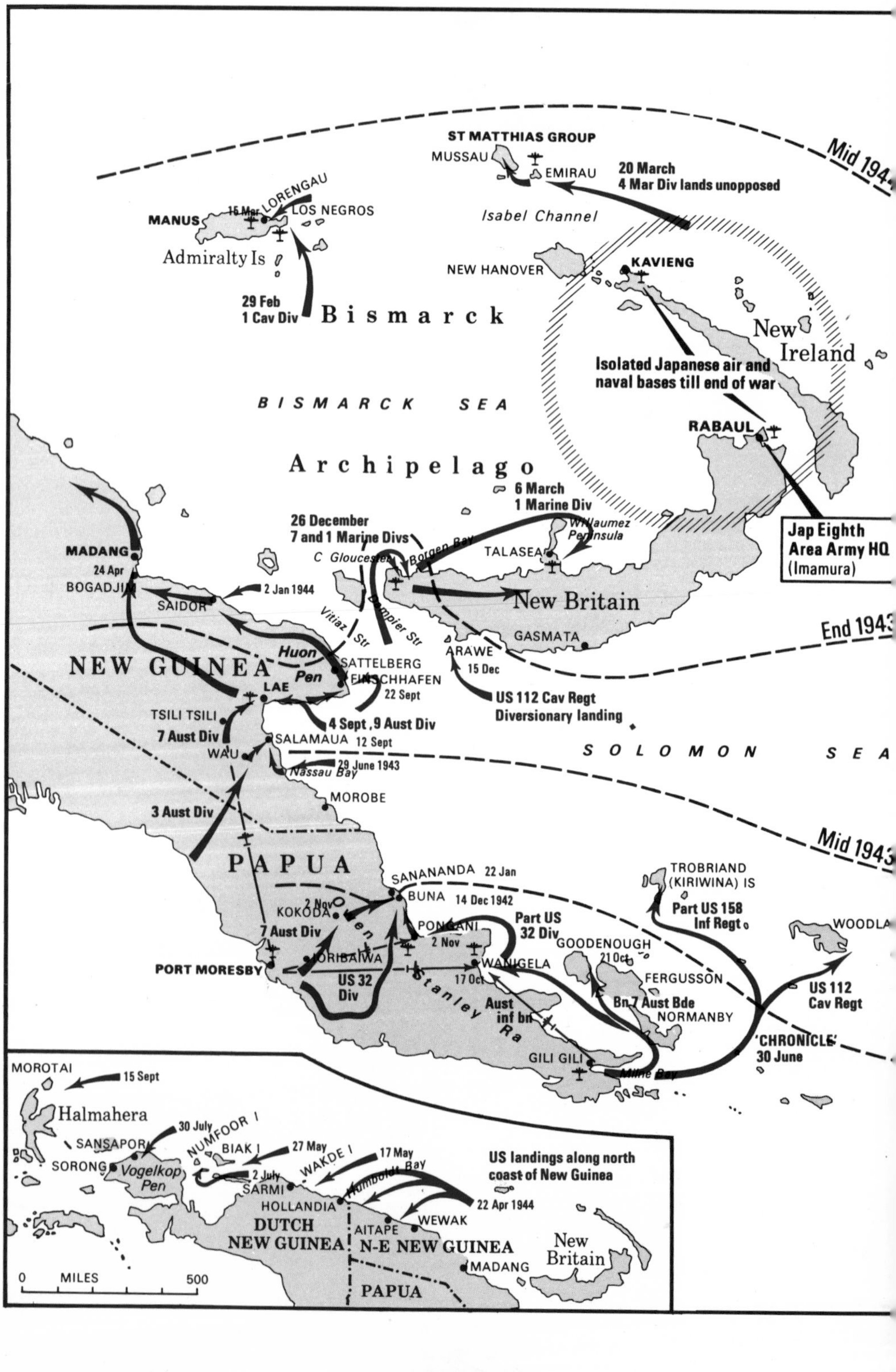

The first of the new men to rise to prominence was Rear-Admiral W L 'Pug' Ainsworth

Above: The USS *Harrison* (DD.573) sends a mailbag by jackstay to her sister *McKee* (DD.575).

'The night bombardment of Munda is . . . the first naval action in which our Navy has co-ordinated surface, submarine and aircraft units in a night bombardment. As an initial venture in this field of operations, this action may be taken as our first lesson in night amphibious warfare.'

Another exploit of Ainsworth's destroyers was the laying of a minefield right in the path of the 'Tokyo Express' route between Arundel Island and Kolombangara. The minelayers were three old flush-deckers, the *Breese*, *Gamble* and *Preble*, which had been converted in the 1930s to 'three-stackers' with mine-rails for laying 80 mines. On the night of 6–7 May 1943 the three old destroyers, with the new *Fletcher* Class *Radford* using her radar to act as a guide, laid 250 mines in the middle of Blackett Strait. Admiral Ainsworth covered the operation with three light cruisers and three fleet destroyers. The whole escapade was accomplished without loss, although a Japanese floatplane spotted the force as it withdrew. The risks were justified sooner than anticipated, for the next morning four enemy destroyers ran straight into the minefield. In quick succession the *Oyashio*, *Kagero* and *Kurashio* were hit, and only the *Michishio* escaped. Packed with survivors, she was strafed by US aircraft from Guadalcanal which had been called up by one of the Australian coastwatchers. Five days later Admiral Ainsworth's force attempted a similar coup, but a series of mishaps gave away the position of the minefield prematurely, so that the Japanese minesweepers were able to deal with it quickly.

Ainsworth's Task Group 36 met the Japanese headlong in the Battle of Kula Gulf on the night of 5–6 July. Once again it was a confused battle in typical Solomons conditions, a moonless and humid night with visibility up to two miles but liable to be suddenly reduced to less than a mile by sudden rain squalls. The Japanese force was a group of ten destroyers under Rear-Admiral Teruo Akiyama, running supplies to Vila-Stanmore, whereas the Americans had the cruisers *Honolulu*, *Helena* and *St Louis* and DesRon 21, the destroyers *Nicholas*, *Jenkins*, *O'Bannon* and *Radford*. Although the Japanese were outnumbered, four of their destroyers were of a new and powerful type known as the *Akizuki* Class, and one of these, the flagship *Niizuki* had the new Type 22 radar set. As all ten also had the 24-inch 'Long Lance' torpedoes with reloads the American advantage of firepower was not as great as it looked on paper.

Although the Japanese lookouts saw the American column at a range of about

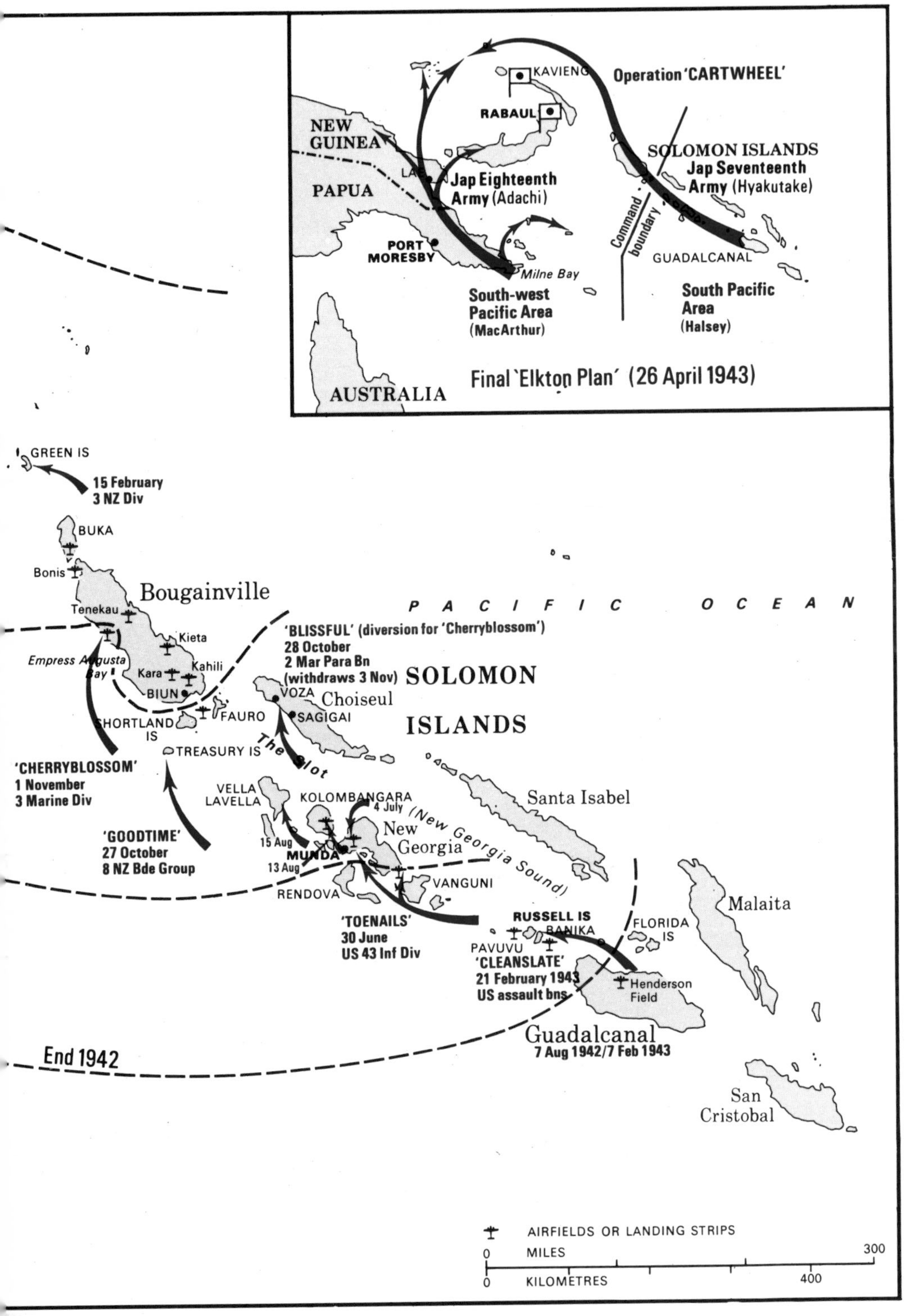

7000 yards American gunnery was good, and the first salvo of six-inch shells from the cruisers crippled Akiyama's flagship *Niizuki*. The *Suzukaze* and *Tanikaze* were hit by apparently 'dud' torpedoes, and when their own torpedoes missed they turned away behind their smoke-screen to reload. This time one of the salvoes ran straight, and the three 'Long Lances' which ripped into the cruiser *Helena* broke her back. So furious was the action by this time that the Admiral and his captains failed to notice what had happened, and did not know until the stricken ship failed to answer her call-sign. Ainsworth kept his formation under control and achieved a crossing of the enemy's 'T', but once again the torpedoes failed dismally and the *Hatsayuki* was hit by three 'duds'. In this first phase the American tactics had been sound but the enormous advantage conferred by the 'Long Lance' got the Japanese out of trouble.

In the second phase the US destroyers made contact once more and inflicted damage on two enemy ships. The *Nagatsuki* was so badly damaged that she later had to be beached near Vila where she was destroyed by bombing. The *Nicholas* and *Radford* were in the middle of rescuing survivors of the *Helena* when they sighted the *Amagiri* which was on a similar errand of mercy for the *Niizuki* survivors. Having chased her off the two destroyers returned to the job of rescue, only to be interrupted again by the *Mochizuki*. With the words, 'If the son of a bitch wants to fight, I'll give him a fight' Lieutenant Commander Hill took the *Nicholas* off at full speed followed by the *Radford*, leaving their boats to continue picking up survivors. The *Mochizuki* having been chased away, they returned and picked up their boats before rejoining Admiral Ainsworth.

The results of the battle were disappointing, but they showed that the Japanese could no longer count on getting the first blow in. The loss of the *Helena* was hardly offset by the sinking of the *Niizuki*, but the loss of Admiral Akiyama was another blow to Japanese morale. Unfortunately the Battle of Kolombangara a week later showed the dangers of using cruisers against the Japanese destroyers. Once again ships were hit at ranges previously thought impossible for torpedo attack, and the cruisers *Leander* (New Zealand), *Honolulu* (Ainsworth's flagship) and *St Louis* were hit. The Japanese light cruiser *Jintsu* was destroyed, killing Admiral Izaki and nearly 500 of her crew, but the attempt to get supplies through the defenders of Vila-Stanmore was frustrated this time. The *Gwin*, the only destroyer which had survived the battleship action at Guadalcanal, was hit by a single torpedo towards the end of the action. With the help of her squadron-mate, *Ralph Talbot*, she was still afloat nearly seven hours later but desperately wounded. US aircraft from airfields in the Russell Islands provided cover against marauding Japanese bombers while the destroyermen laboured to save what was now only a smouldering hulk. At about 0900 the Commander of DesDiv 23, Commander Higgins, decided that nothing further could be done, and ordered her to be scuttled.

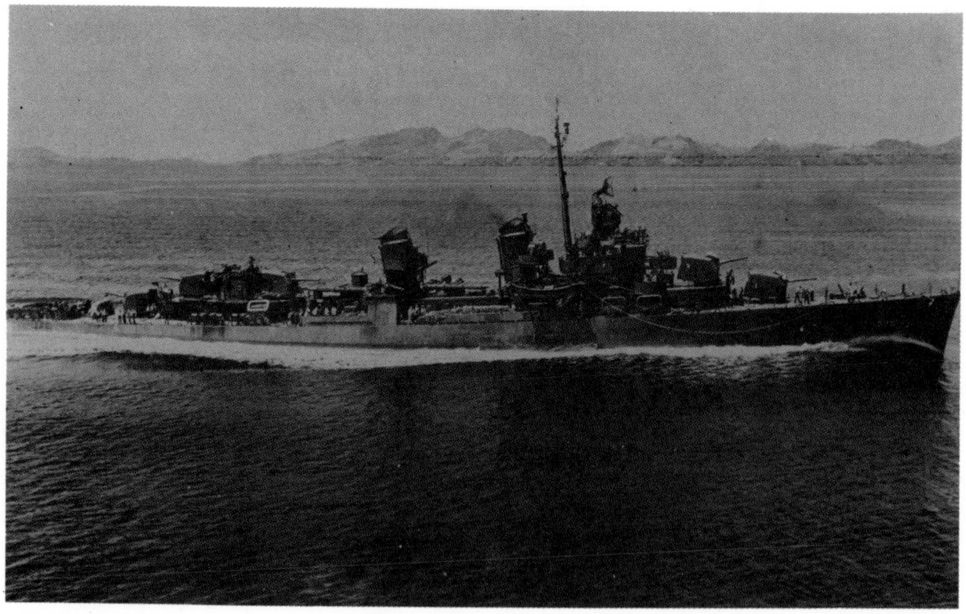

Above: The *Charles Ausburne* (DD.570) returns from an action in the Solomons with empty five-inch shell-cases stacked amidships.
Right: Five-inch 38/cal guns blaze in night action. Flashless cordite helped reduce the dazzling effect on bridge personnel.

The second name to rise to fame in the Solomons was that of Commander Frederick Moosbrugger, who had been given command of DesDiv 12 at Tulagi. When Munda fell at the beginning of August 1943 he was given the job of intercepting another 'Tokyo Express' run in Gizo Strait supported by fighter cover and PT-Boats. Flying his flag in the *Dunlap*, he had the *Craven* and *Maury* under him as well as DesDiv 15, the destroyers *Lang*, *Stack* and *Sterrett*. On the night of 5–6 August the two divisions steamed North up Vella Gulf, between Vella Lavella and Kolombangara. First contact was obtained by the *Dunlap* on radar at 2333 and only three minutes later Moosbrugger gave the order via TBS (the Talk Between Ships short-range radio net), 'Stand by to fire torpedoes'. The range came down to 4000 yards and for once the Japanese seem to have been taken completely by surprise. Within minutes the *Kawakaze* sank after four torpedo-hits from the *Stack*. Then the *Arashi* and *Hagikaze* blew up leaving only the *Shigure* to make her escape at high speed back to Bougainville. This was the Battle of Vella Gulf and it was unusual in that the US Navy suffered no losses at all. But this was not accidental, for Moosbrugger had insisted that his destroyers did not use the unreliable magnetic exploder on their torpedoes' warheads; instead the old and trusted 'contact' setting was used. Another improvement was the fitting of flash-guards to the lips of the torpedo-tubes, to reduce the risk of the flash of the cordite impulse-charge being seen by Japanese lookouts as the torpedoes were fired.

The upshot of all these confused and deadly night actions was the cancellation of the 'Tokyo Express' on the orders of the new Japanese Commander-in-Chief, Admiral Koga. This meant that the outlying garrisons had to be ferried back to Bougainville in landing barges, and so a tempting 'soft-skinned' target was presented to the commander of DesDiv 12 and his fellow destroyer commanders. Between 9 August and 4 October the destroyer squadrons sank some 40 landing barges and escorting gunboats and other light craft. The carnage forced Admiral Koga to reform the 'Tokyo Express', and this quickly brought on another action, the Battle of Vella Lavella, on the night of 6–7 October. This time honours were more even, for three US destroyers took on six Japanese and each side lost one ship to torpedoes. Unfortunately the *O'Bannon* damaged herself by ramming the sinking *Chevalier* in the confusion, but the *Selfridge* managed to limp home after taking a torpedo-hit.

Captain Arleigh A Burke rose to prominence as a result of his leadership of DesRon 23 in the Battle of Empress Augusta Bay on the night of 2 November 1943. The Japanese had despatched the heavy cruisers *Myoko* and *Haguro*, the light cruisers *Sendai* and *Agano* and six destroyers to cover a force of five fast transports heading for Cape Torokina. The American Admiral Merrill was flying his flag in the light cruiser *Montpelier*, with her sisters *Cleveland*, *Col-*

umbia and *Denver* and eight destroyers of Burke's DesDiv 45 and Commander B L Austin's DesDiv 46. It is interesting to note that Merrill's answer to the menace of the 'Long Lance' was to allow his destroyers to attack with torpedoes first to force the Japanese to keep their distance, and then use radar-assisted long-range gunfire to keep the advantage on his side. Unfortunately a turnaway by the Japanese squadron meant that DesDiv 45's torpedoes all missed. As soon as Admiral Merrill realized that the Japanese had spotted his cruisers he countermanded his original plan and ordered the cruisers to open fire. The cruiser *Sendai* reeled under the impact of a number of six-inch shell hits and in the confusion the destroyers *Samidare* and *Shiratsuyu* collided with one another.

The Americans also had their problems. The destroyer *Foote* lost station, was hit in the stern by a Japanese torpedo, and then narrowly escaped being run down by the cruiser *Cleveland*. The *Spence* and *Thatcher* swung together with a crash and sparks flew as the two steel hulls ground side by side at 30 knots. The mishap caused no serious damage to either destroyer but at that moment the enemy heavy cruisers *Haguro* and *Myoko* appeared only 4000 yards away and in the excitement it was assumed that they were American so no torpedoes were fired. The mistake was understandable and shortly

Below: The Japanese destroyer *Sagiri* was a unit of Destroyer Squadron No 10. The original short, level-topped funnels of the *Fubuki* Class were soon raised and given raked caps to keep the funnel gases away from the bridge and controls. Note the 25mm guns between the forward twin five-inch dual-purpose gun mounting and the bridge. The ship is seen leaving Yokosuka in 1931.

afterwards there was a classic exchange between Commander Austin over the TBS:

Austin: 'We've just had another close miss hope you are not shooting at us.'
Burke: 'Sorry but you'll have to excuse the next four salvoes. They're already on their way.'

This misunderstanding had no ill-effects, and when one of Austin's destroyers, the *Spence*, found that she had too little ammunition to finish off the disabled *Hatsukaze*, Burke's division was called up to complete the task. The destroyers were straining at the leash to pursue the Japanese, but Admiral Merrill wisely ordered them to fall back on his cruisers once more, with the result that they escaped damage from a determined air attack next morning.

Arleigh Burke was soon christened '31-knot Burke' and the 'cans' of Destroyer

Below: The USS *Selfridge* (DD.357) displays the mangled remains of her forward twin five-inch gun mountings. She was lucky to escape after being hit by a Long Lance torpedo during the Battle of Vella Lavella on 7 October 1943.

Above: Captain Arleigh A Burke USN receives the Navy Cross from Rear-Admiral Merrill in February 1944.
Right: Captain Burke and bridge personnel on board the *Charles Ausburne* take a rare moment of relaxation. Note the 'Little Beaver' insignia of DesRon 23 painted on the bridge wing.

Squadron 23 were known as the 'Little Beavers' from their unofficial insignia. The flagship was the *Fletcher* Class *Charles Ausburne,* which won 11 Battle Stars in three years. The nickname was won in November 1943, when DesRon 23 was refuelling at Hathorn Sound in Kula Gulf. Orders came through to steam at top speed to intercept a Japanese convoy evacuating air force personnel, and the *Charles Ausburne* confirmed that she and her three squadron-mates would make the arranged rendezvous by a specified time. Back at Admiral Halsey's headquarters the operations officer worked out the average speed needed for the run as 31 knots and remembered that Burke had recently insisted that his squadron could only make a maximum formation speed of 30 knots. With this in mind Admiral Halsey's next order to Burke read:

'Thirty-one knot Burke get athwart the Buka-Rabaul evacuation line about 35 miles west of Buka X If no enemy contacts by 0300 . . . 25th . . . come south to refuel same place X If enemy contacted you know what to do.'

The result was the Battle of Cape St George, fought in the early hours of 25 November 1943 between the *Charles Ausburne*, *Dyson*, *Claxton*, *Converse* and *Spence* and the Japanese *Onami*, *Makinami*, *Amagiri*, *Yugiri* and *Uzuki*. In Burke's own words the moonless night was ideal 'for a nice quiet torpedo attack', and so it proved. The first attack hit two Japanese destroyers, the *Onami* and *Makinami*, and then the American destroyers settled down to a long stern-

chase as the remaining three enemy destroyers fled to the North. Such was Burke's instinct for destroyer tactics that after 15 minutes he suddenly ordered his squadron to swing to starboard to avoid a possible torpedo attack. As the five destroyers swung back on to their original course three 'Long Lances' exploded astern, detonated either at the end of their run or on running into the wakes of DesRon 23. Under such circumstances it is hardly surprising that the 'Little Beavers' came to regard themselves as a lucky formation, and they responded by adding the *Yugiri* to their night's score.

The struggle for the Solomons was over and the destroyers had contributed greatly towards that achievement. From the first days of trial and error, when the Japanese destroyers and cruisers held the whip hand, destroyers had done all the hardest fighting. Their losses had been heavy but gradually they had learned to beat the Japanese at their own game, and had become more cunning and resourceful. As one anonymous destroyerman said, 'in the Solomons everyone felt they were living on borrowed time'.

Leyte Gulf

Admiral Halsey's Third Fleet was given the task of delivering the long-awaited blow against the Philippines in the Autumn of 1944. He was to strike at the Northern part of the island group and use his fast carriers to support the invasion of Leyte Gulf in the Central Philippines. To do this he had the largest and most powerful fleet ever assembled: five battleships, 13 fleet carriers, 14 cruisers and 58 destroyers. General MacArthur's invasion forces would also have the close support of Admiral Kinkaid's Seventh Fleet, a further six battleships, 18 escort carriers, 11 cruisers, 86 destroyers and 25 destroyer escorts (DEs). Against this mighty armada the Japanese Navy could only field nine battleships, four carriers, 23 cruisers and 63 destroyers, but a combination of daring and slipshod communications nearly brought off a Japanese victory.

Left: A *Fletcher* Class destroyer lays a smokescreen to hide one of the battleships during the bombardment for the landings in Leyte Gulf, October 1944.
Below: Destroyers fire phosphorous shells during the invasion of Guam. On the right can be seen an ex-flush-decker APD (fast transport).

The Battle of Leyte Gulf is only a convenient name for a series of four big battles which took place over a period of four days. Together they amount to the greatest sea battle in history and, for the only time in the Pacific, all warship-types played the role for which they had been designed: battleships fought battleships while destroyers attacked with torpedoes and defended their own fleets. It opened with a landing in Leyte Gulf on 20 October 1944, but three days previously the Japanese had initiated their *Sho* or 'Victory' Plan when they learned that demolition teams and battalions of Rangers had reconnoitred the Leyte beaches. Under the *Sho* Plan there were four fleets:

1. The Main Body under Vice-Admiral Ozawa, composed of four carriers, two battleship-carrier hybrids, three cruisers and eight destroyers, coming from the Inland Sea.
2. Force 'A' under Vice-Admiral Kurita, composed of five battleships, 12 cruisers and 15 destroyers, coming from Borneo.
3 & 4. Force 'C', which was in two parts, the Van Squadron under Vice-Admiral Nishimura with two battleships, one cruiser and four destroyers, and the Rear Squadron under Vice-Admiral Shima. This last body included three cruisers and four destroyers, and although both sailed from Borneo they were under separate commands.

To the Americans they were known merely by the areas in which they were first spotted, so that the Main Body was labelled the 'Northern Force', Force 'A' became the 'Centre Force' and the two squadrons of Force 'C' became the 'Southern Force'.

Admiral Ozawa and the Northern Force were merely a decoy to lure Halsey's Fast Carrier Task Force away from the invasion area, which in turn would

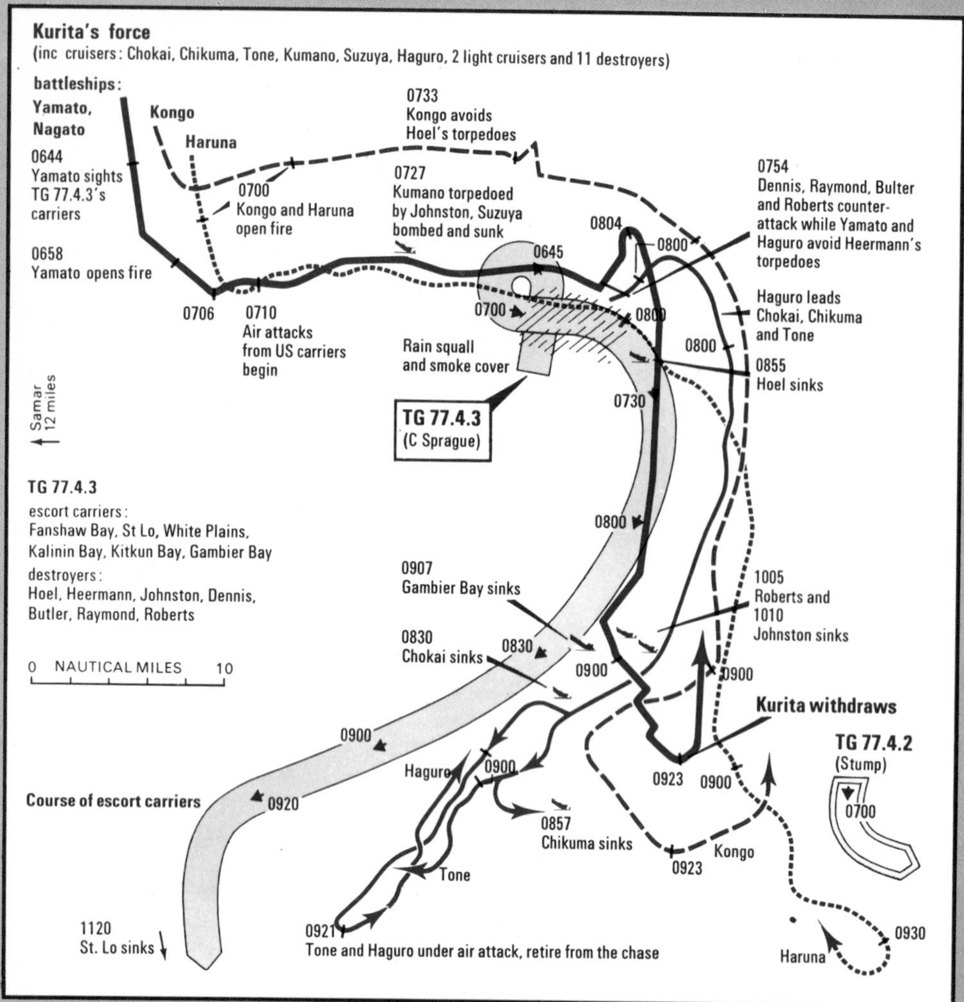

allow Kurita to unite his Centre Force with Shima's Southern Force to sweep into Leyte Gulf and destroy the invasion fleet. The Centre Force was to reach Leyte Gulf by passing through the San Bernardino Strait between Luzon and Samar and the Southern Force would pass through Surigao Strait between Leyte and Mindanao. Things went wrong on both sides. At first the departure of Ozawa's Northern Force was undetected and so it did not function as a decoy as early as had been hoped. Then Kurita lost three heavy cruisers in an ambush by US submarines off Palawan on 23 October. Next day carrier planes attacked the Centre Force and sank the giant battleship *Musashi*, and a temporary turnabout by Kurita was mistaken for a complete withdrawal. As Ozawa's Northern Force had now been located a jubilant Halsey decided that it was the main Japanese striking force and set off in pursuit. At 1512 on 24 October he signalled his *intention* of forming a new task force of battleships and carriers to guard the exit of the San Bernardino Strait. Although nothing was done about it, the Seventh Fleet, which had the responsibility of guarding the invasion fleet assumed that the task force had been formed and that the exit was guarded. The other exit, Surigao

Above: Kurita's heavy cruisers in action off Samar in the Battle of Leyte Gulf.
Below: American destroyers and escort carriers take the full weight of Japanese fire power as Admiral Kurita's Centre Force breaks through the San Bernardino Strait.

Strait, was guarded by the six old battleships, eight cruisers with 20 destroyers in attendance, but the failure to watch the San Bernardino Strait put the entire invasion armada at the mercy of Admiral Kurita's powerful force.

Oldendorf had been warned at midday to expect a night engagement and he had laid a cunning trap. He sent 30 PT Boats forward to give early warning of Nishimura's approach. Further in he put the destroyers of DesRon 54, the *McDermut* and *Monssen* of the right flank and the *Remey*, *Melvin* and *McGowan* on the left flank. Tucked away close to the coastline of Leyte was the third line of defence, the *Hutchins*, *Bache*, *Dale*, *Arunta* (Australian), *Beale* and *Killen* of DesRon 24. The final element of the trap was a double line of five cruisers and six battleships, with the remaining nine destroyers of DesRon 56 in the centre. The Strait is 12 miles wide at this point, and so the cruisers were used to extend the patrol line in case the Japanese tried to slip past. Although nothing much was expected of the PT Boats, they were stationed as far down the Strait as possible so that their surface-warning radar sets could give accurate coverage.

The PT Boats made contact at 2230 and although they did their best, the Japanese brushed them aside and steamed on. DesRon 54 did not catch sight of them until 0300 but their first torpedo attacks had no effect either, and they had to retire at high speed, zigzagging and making smoke. But three out of the 47 fired hit, two against the battleship *Fuso*'s side and one against the destroyer *Michishio*. It must have been a majestic sight, four destroyers leading the flagship *Yamashiro*, the *Fuso* and the cruiser *Mogami* at one-kilometer intervals, weaving to dodge the torpedoes and trying to pick off the attacking destroyers in the glare of searchlights.

At 0349 the *Fuso* finally blew up, and the two halves of the battleship drifted crazily down the Strait for some time

Above: A heavily retouched photo of the *Nenohi* taken when newly completed.

before sinking. But Nishimura ploughed on doggedly, and his flagship seemed to be impervious to the hail of torpedoes and shells fired at her by DesRon 24. Another destroyer, the *Yamagumo* had been sunk, but still the Japanese advanced. One of DesRon 24's destroyers, the *Killen* is credited with a killing torpedo-hit on *Yamashiro*, for her skipper Commander Corey, decided to order a depth-setting of 22 feet on the torpedoes to inflict maximum damage. The salvo ran straight, but the blazing battleship still careered on towards Oldendorf's waiting battleships. Although the plan was to finish off the Japanese by gunfire some of the destroy-

ers of DesRon 56, held in reserve between the battleships and the cruisers, took a hand in the action. One of their torpedoes hit the destroyer *Asagumo* but the *Albert W Grant* was hit by six-inch shells from her own side before she could get out of range. In all she was hit by seven Japanese 4.7-inch shells and 11 US six-inch, and suffered heavy casualties.

It was left to the battleships to administer the *coup de grâce* to the *Yamashiro*, and the tortured battleship finally capsized at 0419. The cruiser *Mogami* and the destroyer *Shigure* fled at high speed, and when Admiral Shima learned of the disaster he withdrew. Air attacks and PT Boats accounted for the cruisers *Abukuma, Nachi* and *Mogami* and two of his destroyers, with the result that only three destroyers out of the whole Southern Force survived the Battle of Surigao Strait. The victors emerged almost without a scratch, apart from the sorely tried *Grant*, and even she lived to fight another day.

As Admiral Oldendorf's ships finished their work the news came through of desperate fighting off Samar. Not until 0645 had anyone been able to ascertain the unwelcome news that no ships were guarding the San Bernardino Strait. In another ten minutes Rear-Admiral Sprague's escort carriers learned the awful truth, as 18-inch shells from the giant battleship *Yamato* began to fall around them. Kurita's Centre Force had got within 17 miles of the escort carriers which were providing air cover for the massive fleet of transports and landing craft in Leyte Gulf. The six 'jeep carriers' were escorted by only three destroyers and four DEs, the *Hoel, Heermann, Johnston, Dennis, John C Butler, Raymond* and *Samuel B Roberts*, and they were all that stood between Kurita and a slaughter of the defenceless transports. The alarm had been sounded and reinforcements were on the way, but they were too far away to be of any immediate help. The DEs were not designed to fight anything but submarines, but fortunately most of the earlier vessels of this type had been completed with a set of triple torpedo-tubes, which gave them some offensive capability. In speed and manoeuvrability, however, they were not in the same class as the destroyers, and would not be able to look after themselves so well. As for the escort carriers, their small hulls were built to mercantile standards and they were even slower than the DEs, to say nothing of their stores of highly inflammable aviation gasoline.

Admiral Sprague in his flagship *Fan-*

Below: The USS *Johnston* (DD.557) was sunk by Japanese gunfire in heroic action off Samar on 25 October 1944.

Above left: The commissioning ceremony at Seattle on board the *Johnston* on 27 October 1943. *Above:* Lieutenant Commander Ernest E Evans at the commissioning of the *Johnston*.

Above: A *Fletcher* Class destroyer and the light cruiser *Birmingham* pull away from the aircraft carrier *Princeton* after an explosion wrecked the carrier's stern and killed 200 men on her deck. *Left:* Cleaning a five-inch gun on the spray-drenched fantail of a destroyer.

shaw Bay led the other carriers to the South, heading into a rain squall in a frantic attempt to hide from the Japanese battleships and cruisers. All available aircraft had been launched, but as they had been expecting to attack shore targets they were not provided with the armour-piercing bombs or torpedoes which were needed against surface ships. Despite this the pilots attacked as best they could, and when their bombs were spent they made dummy passes at Kurita's ships, anything which would distract them from their prey. Fortunately Kurita chose to waste precious time by manoeuvring to hem the carriers in on three sides, instead of dashing forward to get to his main objective beyond them. But the threat of being boxed in presented Sprague's destroyers

Below: The destroyer *Heermann* (DD.532) lays a smoke-screen to protect the escort carrier *Kalinin Bay* off Samar.

with no choice but to stand and fight, for if the 'box' was closed the escort carriers would be wiped out with ease.

The *Johnston* under Commander Ernest E Evans found the heavy cruiser *Kumano* within range and rushed to the attack. She launched a salvo of torpedoes but staggered in the water as a salvo hit her. With her speed severely reduced she continued to fire at her opponents, which included the battleship *Kongo*. She gamely followed the *Hoel* and *Heermann* as they obeyed Admiral Sprague's call for a torpedo attack, but by 0830 her speed was down to 15 knots and only two five-inch guns were firing. The *Johnston* clung to life grimly but the Japanese shells were reducing her to a shambles. Only one shaft was turning, the gyro-compass had been knocked out, and the ship was so helpless that she could not take avoiding action when the *Heermann* collided with her. The *Hoel* (Commander Leon Kintberger) suffered a similar fate, being hit by two of the *Kongo*'s 14-inch shells while racing in to fire her torpedoes. She tried to get clear but found enemy battleships to port and cruisers to starboard. An hour later the destroyer was still afloat after being battered by 40 hits, but when she sank shortly afterwards 253 officers and men died. The attack was not in vain, as one torpedo hit the eight-inch gunned cruiser *Kumano* and ultimately influenced the outcome of the battle.

Sprague used the phrase 'men' to signify escort carriers and 'small boys' for his destroyers and destroyer escorts, which accounts for the signal:

'Small boys on my starboard quarter interpose with smoke between men and enemy cruisers.'

The DEs began to lay a smoke-screen but three of them were ordered to make a torpedo attack as soon as the three destroyers had finished theirs. The *Samuel B Roberts* was soon hit, but not before her salvo of three 'fish' had been fired. Soon her forward five-inch guns were knocked out – half her armament – but the after gun continued to fire for an hour. Over 300 rounds were fired, and even the starshell and practice rounds were fired when nothing else was left. Even though the air-blast had failed, making the gun dangerous to load, the gun-crew continued to load by hand until the heat of the breech 'cooked off' a cordite-charge and wrecked the gun-house. The fire-party which entered the smoking ruin was met by a horrifying but moving sight, the horribly mutilated captain of the gun holding a 54lb shell in his hands and trying to load it. Even when kindly hands removed the shell and tried to give him some comfort, the dying gun captain, named Carr, struggled to his

Left: An *Akizuki* Class destroyer and *Ise* Class carrier-battleship manoeuvre under attack from the aircraft of USS *San Jacinto*.

knees and lifted the five-inch shell in a pathetic last effort to load it. He was among the 89 officers and men who died before the *Samuel B Roberts* gave up the unequal fight.

The *Dennis* was damaged during her torpedo attack, but the *Raymond* escaped, like the *Heermann* before her, with only slight damage. The *John C Butler* was ordered to continue laying the smoke-screen, and the *Dennis* thankfully took cover behind it with the carriers. The carrier *Fanshaw Bay* was hit by four eight-inch shells but they did not stop her. The *Gambier Bay*, however, was hit and set on fire, and had to be abandoned. But the carriers were to undergo a further ordeal, for what Kurita's guns could not achieve, land-based aircraft from Luzon could. At about 2300 the *Saint Lô* and the *Kitkun Bay* were hit by aircraft diving onto their flight decks, a foretaste of the *kamikaze* attacks to come. The *Kitkun Bay* survived the blast of two Zeros but the *Saint Lô*'s gasoline and bomb store exploded and tore her flimsy hull apart.

Sprague's small force had been nearly annihilated, but the Japanese never got through to the invasion fleet off Leyte. If there is a chapter in destroyer-operations to match the heroism of Guadalcanal it must surely be the Battle of Samar. With the fate of the entire Philippines campaign depending on them, the seven small ships never flinched. Even if they had been defeated their courage would have been memorable, but they managed somehow to hold off a vastly superior force and save the day. It was a glorious contribution to the destroyer tradition.

The Terror of the Kamikazes

On the first day of April 1945 a huge invasion force prepared to capture the island of Okinawa in the East China Sea. It was the last step before the invasion of the Japanese home islands; possession of

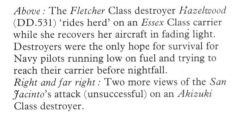

Above: The *Fletcher* Class destroyer *Hazelwood* (DD.531) 'rides herd' on an *Essex* Class carrier while she recovers her aircraft in fading light. Destroyers were the only hope for survival for Navy pilots running low on fuel and trying to reach their carrier before nightfall.
Right and far right: Two more views of the *San Jacinto*'s attack (unsuccessful) on an *Akizuki* Class destroyer.

the precipitous volcanic island and the rest of the Ryukyu group was vital. Yet, as the minesweepers swept the approaches and the bombarding ships 'softened up' the defences there was an ominous silence.

For Operation Iceberg the US Navy had mustered over 1500 ships, including 40 aircraft carriers and 18 battleships. Most of these were allocated to Admiral R K Turner's Task Force 51, the Okinawa Expeditionary Force: 10 battleships, 18 escort carriers, eight heavy cruisers, 82 destroyers and 54 destroyer escorts.

The majority of destroyers and DEs were to screen the invasion area, either by patrolling or maintaining a 'picket line' to give early radar warning of the approach of Japanese aircraft. The threat from *kamikazes* was known, and it was expected that the Japanese would spare no effort to destroy ships.

The 'radar picket' was an innovation suggested by previous experience, and its purpose was to give early warning of raids by aircraft or surface warships, and in addition to provide fighter-direction. Distant radar pickets were stationed 40–70 miles away from the transport area, but there was also a close picket line only 20–25 miles out. There were also destroyers and DEs assigned to radar picket 'stations' in the outer and inner anti-submarine screens. The distant picket line was composed of groups, each of which had one Fighter-Director (FD) destroyer and two Landing Craft Support (LCS) equipped with radar to extend the radar range. The FD destroyers could control any aircraft of the Combat Air Patrol (CAP) assigned to them by the central fighter-direction unit to deal with hostile aircraft in their area. The force was known as Task Flotilla 5, and it was commanded by Commodore Moosbrugger.

Although the defenders of Okinawa fought tenaciously from the warren of caves and pillboxes on the island, the land fighting was soon outmatched by the ferocity of the sea battle. It was soon realized that the main weight of Japanese air attack was falling on the picket line, and that one destroyer to each picket station was not enough. Yet the DEs did not carry enough anti-aircraft guns to stand up to continuous air attack. The picket groups were strengthened and eventually comprised three or more destroyers and four LCSs and strenuous efforts were made to keep a CAP over as many stations as possible. As radar stations were established ashore the 16 floating stations were reduced, and after six weeks only five were in use. Another problem was the small number of FD destroyers available and, as ships were damaged or sunk, it became necessary to equip fresh ships as rapidly as possible.

The onslaught on the destroyers began on 6 April, D+5, when the *Bush* and *Colhoun* were sunk by *kamikaze* aircraft diving onto them. Seven more destroyers and a DE were badly damaged in attacks of an intensity never seen before. The *Colhoun* was hit by no fewer than four *kamikazes*, but stayed afloat for more than seven hours. The problem of dealing with *kamikazes* was the human guidance system, which made them in effect operational air-to-surface guided missiles. Once the aircraft had been steered into its final dive the target ship had to destroy it by literally shooting it apart. This the 40mm Bofors anti-aircraft gun could not do as it did not fire proximity-fused (VT) ammunition; nor did the five-inch dual-purpose gun fire fast enough to do the job. It was found that the best tactics for destroyers was not to weave and zigzag, as they normally did under air attack, but to remain steady to maintain a steady gun-platform as long as possible to give the AA guns the best chance. Destroyers are such lively craft that the motion and vibration of being thrown about at high speed was too much for their fire-control, whereas larger warships could cope with evasive manoeuvres with no loss of accuracy.

But all this was academic, for the immediate problem of the destroyers was to survive the 'divine wind' which was striking them down in ever-increasing numbers. Added to the obsolescent aircraft was the *Ohka* or 'Baka' bomb, a small piloted rocket bomb which achieved a diving speed of 535mph. The attacks continued right through to the end of July and, in all, 13 destroyers and DEs were sunk off Okinawa and another 88 damaged. In many instances the casualties were on a terrible scale – as many as a third of the entire complement; in others the loss of life was miraculously light. One of the worst cases was, ironically, not a *kamikaze* attack. On 18 May the *Longshaw* was on the fifth day of a gruelling routine of fire-support off the beaches when she ran aground on a reef. Japanese shore-batteries ranged on her and began to demolish her methodically until her superstructure was a mass of tangled steel. The captain gave the order to abandon ship, but the casualties continued to mount up. The wrecked destroyer resembled a slaughterhouse, with dead and wounded trapped in every corner. Thirteen officers and 73 enlisted men were killed and 90 wounded.

The final suicide run of the Okinawa campaign was the most spectacular of all, a one-way trip proposed for the giant battleship *Yamato* in which she hoped to smash her way through the destroyer-screen to get at the invasion fleet off Okinawa, and even run herself on shore and use her 18-inch guns to pound the American troops ashore. But inevitably she was spotted by submarines and heavily attacked by Admiral Mitscher's carrier aircraft. This was one of the last operations of the once-powerful Japanese destroyer flotillas, and eight destroyers under the cruiser *Yahagi* were given some of the dwindling reserves of fuel oil for the trip to Okinawa. It was called the Battle of the East China Sea but in fact it was nothing more than a prolonged

Above: The USS *Haraden* (DD.585) is assisted by one of her sister *Fletchers* after being struck amidships by a *kamikaze* plane while en route to Mindoro Island in December 1944.
Below: The destroyer-minelayer *Aaron Ward* (DM.34) is almost unrecognizable as a *Fletcher* after being hit by no fewer than five *kamikazes* off Kerama Retto on 3 May 1945.

live target practice for the experienced American aircrews, for there were no defending fighters to distract them. The *Yamato* went down in the afternoon of 7 April in company with the *Yahagi* and the destroyers *Asashimo*, *Isokaze*, *Hamakaze* and *Kasumi*.

After the battle was over Moosbrugger paid tribute to his destroyers:

'The performance of the personnel of the screening and radar picket ships, both individually and collectively, was superb through the Okinawa campaign. Acts of heroism and unselfishness, fighting spirit,

Above: The *Umikaze* of Destroyer Squadron No 24 runs at high speed, possibly on her acceptance trials in 1937.

coolness under fire, unswerving determination, endurance and qualities of leadership and loyalty exceeded all previous conceptions set for the US Navy. The radar picket station groups took every blow that the Japs could inflict and absorbed terrific punishment in personnel casualties and material damage, . . .'

The Sinking of the *Haguro*

While the American destroyers were locked in their terrible struggle with the *kamikazes* four British destroyers of the East Indies Fleet fought what turned out to be the last classic destroyer action in history. On 9 May two submarines in the Malacca Strait sighted the heavy cruiser *Haguro*, a destroyer and two patrol craft heading North-West. The small Japanese force was carrying supplies to the Andaman Islands and Vice-Admiral H T C Walker RN detached escort carriers and the 26th Destroyer Flotilla under Captain Manly Power to search North of Sumatra for it. On the morning of 15 May an aircraft from HMS *Shah* signalled that she had sighted the *Haguro*, and at 2300 that night the flotilla leader HMS *Saumarez* picked up a radar contact at a distance of 34 miles. Captain Power planned his attack with care ensuring that whichever way the *Haguro* turned she would be caught.

Even at this late stage the Japanese had not lost their boldness, and while the four destroyers were moving into position the cruiser suddenly reversed course. There was a brisk flurry of gunfire during which the *Saumarez* was hit several times. She and HMS *Verulam* fired their torpedoes, and when the *Haguro* turned away to avoid these she ran into the torpedoes from the *Venus* and *Virago*. The cruiser sank just before 0200 on 16 May, about 45 miles South-West of Penang, but her escorting destroyer, the *Hamikaze*, escaped and was able to pick up survivors when the 26th Flotilla had left the scene. Although only a minor action it was appropriate that destroyers should finish their long and distinguished war career with a text-book operation.

Above: The USS *O'Brien* (DD.725) was one of the first *Allen M Sumner Class* to be completed. She had twin five-inch 38/cal gun houses and heavy AA armament but otherwise maintains a family resemblance to the *Fletcher* Class. She was launched on 7 December 1943.

Below: Two *Allen M Sumner* Class destroyers of Task Force 77.4 in an idyllic setting in the Mindanao Sea in January 1945. The reconquest of the Philippines was the beginning of the end of the Japanese empire.

The Changing Destroyer

No other type of warship proved as adaptable as the destroyer, and throughout World War II it was used for every purpose imaginable. Yet by 1945 its *raison d'être*, torpedo attack against an enemy fleet, had disappeared. With the disappearance of the battle-fleet there were no battleships to attack, and in any case radar-controlled gunfire made even night attack suicidal.

The British had tried to build destroyers equipped primarily for surface action, and this policy had been wrong as witnessed in the Norwegian campaign in 1940. Although dive-bombing was not the most accurate form of air attack against ships it was very easy if no serious opposition was offered. This led to an immediate increase in close range weapons, principally the 20mm Oerlikon gun from Switzerland and later the 40mm Bofors gun from Sweden. Unlike the US Navy, the RN had not invested any money in developing a suitable medium-calibre (four to six inch) gun-mounting and fire-control system, and so nothing much could be done. Some destroyers were given four-inch twin AA guns but the mounting had many disadvantages in surface action. In 1942 dual-purpose mountings were introduced but a true high-angle mounting designed for destroyers did not appear until 1945. So desperate was the shortage that in 1941 serious thought was given to arming new destroyers with the US Navy's five-inch/38 calibre gun.

The pressing need for escorts meant that the British tended to use a large percentage of their fleet destroyers as escort destroyers. Provision had been made pre-war, and all fleet destroyers had been fitted with Asdic (Sonar) but the depth-charge stowage had to be increased, usually accomplished by taking out 'Y' gun and using the shell-room for stowing reload charges. The difference between the fleet destroyer and one reclassified as an escort destroyer was that the fleet destroyer operated with her flotilla whereas the escort destroyer was merely one of a large number attached to one of the anti-submarine commands. However, fleet destroyers were so often detached for special duties that the flotillas were rarely at full strength.

The pre-war notion of building smaller versions of the fleet destroyers as escorts proved a great success. In 1938 the Admiralty had been desperately worried by the shortage of destroyers and had asked Andrew Cunningham, then R-A, D (Rear-Admiral Commanding Destroyers), to advise on the best remedy. Cunningham advised the building of small 'utility' destroyers with only a light torpedo armament but a heavy anti-aircraft gun armament and depth-charges as mounted in the latest type of escort. Even though the war clouds were gathering the British Treasury still kept the purse strings tightly drawn, and it was necessary to disguise the first 20 of the new type as 'fast escort vessels' to get Parliamentary approval, but they were clearly scaled down versions of the latest *Javelin* Class, and when they came into service they were known as the 'Hunt' Class escort destroyers. For once the conservative British designers overreached themselves, and the prototype HMS *Atherstone* was so top-heavy that she had to sacrifice a twin four-inch high-angle gun mounting and the triple 21-inch torpedo-tubes. They were about ten years ahead of their time in having fin-stabilizers, but such a novelty was too much for the average destroyer-officer, who cursed them as an unmitigated nuisance.

The faults of the 'Hunts' were quickly remedied in a second group by adding 2.5 feet to the width of the hull; this allowed the third twin four-inch gun to be put back. The smaller hull and simpler

armament enabled building time to be cut, and by 1942 55 had been built. They proved so useful, despite their small size and lack of endurance, that they were often used on fleet operations. This inevitably led to criticism that they had no torpedo-tubes, and in an action like the Second Battle of Sirte it will be remembered that the 'Hunts' had to stay with the convoy because they could not attack the Italian Fleet. As a result a further 19 were built with a pair of torpedo-tubes in lieu of a four-inch mounting, and these were known as the 'Hunt' Type III. Two more were built to a special design by the well-known destroyer building firm of John I Thornycroft to achieve what they regarded as the design of the future. In this 'Hunt' Type IV the traditional characteristics of the destroyer almost disappeared, for Thornycrofts' designers used a fuller hull-form to improve endurance (at the expense of top speed) and to reduce rolling. The weak point of destroyers had always been the break of the forecastle but instead of the flush deck chosen by US destroyer designers, the British chose to extend the forecastle deck back three-quarters of the length. This gave an enclosed fore-and-aft passage allowing under-cover access to all parts of the ship and for the first time in the 'Hunt' series, the originally designed armament of six four-inch AA guns, a quadruple pom-pom and three torpedo-tubes could be mounted. The only disappointment for the builders was that they were forced to keep the power down to the 19,000hp of the earlier 'Hunts', and so the *Brecon* and *Brissenden* were no faster.

German destroyers were much less involved in escort work apart from screening their heavy ships at sea, and so they continued to be equipped primarily for surface action. Like the British they found the pre-war scale of anti-aircraft armament inadequate, even though they had adopted the efficient 3.7cm and two-cm automatic guns. By 1945 those few destroyers still afloat mounted as many as 12 3.7cm and six two-cm guns. In 1938 the *Kriegsmarine* tried to remedy the problem of its lack of cruisers by reviving the concept which it had initiated 20 years earlier; the eight destroyers authorized that year were armed with 15cm (5.9-inch) guns in place of the 12.7cm (five-inch) guns in the previous classes. None of these super-destroyers was in service before the end of 1940, and they formed the Narvik Flotilla, so named in honour of those killed at Narvik in April that year.

Above: The 'Elbing' or *T.22* Class of 1300-ton torpedo boats were the most successful German design. This is *T.26* as completed.

Only 17 of the 'Narvik' Type were completed by 1945, which underlines the danger of trying for quality at the expense of numbers. They served with distinction in the Bay of Biscay and the Arctic, but just as it had in the *S.113* and *V.116*, the 15cm gun caused more problems than it solved. Not only was it clumsy to load, but the twin turret (when at last it was available in 1942) was too heavy and was badly cramped to fit into the narrow forward section of the hull. In most of them the third gun had to be replaced by extra light AA guns and thereby reduced the weight of broadside to that of the earlier five-inch gunned destroyers. To add to their disadvantages the big destroyers suffered from the same machinery problems as their predecessors, and this seriously hampered operations against Allied convoys in the Arctic. For some reason they reverted to Z-numbers in place of names and were sometimes known to the Allies as the 'Z' type.

Lack of numbers caused the *Kriegsmarine* to build torpedo boats of about

Below: HMS *Brissenden* and her sister *Brecon* were a complete break with destroyer tradition, with the forecastle deck well-extended for added strength and improved habitability. They were the fore-runners of the anti-submarine escorts of the 1950s.

Left: British destroyermen pose for a photograph after a successful action against a Japanese convoy in the Andaman Sea in March 1945.
Right: German destroyers lying at Kiel after the unconditional surrender in May 1945.

half the size of the destroyers and, like the British 'Hunt' Classes, these proved a useful addition to the strength. The first types were armed with two triple banks of torpedo-tubes but only one 10.5cm gun and had a good turn of speed rather than radius of action. They were given T-numbers up to *T.21*, and in 1941 they were superseded by a new type known as the 'Elbings'. These 1300-tonners were nearer to the destroyer category, with a good gun-armament of four 10.5cm (4.1-inch) guns to match the same torpedo armament as before.

The 'Elbings' had a flush deck and two widely spaced funnels, a silhouette which became painfully familiar to the British light forces operating in the English Channel. They showed their capabilities in an action off Brittany in October 1943, in which *T.23* and *T.27* sank the cruiser HMS *Charybdis*. The British ship had left Plymouth on the evening of 22 October to try to intercept the merchant ship *Munsterland*, which was trying to get to Cherbourg from Brest, and she had two fleet destroyers and four 'Hunts' as escorts. The British force acted without cohesion, for the cruiser did not appear to have alerted her destroyers when she made radar contact. At 0130 the *Charybdis* increased speed, and 15 minutes later she was in action at only 4000 yards. The five German torpedo boats immediately turned towards her and scored several hits with torpedoes, sinking her and the destroyer *Limbourne* with heavy loss of life. It was all too reminiscent of the early actions in the Solomons, the advantage of radar being nullified by poor tactics. It also showed up the weaknesses of the early 'Hunts' in surface actions against destroyers: modest speed and, even more important, no torpedoes.

The Japanese seem to have taken the first step in building a destroyer capable of protecting the Fleet against air attack as well as underwater and surface attack. In 1939 the so-called Type 'B' design was completed, a huge destroyer displacing nearly 3000 tons and armed with a new long-barrelled 100mm (3.9-inch) twin AA mounting. The new gun also had a surface capability and could outrange the USN five-inch gun at 20,000 yards. Two enclosed mountings were provided forward and two aft, with two fire-control directors. At a late stage in the design it was decided to give them an offensive armament as well, and so they were given a quadruple bank of 24-inch torpedo-tubes amidships. The new destroyers, known as the *Akizuki* Class, appeared in 1942, and with their four boiler uptakes trunked into one large raked funnel they bore a strong resemblance to the small light cruiser *Yubari*. For many months puzzled US Navy intelligence officers sifted through sighting reports of the *Yubari* thousands of miles apart.

Only 12 of the *Akizuki*s were completed, and such was the ferocity of the fighting in the Pacific that half were sunk by the end of 1944. Although there were plans to build more, the disasters of 1942 led to the recasting of the construction programme, and in any case the Type 'A' or *Yugumo* Class order was repeated under the 1941 Programme, to form a new class called the *Hayanami*s. The main improvement in the *Yugumo* Class was to give the five-inch guns 75° elevation and by the time the first vessels were ready early in 1942 the first Japanese radar sets were also available. Another type of destroyer was building in 1941, the prototype Type 'C', called *Shimakaze*. This remarkable destroyer had a layout similar to previous classes, but had quintuple 24-inch torpedo-tubes, and her very advanced turbines and boilers produced a maximum speed of 39 knots. The steam temperature was 400° C and and pressure was 40 kg/sq cm, enabling 76,000 hp to be developed. On one occasion the *Shimakaze* reached 40 knots with 79,000 hp, but there was no justification for continuing to build such a complex type of destroyer in wartime, and the rest of the class were cancelled in 1942.

The Japanese only belatedly realized the need for escort destroyers, and it was not until 1943 that a new, simplified type appeared. Known as the *Matsu* Class, these destroyers were also the first to adopt the unit system of alternate boilers and machinery to improve the chances of surviving torpedo damage. Speed was a modest 28 knots and, although the torpedo armament was also weak, they carried a heavy battery of AA guns. A repeat design was even simpler, with curves and flares in the plating replaced by flat sections to simplify welding, but very few of them were completed by the end of the War. The distances in the Pacific did not justify small destroyers, and the *Matsu* and *Tachibana* Classes were as big as many other navies' fleet destroyers. Despite their simple design they proved to be

Below: The ultra-fast Japanese destroyer *Shimakaze* running trials at 39 knots in May 1943.

robust and many limped home after severe damage. One was refloated in 1955 to serve in the post-war Maritime Self Defence Force.

In contrast with most other navies the US Navy made the minimum of alterations to its destroyers. Most of the second group of *Fletchers* had ten 40mm Bofors guns in five twin mountings to cope with the great weight of air attack in the Pacific, but retained their full outfit of two quintuple banks of torpedo-tubes. In 1942 they were followed by the *Allen M Sumner* Class, which had three twin five-inch/38 calibre gun mountings but otherwise differed little in basic design from the *Fletchers*. The hull was the same length but there was a slight increase of beam to allow for the extra topweight. This allowed two quadruple 40mm Bofors gun-mountings to be carried abaft the second funnel. After only 70 had been ordered the design was lengthened by 14

Above: The destroyer *Svobodny* of the Soviet Black Sea Fleet sinking at her moorings after a German air attack.

feet to give more space between decks, and the new 'long hull' variant was known as the *Gearing* Class. Many of them had the after-bank of torpedo-tubes replaced by an extra quadruple 40mm Bofors mounting, and others had the forward tubes replaced by a big tripod mast carrying a long-range air-warning radar antenna to allow them to function as radar pickets. Over 50 were incomplete in 1945 and had to be cancelled.

In 1941 the US Navy started to build destroyer escorts or DEs to meet British requirements for North Atlantic escorts. They bore the same relation to contemporary USN destroyers as the little 'Hunts' did to the Royal Navy's *Javelin* Class, but unlike the 'Hunts' they were normally restricted to anti-submarine and escort duties. The British had originally asked for a set of triple torpedo-tubes to be included in their DEs but later changed their minds. The USN decided to keep them, and at Leyte Gulf the four DEs had to use them against Admiral Kurita's force. A leaf was taken out of the Japanese book in 1942, when many DEs were earmarked for conversion to fast transports (APDs) for carrying troops. The superstructure amidships was carried out to the ship's side, and four assault landing craft (LCAs) were carried in davits. Some of the old flush-deckers were also converted for this role, with the two forward boilers and funnels removed.

The British built 14 groups of destroyers to one basic design for European and Mediterranean operations, single-funnellers with four single guns, but in 1942 they started to build a new class for the Pacific. Although still single-funnelled, the new destroyers marked a considerable advance over previous craft. Known as the 'Battle' Class, they were nearly 20 feet longer and five feet beamier which allowed a heavier scale of armament. A new twin dual-purpose 4.5-inch twin gun mounting was provided and, for the first time, both twin mountings were concentrated forward, leaving astern fire to a dozen 40mm Bofors guns. These guns were in four twins (each with its own radar control) and four singles, and eight 21-inch torpedo-tubes were carried.

The next three classes had more in common with the Japanese *Matsu* Class and the *Fletcher*s for they adopted the unit system of machinery. In the 'Weapon' Class the opportunity was taken to make up some of the leeway lost in British machinery by adopting higher temperatures and steam pressures and, for the first time, the twin four-inch high-angle gun mounting was used as the main armament. Although a full torpedo armament was still mounted, this marked the transition to a fleet escort, and the 'Weapons' were clearly not expected to engage in a surface gun action. The fol-

Below: The destroyer-minesweeper USS *Butler* (DMS.29) having been hit by a *kamikaze* is aided by a tug off Okinawa.

lowing class, the 'Gs', had a dual-purpose gun armament and adopted the well-tried US Navy Mk.37 fire-control director which had been supplied to the RN. All the war lessons were incorporated in a third design, the 'D' or *Daring* Class, which combined elements of the 'Battles', 'Weapons' and 'Gs' in a big hull. None of this group was completed by the end of the War, but they mark the summit of British destroyer development.

War Losses

Destroyers fought a hard war, and the statistics reflect this. In all the Allies lost 324 destroyers, while the Axis lost 293. The causes of the losses are shown below.

With their fragile plating no more than .125-inch (three-mm) thick destroyers could be sunk quite easily but the stories of the punishment that destroyers survived seem to contradict that statement. The USS *Cassin* and *Downes*, for example, were burnt out and apparently beyond repair after the Japanese had finished with them at Pearl Harbor. Yet it was still considered worthwhile to salvage the machinery and some of the fittings, as destroyer-turbines took so long to manufacture. New hulls were built from the original drawings at Mare Island Navy Yard, Vallejo, and in April 1943 the new *Downes* was launched, followed by the *Cassin* in June. The two destroyers reached the Pacific in 1944, considerably more up-to-date than their sisters as the opportunity had been taken to update their fire-control, communications and radar.

Another 'phoenix' was Lord Louis Mountbatten's *Kelly*. On the night of 9–10 May 1940 she was hit by a torpedo from a German 'E-Boat' in the North Sea. The hull was badly twisted and bent, and she looked more like a submarine than a destroyer when she was finally towed home. So severe was the damage that the *Kelly*'s hull needed to be realigned with hydraulic jacks and shores, and the entire midship section had to be rebuilt. Previously a destroyer would have probably broken in two under such stresses but the *Kelly* and her sisters were built on the new principle of longitudinal framing in which the main strength-members ran lengthways, not transversely. Longitudinal framing was usual for larger ships, but had not been applied to small craft such as warships partly on grounds of cost but mainly because of its complexity. Ironically it had first been tried in a British destroyer, HMS *Ardent*, as long ago as 1913, but had not found favour as it would have slowed destroyer production at a crucial time. In World War II longitudinally framed destroyers survived heavy damage again and again, and it saved as many ships as the unit system of machinery.

Not until the end of the war was in sight did any navy dare to write off a destroyer as a total loss if she could be saved. Even a 25-year-old like HMS *Wolfhound*, which was cracked in half by a pair of bombs bracketing her, was rebuilt. The *Wivern* was rescuing survivors from the Canadian corvette *Weyburn* in 1943 when the sinking ship's depth-charges went off 25 feet down. The destroyer's turbines and boilers were lifted off their mountings and the keel was split open but she returned to duty in 1944. When the flush-decker USS *Blakeley* was torpedoed off Martinique in 1942, Philadelphia Navy Yard was able to give her a new bow by the simple expedient of cutting one off her stricken sister *Taylor*. But nobody tried to repeat the trick of joining two destroyers together to make a third, as with HMS *Zubian* in 1918.

In the final analysis nature was the worst enemy of all. In the Atlantic and the Arctic there were gales capable of capsizing a destroyer and in the misnamed 'Pacific' there were typhoons of unparalleled ferocity. On 17 December 1944 the US Third Fleet was hit a harder blow than any the Japanese could have struck at that time.

It was the morning of 17 December about 500 miles East of Luzon and the Fleet's destroyers were refuelling from the battleships *New Jersey* and *Wisconsin* in a moderate swell, with wind speed varying from 20 to 30 knots. As destroyers were prone to do under these conditions, they began to plunge heavily like porpoises, and soon fuelling hoses were part-

Top: The *Soobrasitelny* takes off survivors from the sinking *Tashkent*.
Right: HMS *Crossbow* of the 'Weapon' Class incorporated all the wartime lessons in her design.

	Air Attack	Surface Torpedo	S/marine Torpedo	Gun-fire	Mines	Misc.*	Total
Royal Navy	56·5	14	38	13·5	26	21	169
Free French†	5	3	—	—	2	4	14
Dutch Navy	4	1	1	2	—	1	9
US Navy	49	6	10	9·5	7·5	17	99
Soviet Navy	16	—	1	—	14	2	33
German Navy	5	6	—	9	4	1	25
Italian Navy	37·5	5·5	13	23	22	33	134
French Navy†	1	—	—	9	—	36	46
Japanese Navy	48·5	12	43	15·5	8	7	134

*Includes scuttling, stranding etc.
†For convenience 'Free French' includes French Navy losses before the June 1940 armistice and after French units had rejoined the Allies at the end of 1942.

G96

ing. Admiral Halsey prudently ordered refuelling to stop and took the Third Fleet North-West to try to avoid the storm which the meteorologists predicted. Late in the afternoon the storm, or to give it its proper name, the typhoon, changed direction, and the Fleet turned South-West. But the typhoon veered again and relentlessly overhauled Halsey's ships. By the following morning the whole Fleet was trapped in a seething maelstrom of wind and giant waves, only 150 miles from the typhoon's centre.

Not even battleships and carriers could cope with 70-foot waves and 90-knot winds. Just after midday the eye of the typhoon came closer until it was only 35 miles distant. For the destroyers it was a horrifying ordeal. Although US destroyers had self-compensating fuel tanks which took in sea-water to replace oil fuel, this had to be pumped out before refuelling, leaving them very 'tender' and riding light. Having failed to refuel 24 hours before the thirsty destroyers were desperately overdue to top up, and even less able to cope with the deteriorating weather. Two of the *Farragut* Class, the *Dewey* and *Aylwin*, reported that their engine room inclinometers had registered a roll of 70° or more, and veterans remember vivid impressions of destroyers lying on their sides, with the lips of their funnels touching the surface of the water in a series of terrifying rolls.

For a destroyer severe rolling entails more than the obvious risk of capsizing. Water spewing through ventilators and boiler-intakes caused short-circuits and cut off electric power, while sea-water down the funnels could easily put out the boiler furnace. A destroyer without steam or electricity could only wallow helplessly until the storm blew itself out. And if the ship sank there was little chance of sur-

Above: The rebuilt USS *Downes* (DD.375) bears little resemblance to the shattered wreck which was salvaged from Pearl Harbor.
Right: USS *Halford* (DD.480) under refit at Mare Island Navy Yard in May 1945. Note the new radar directors on her 40mm Bofors guns, and the *Allen M Sumner* Class in the floating dock in the background.
Far right: The Mark 37 director control tower of the destroyer *Nicholas* at Mare Island 1944 had 40mm directors added on the roof of the bridge.
Below: The Japanese escort destroyer *Hatsuzakura* seen from the USS carrier *Shangri-La* in Sagami Bay on 27 August 1945. These *Matsu* Class destroyers had a unit arrangement of machinery and boilers to reduce the risk of a single hit which could conceivably put all machinery out of action.

Below: HMS *Quickmatch* and her seven sisters of the 'Q' Class were the third group of destroyers built to the wartime Emergency Design, using the single funnel and longitudinal framing of the 'J' Class but single guns.

Above: The *Momo*, another *Matsu* Class running trials off Myazu Bay, is making 28.59 knots at 1534 tonnes.

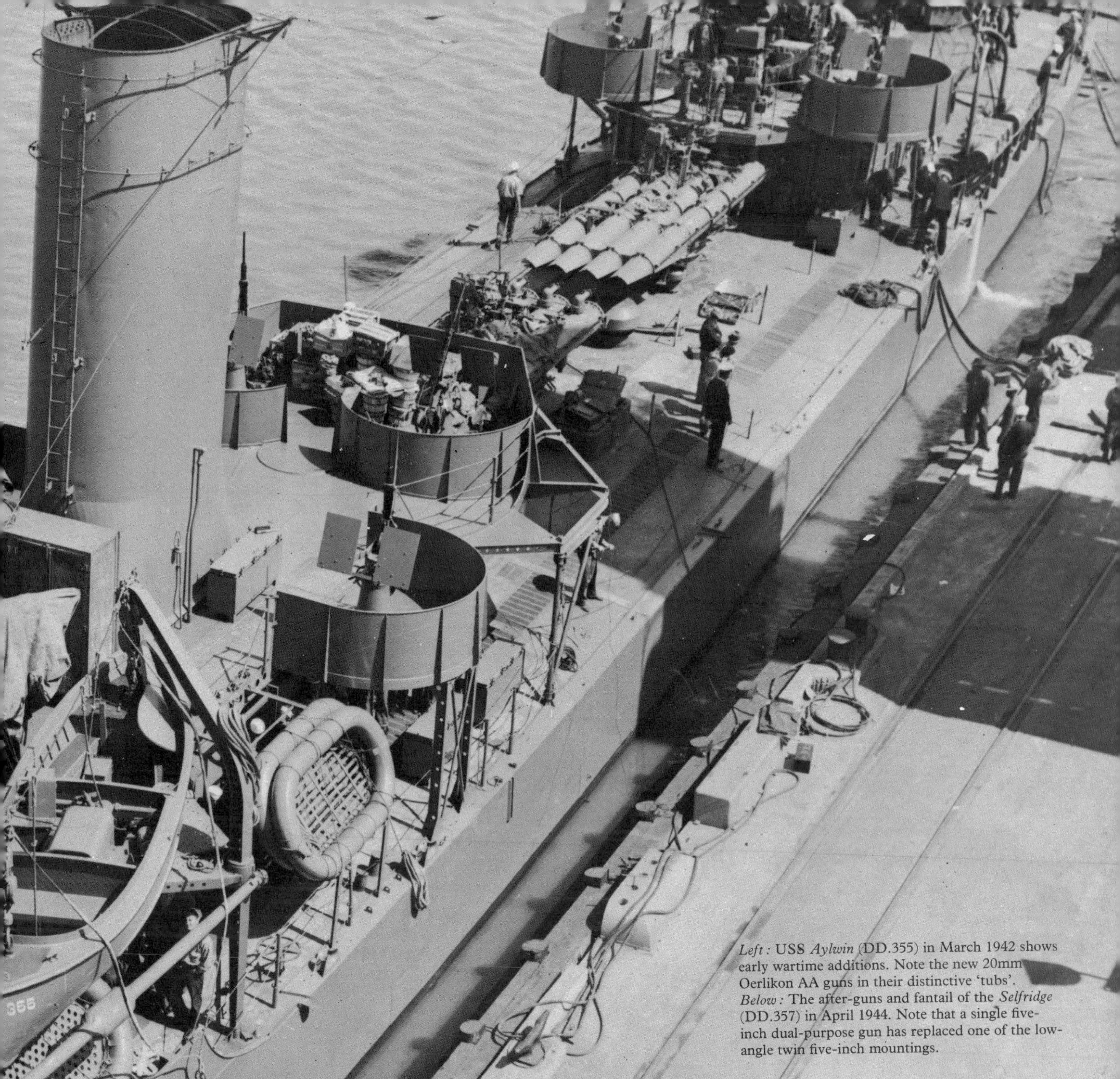

Left : USS *Aylwin* (DD.355) in March 1942 shows early wartime additions. Note the new 20mm Oerlikon AA guns in their distinctive 'tubs'.
Below : The after-guns and fantail of the *Selfridge* (DD.357) in April 1944. Note that a single five-inch dual-purpose gun has replaced one of the low-angle twin five-inch mountings.

Far left: Gunners loading the forward five-inch guns aboard the USS *Downes* during the bombardment of Marcus Island, 9 October 1944. Note that the cartridge case is separate.
Left: On 24 August 1944 Beaufighters of the RAF and RCAF attacked German destroyers off Le Verdon at the mouth of the Gironde River. *T.24* (foreground) was sunk that day and *Z.24* (background) ran ashore the next day. The German light forces trapped West of the Normandy invasion area were all completely wiped out.

viving in the seething water, even if the boats and life rafts had not been torn away by the waves. Several destroyers reported deck fittings torn out, boats smashed and even radar aerials and depth-charge racks bent and twisted. The destroyers *Hull*, *Monaghan* and *Spence* turned turtle that day, and only 91 officers and men survived out of the 790 who formed their crews. It was not possible to begin a search for them until nightfall and the survivors were not found for two days. As Admiral Nimitz pointed out in his comments on the disaster, 'the time for taking all measures for a ship's safety is while able to do so'. All three destroyers were overwhelmed because they had been trying to maintain station, and it was felt that they should have been free to abandon their stations to give themselves a free hand in manoeuvring. The fact that the path of the typhoon had not been accurately predicted, and that the destroyers were low on fuel, also played parts in the catastrophe.

It is difficult to establish the last action fought by destroyers, but in the European theatre it was probably between German destroyers or torpedo boats and Russian aircraft as the *Kriegsmarine* struggled to evacuate Eastern Prussia in the face of the Russian advance. On 5 May 1945 the *Hans Lody*, *Friedrich Ihn*, *Theodor Riedel*, *Z.25*, *T.17*, *T.19*, *T.28* and *T.35* fought off attacks by Soviet motor torpedo boats to escort a convoy with 45,000 refugees to Copenhagen. It was the *Kriegsmarine*'s swansong, and as at Dunkirk and Guadalcanal, destroyers bore the brunt; a dozen were lost and another dozen were damaged by Allied bombing of their bases. In the Pacific, the situation was similar but on a much larger scale as US carrier aircraft wiped out the remnants of the Imperial Japanese Navy in each and every anchorage. The last amphibious landing was in Borneo, and on 30 June, just six weeks before the surrender, US destroyers fired 18,820 rounds of five-inch ammunition at Balikpapan. It was appropriate that they should be at the scene of DesDiv 59's heroic action in January 1942.

Below: An unusual view of the USS *Drayton* (DD.366) and her torpedo-tubes, June 1944 – she has just had two twin 49mm AA mountings added.

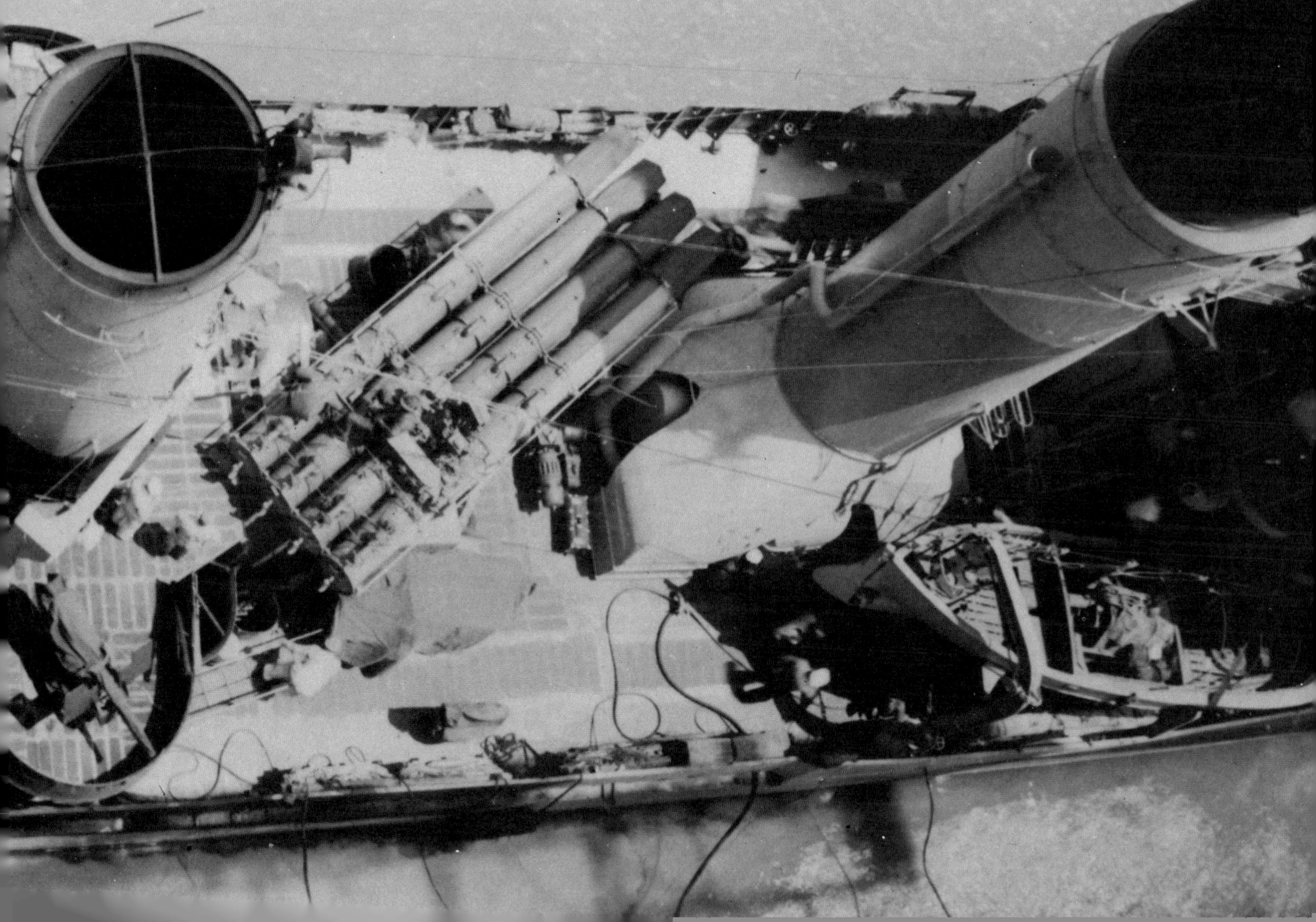

The Final Phase

When the Royal Navy took delivery of HMS *Daring* in March 1952 it was so nonplussed by her size that for a while there was talk of her being too big to be a destroyer. At 2600 tons she seemed to have gone from the category of the hunter to the hunted, but she was merely the first of a new series of super-destroyers, and within a few years the destroyer as warship-type had changed completely.

It was not just in size that the destroyer changed. Radar-assisted fire-control had already made torpedo attack a thing of the past and, although this was not recognized for some years, the implications of air-attack had been recognized. The weight needed to accommodate truly dual-purpose guns as well as the bulky fire-control to make those guns effective made the jump in size inevitable. But there was a tendency in the opposite direction as well, to reduce the destroyer to an anti-submarine escort in which only self-defence weapons were carried so that a full outfit of anti-submarine sensors and weapons could also be carried.

For some years after 1945 no new destroyers were built for the victors had more than enough destroyers to meet their needs. The US Navy completed several *Gearing*s in leisurely fashion as DDKs or 'Hunter–Killer' Destroyers, reducing the five-inch guns and in some cases removing them entirely, suppressing the torpedo armament and giving them Hedgehogs and anti-submarine rocket launchers. In the post-Hiroshima era the principal obsession concerned a Soviet attack on the United States, and so many destroyers were converted to radar picket or DDRs. Their role was to extend the flanks of the early-warning radar network across the North American Continent as a defence against Russian nuclear bombers.

Sadly it was the British, who having invented the name 'destroyer', took the initiative in getting rid of it. Aware that their standard 'Emergency' type of destroyers built during the war had a hotchpotch of unsuitable weapons and fire-control, they decided to convert two prototypes for anti-submarine warfare. When HMS *Relentless* and HMS *Rocket* appeared in 1941 there was a gasp of horror from every destroyer-lover. Gone was the sleek silhouette bristling with guns; in its place was a block structure amidships and a forecastle deck extended

Below: HMS *Whelp* was transferred to the South African Navy in 1953 and was renamed *Simon van der Stel*. She is seen here leaving Capetown.

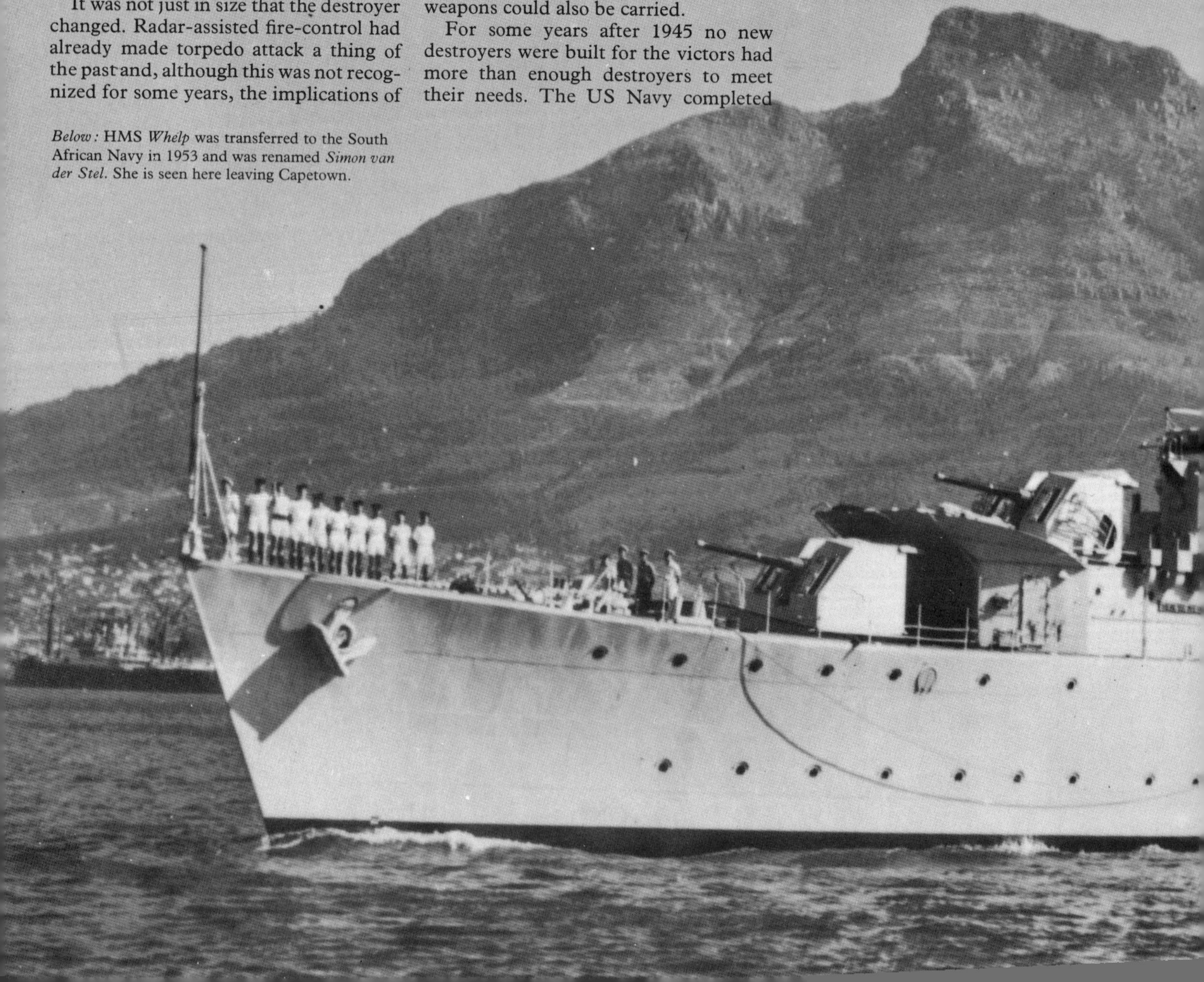

Right: HMS *Barrosa* and the 'Battle' Class were designed in 1943 for service in the Pacific.
Below right: The British *Daring* Class were completed in the early 1950s and were the largest destroyers in the world at the time. HMS *Dainty* was launched at Cowes on 16 August 1950.

aft nearly to the stern. The only guns were a twin 40mm anti-aircraft mounting forward and a twin four-inch aft, although a pair of triple depth-charge mortars were also carried aft. They were now to be known as 'frigates', a term which had been revived in 1943 by the Canadians for a new type of twin-screw escort, and within a few years another 30 destroyers had undergone similar conversions or had become less sophisticated editions.

Time mellowed opinions of the Type 15 frigates, as they were known, and they certainly had more ability to cope with the submarine threat facing Western Navies in the 1950s than the destroyers

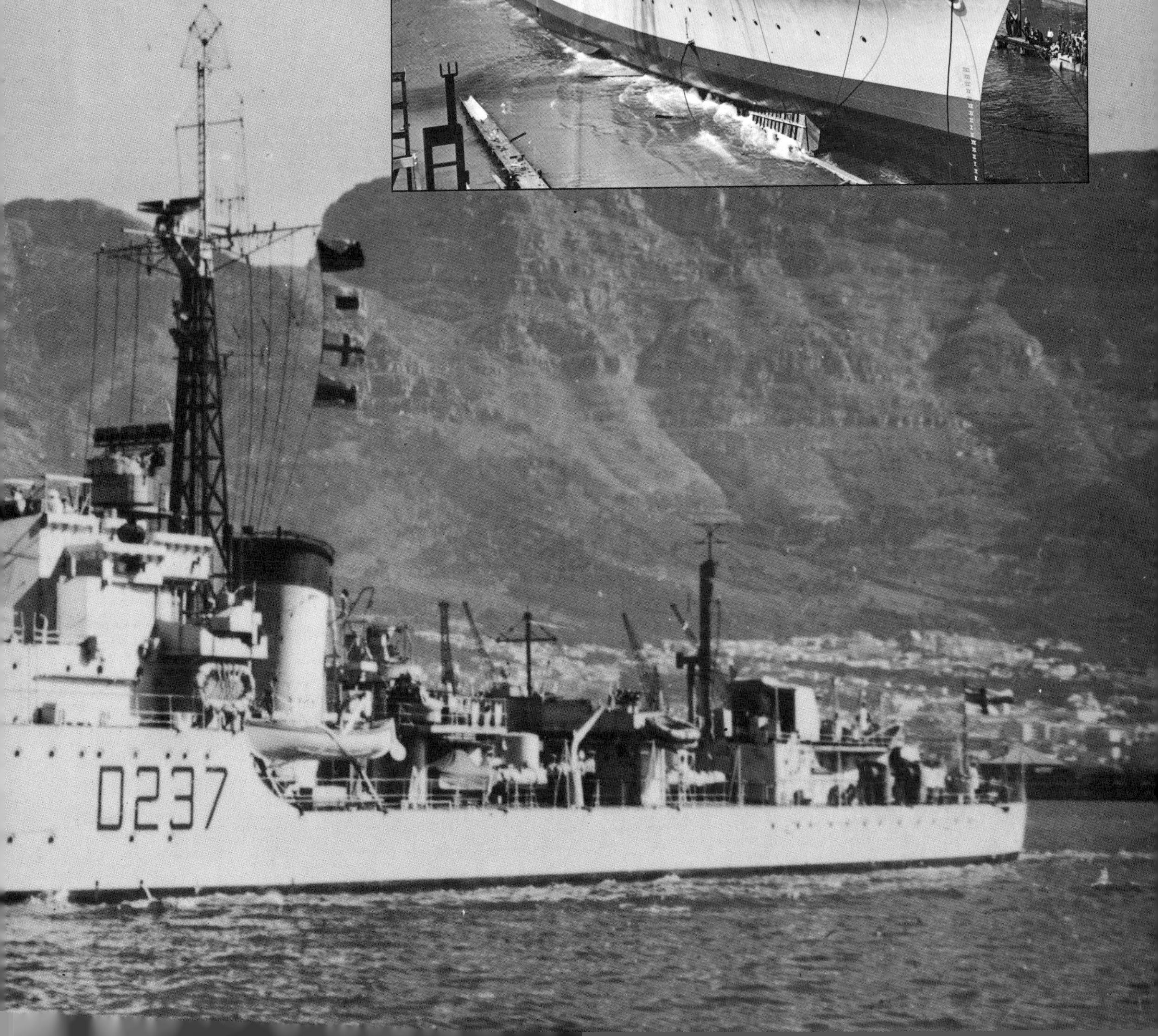

Above : The *Fletcher*, *Sumner* and *Gearing* Class destroyers in commission in the 1950s were refitted with tripod masts to carry additional radar.
Above right : On 26 October 1946 the British destroyers *Saumarez* (foreground) and *Volage* of the 3rd Flotilla were badly damaged by Albanian mines in the Corfu Channel.
Left : The Swedish destroyer *Halland* fires her 12cm guns while turning at high speed.

that they had once been. They incorporated many lessons from the war, notably the long enclosed forecastle which had been so successful in Thornycroft's *Brecon* and *Brissenden*. If they seemed under-armed by comparison with older destroyers, it was because it was clear by 1950 that guns had to be accompanied by fire-control if they were to be effective against aircraft. Unfortunately a decision was made in the UK to retain the term 'frigate' for ships designed for purely escort duties, unlike the US Navy, which justified the retention of the emotive type-name, destroyer, on the grounds that it could mean 'submarine destroyer' just as easily as 'torpedo boat destroyer'.

Above: Radar picket destroyers were used in the 1950s to extend the early warning defences of the North American continent. The USS *Higbee* (DDR.806) is seen here.
Left: The Brazilian *Piaui* was formerly the *Fletcher* Class *Lewis Hancock* (DD.675) and was transferred in 1967.

However the US Navy was not blameless in altering names either. In 1948–49 an experimental 'Hunter–Killer Ship' (CLK) of light cruiser size was started, the first of a class of four very large destroyers. During construction both the 5600-ton *Norfolk* and the 3675-ton *Mitscher* Class were re-rated as Destroyer Leaders, but in 1955 the term 'frigate' was revived for them. Although more correct historically than the British and Canadian use of the term, it complicated matters even further. Fortunately destroyers continued to be built, and in 1943–58 the 18 *Forrest Sherman* Class joined the Fleet. They incorporated no radical improvements over wartime destroyers, but had an armament of single five-inch guns of new design and the four 21-inch torpedo-tubes amidships fired only homing torpedoes against submarines. As a result the distinction between the DL and DD became one of size rather than type, and when guided missiles were introduced as the main defence against aircraft they became DLGs and DDGs.

The Royal Canadian Navy spurned the idea of turning its destroyers into frigates, and adopted the term 'destroyer escort' to conform with the US Navy's reclassification of its DDKs. The French abandoned the *contre-torpilleur* idea, and in 1954–55 built a new class of *escorteurs d'escadre*, handsome ships built on traditional destroyer-lines with a heavy gun armament and torpedo-tubes capable of firing both anti-submarine and conventional torpedoes. The *Surcouf* Class commemorated famous French privateers and captains, and with typical Gallic shrewdness, their five-inch guns were chambered to take the standard US five-inch shell to ensure a supply of cheap ammunition.

Although Italy had ended up on the winning side in World War II little remained of the glittering fleet built up by *Il Duce*. Those ships which had not been sunk were scuttled or seized by the Germans, handed over to the victors as reparations or scrapped under the terms of the Peace Treaty. All that were left were three destroyers and five torpedo boats, but it was not long before Italy was asked to bear some of the burden of building up NATO's naval strength. To help train personnel the USN handed over two pre-war destroyers in 1951, and in 1958 the *Impetuoso* and *Indomito* were completed in Italian shipyards. They were about the same size as the *Forrest Shermans* and the five-inch guns and fire-control were supplied by the USA. As always, they looked good and were fast, reaching 35 knots on trials.

The Japanese were the next 'former enemy' to be helped to their feet sooner than expected, thanks to the pressure of the Cold War. The so-called 'Maritime Self-Defence Force' was given two old US destroyers, and in 1956 the *Harukaze* and *Yukikaze* came into service, clearly owing a lot to the *Fletcher* design. At the same time the sunken *Matsu* Class *Nashi* was raised and repaired for service as the radar training ship *Wakaba*. A number of other destroyers had survived the War but after a few months of repatriating Japanese troops from the outlying Pacific islands in 1946–47 all were handed over to China and the Soviet Union as reparations or used by the British and Americans as targets. The *Yukikaze*, which had come through the war without a scratch,

Below: The big French destroyer *Duperré* was converted to a sonar trial ship and is seen here in 1968 with an enormous variable-depth sonar aft.

Above : The French *D'Estrées* and her sisters were originally armed with five-inch guns using standard USN ammunition but they have since been re-armed with a powerful Franco-German 100mm gun.
Above right : In the 1950s the Dutch built two classes of big destroyers, the *Hollands* and the *Frieslands*.

was handed over to China in 1947 and was one of the few ships which did not fall into Communist hands in 1949. As the *Tan Yang* she was the largest combatant unit in the Nationalist Chinese Navy for some years and was not scrapped until 1971.

The last of the Axis navies was reborn in 1955, when the *Bundesmarine* was established as part of NATO. Three years later the first of six *Fletcher* Class destroyers was handed over at Bremerhaven. As *Z.1–6* they were to provide training for the new personnel during the five-year loan period but in 1977 four

Above : The *Impetuoso* (above) and *Indomito*, Italy's first post-war destroyers, were armed with twin five-inch 38/cal and 40mm Bofors guns and Mark 37 fire-control supplied by the USN.

were still in service. None of the destroyers of the *Kriegsmarine* survived, as those still afloat in 1945 had been incorporated into the Soviet and French Navies. Four new destroyers were built for the *Bundesmarine* in 1959–68 known as the *Hamburg* Class and they bore little resemblance to any contemporaries. With two massive funnels and a superstructure which towered up deck upon deck, they were known as the 'high-rise' class. The armament was a strange assortment from various countries: 100mm guns from France, 40mm guns from Italy, fire-control from Holland and homing torpedoes from Sweden.

Sweden had always taken an interest in torpedo-warfare, particularly as the Baltic is ideal for hit-and-run tactics. Until the end of the war Swedish destroyers had been on the small side, but the *Öland* and *Uppland* completed in 1947–48 were comparable to those in bigger navies. They were followed by the much bigger *Halland* and *Småland*, which made history in 1957 as the first destroyers equipped to fire surface-to-surface guided missiles. A ramp was mounted over the after-bank of torpedo-tubes, but unfortunately the missile, the Saab-Scania Rb 08A did

Right and below : As the Soviet Navy expanded its captains became more aggressive and took to harassing NATO warships. On the right the 'SAM-Kotlin' destroyer No 365 rashly approaches the 44,000-ton carrier HMS *Ark Royal* while she is recovering aircraft; below a collision takes place leaving the Soviet ship badly damaged. *Bottom right :* A heavily retouched photograph of a Soviet 'Kashin' Class guided missile destroyer, the first major warships in the world to be propelled by gas turbines.

not become operational for another ten years. It was not very successful either, and was only in production for three years, but it pointed the way to future developments.

The Russians, the cause of much of this flurry of destroyer-building, had not so far shown any great ingenuity in the destroyer field. Their pre-war fleet had been largely composed of pre-Revolution destroyers completed laboriously many years later; any new construction was based on Italian designs. Their only outstanding vessel was the 2890-ton leader *Tashkent*, built in Italy and having the distinction of being the only Soviet warship to be blessed by a Roman Catholic priest on launching. The weaknesses of the Italian-designed *Gnevny* Class or Type VII led to the more robust *Silny* type being started in 1937, and although they proved better able to cope with Arctic conditions their operations were so circumscribed that it is hard to assess their fighting value. The solitary attempt to be adventurous, the 42-knot *Opitny* (ex-*Serge Ordzhonikidze*), was a total flop. She vibrated so much that it was impossible to work the guns and she only commissioned in June 1941 for service as a floating battery in the defence of Leningrad.

Following developments in other navies, the firepower of the *Silny* was increased by the adoption of twin gun mountings in the *Ognevoi* Class, most of which were not finished until the War was over. They served as the basis for Stalin's massive expansion of the post-1945 Soviet destroyer strength. The *Skoryi* Class, completed in the 1950s, was not outstanding in any particular way, but as some 70 were built at a time when NATO navies were adding very few destroyers and scrapping far more, they posed a considerable threat. In 1955 there was further consternation when Western observers sighted a new type, codenamed *Tallinn* as that was the area in which she was first sighted. As it turned out only one of the class was built, the *Nastoichivy*, an indication that Western suspicions about her excessive topweight might be well-founded. Next came the *Kotlin*

Class, built between 1954 and 1958. Like the *Tallinn* design they were flush-decked, but in other ways they were a reversion to the layout of the *Skoryi*, with two sets of quintuple torpedo-tubes and two twin 130mm (5.1-inch) dual-purpose gun mountings. Although fitted with radar control for their guns and credited with 36 knots maximum speed they did not mark any startling advance.

While the *Kotlins* were being built the US Navy was pondering its next step. All wartime experience and post-war trials had shown that gunfire was of limited use against air-attack. The rapid firing three-inch/50 calibre guns installed in US destroyers were far more effective than the 40mm Bofors, but something better was needed to down the high-flying aircraft, which in all probability would launch a 'stand-off' guided missile against ship targets. The protracted 'Bumblebee' programme had eventually produced the first operational shipboard anti-aircraft guided missile, the 'Terrier', which was capable of destroying a supersonic aircraft at a range of up to 22 miles. 'Terrier' was currently being installed in two heavy cruisers, and it was decided to test the feasibility of installing a twin missile launcher and magazines in a destroyer. The guinea pig was the *Gearing* Class *Gyatt* (DD.712) which became DDG.1 on 1 December 1955, and she commissioned a year later with a missile launcher and loading gear in place of her after twin five-inch gun. To provide a stable launching platform she also incorporated that

Left: The handsome Italian guided-missile destroyer *Impavido* at full speed in the Mediterranean in March 1971.
Right: The Soviet naval replenishment tanker *Boris Chilikin* refuels two 'Kashin' Class destroyers in the Mediterranean East of Sardinia in 1975.

unpopular feature of the British wartime 'Hunt' Class destroyers, retractable fin stabilizers.

As the *Gyatt* lacked proper missile fire-control she was little more than a test-bed for the idea of a guided-missile-armed destroyer, but she proved the feasibility of such an idea. In Fiscal Year 1956 six 4770-ton DLGs were ordered, followed by four more the following year, and eight smaller DDGs. The DLGs became the *Coontz* Class, all named after famous captains and admirals, while the DDGs were known as the *Charles F Adams* Class and have been the USN's standard destroyer design for some years. Three more were built for Australia, the *Brisbane*, *Hobart* and *Perth*, and three for the Federal German Navy, the *Lütjens*, *Mölders* and *Rommel*. They bear no worthwhile comparison to the humble destroyers of 30 years ago, with hulls 437 feet long, air-conditioned living spaces and bewildering arrays of electronics.

The next generation of DLGs, the 5670-ton *Leahy* Class, stretched credibility too far, and in 1975 they and their successors, the *Belknaps*, were reclassified as guided missile cruisers (CGs). The Royal Navy suffered the same *frisson* with its first guided missile ships, the 5440-ton 'County' Class, which were rated as destroyers when the lead-ship HMS *Devonshire* commissioned in 1962. Anyone who appreciated the RN's respect for tradition knew that names like *Devonshire*, *Hampshire*, *Kent* and *London* belonged to cruisers, but the politicians did not. As those same politicians and the Treasury also regarded destroyers as cheaper and less contentious than cruisers, it was a way of getting parliamentary approval without too much acrimony. The 'Counties' were eventually reclassified as DLGs, but are unofficially referred to as light cruisers. However the most preposterous misuse of the term DLG must still be for describing the 7–8000-ton nuclear cruisers *Bainbridge* and *Truxtun* completed in 1962 and 1967 respectively. Like the other DLGs, the only point they had in common with destroyers was the fact that the hulls are subdivided principally by transverse bulkheads rather than the longitudinal bulkheads associated with larger warships.

The Russians were not slow to respond with guided missile destroyers of their own but there was a significant difference. Four *Kotlins* lying on the stocks were built to fire a surface-to-surface missile known to NATO as the SS-N-1 or 'Strela'. The Russians were convinced that long-range missiles (150 miles) could force US and NATO carrier task forces to keep a more respectful distance, and 'Strela' (later renamed 'Scrubber') was the first of a series of cruise missiles developed to that end. To distinguish them from the original *Kotlin* type the four were dubbed *Kildins*. In 1967 another new destroyer appeared, the *Krupny* type (NATO had now settled on 'K' names for Soviet ships), with 'Scrubber' launchers forward and aft. Apparently the 'Scrubber' was not all that was hoped, and only one ship of the class, the *Gordy*, is believed to have been completed. Seven others were completed as the *Kanin* type, with surface-to-air missiles (SAMs) of the 'Goa' SA-N-1 type. They were a development of the SAM-*Kotlin*, which had first been seen in 1962, with a 'Goa' launcher aft in place of the 130mm guns.

Although the respective merits of all these DDGs depended on the unpublicized performance of their respective weapons, the various navies seemed to be in agreement that defence against aircraft was now the primary role for destroyers. However, on 21 October 1967 an event of great significance caused a complete upheaval in naval thinking. On that day, during the Six-Day War between Israel and the United Arab Republic, the old Israeli destroyer *Eilat* was patrolling close inshore off the Sinai Peninsula. Suddenly the radar set picked up airborne contacts heading from a position close to the shoreline, and within a space of seconds it was realized that they were

Below: The four large angled uptakes of the 'Kashin' Class are needed to provide cooling for the four gas turbines.

four missiles flying close to the speed of sound. They were Soviet-designed 'Styx' SS-N-2 surface-to-surface missiles, fired by two Egyptian fast patrol boats of the Russian *Komar* type. The *Eilat* opened fire with her 40mm guns but it was hopeless, and she was hit by three of the missiles amidships, homing apparently on the heat of her funnel gases. The destroyer sank quickly with heavy loss of life.

It was hardly surprising that three hits from heavy warheads fitted with semi-armour piercing fuzes would sink a destroyer. The *Eilat* was the former HMS *Zealous*, launched in 1944 and lacking any modern equipment or armament for dealing even with manned aircraft, let alone missiles. Yet, as far as the world was concerned, a tiny patrol boat had blown a mighty destroyer out of the water, and no ship was safe. The crudities of the Styx were forgotten, and the fact that they were travelling slowly enough for the *Eilat* to engage them with her Bofors guns using a simple tachymetric director. But the *Eilat* sinking had one beneficial effect for Western navies; it persuaded politicians to loosen the purse strings and permitted the development of surface-to-surface guided missiles in reply to the Russians.

In the surprisingly short space of five years France produced the Exocet surface-to-surface missile, with better range and far superior guidance to the Styx. Exocet was immediately snapped up by the British, who started to convert their 'County' Class DLGs to carry four of them. Other navies followed suit, and a number of destroyer-sized vessels now carry an outfit of these light and effective weapons to increase their surface strike capability, a reversion to the original purpose of destroyers. One important advantage of a weapon like Exocet is that it has no recoil, and so the boxlike container is merely bolted on deck wherever there is sufficient space. The target is located by the same radar sets which track and indicate targets for other weapons on board, and once Exocet is fired it skims across the surface of the sea using a radio altimeter to keep a constant height until it is close enough to track the target with its own radar homing head.

One more technological advance altered the destroyer beyond recognition. In 1962 the Soviet Navy introduced a new destroyer with an unusual profile, *four* funnels angled outwards in pairs. She was called the *Kashin* type by NATO, and was the world's first major operational warship to be powered by gas turbines. The reason for the big angled uptakes was to disperse the intense heat generated by four large gas turbines developing 15,000

horsepower or more; unlike steam machinery, in which much of the heat is dissipated through the boiler feedwater, about 90 per cent of a gas turbine's heat goes 'up the chimney', where it can play havoc with radar aerials. Although gas turbines are heavy on fuel they give such quick getaway and acceleration that they confer important tactical advantages for modern sea warfare.

The British had already gone part of the way in their 'County' Class, which had a combined steam and gas turbine (COSAG) plant. This was repeated in the DLG *Bristol*, but in 1975 HMS *Sheffield* appeared as the first of a class of eight DDGs driven by four gas turbines at a maximum speed of over 30 knots. Later the same year the US destroyer *Spruance* (DD.963) became the first American all-gas turbine warship. The *Sheffield* represents an attempt to keep size down to a minimum, whereas the *Spruance* does exactly the opposite. The British ship had its displacement pared down to 3150 tons, whereas the designers of the *Spruance* deliberately allowed for future developments in weapons and sensors not yet even on the drawing board. The result was a destroyer of 7800 tons armed with only two five-inch guns, an ASROC anti-submarine missile system, six torpedo-tubes and an anti-submarine helicopter. A short-range 'Sea Sparrow' missile launcher will be fitted, and possibly some light guns.

There has been considerable heat generated in the discussions over the *Spruance* and her 29 sisters. In size they are as big as the original DLGs, and yet they have no area-defence guided missile system. The 20mm Phalanx 'Gatling' gun may be installed as a last-ditch defence against surface missiles, putting up

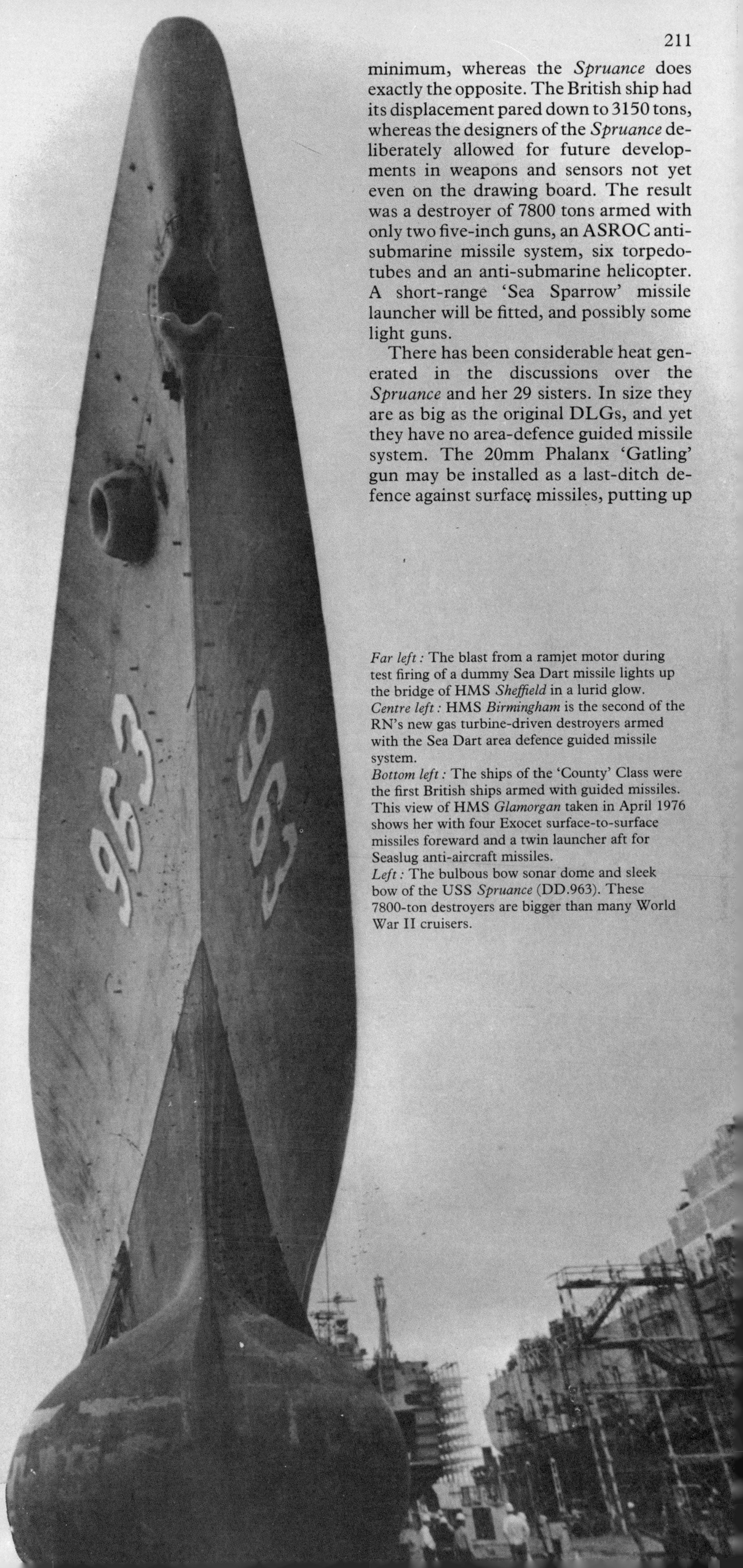

Far left: The blast from a ramjet motor during test firing of a dummy Sea Dart missile lights up the bridge of HMS *Sheffield* in a lurid glow.
Centre left: HMS *Birmingham* is the second of the RN's new gas turbine-driven destroyers armed with the Sea Dart area defence guided missile system.
Bottom left: The ships of the 'County' Class were the first British ships armed with guided missiles. This view of HMS *Glamorgan* taken in April 1976 shows her with four Exocet surface-to-surface missiles foreward and a twin launcher aft for Seaslug anti-aircraft missiles.
Left: The bulbous bow sonar dome and sleek bow of the USS *Spruance* (DD.963). These 7800-ton destroyers are bigger than many World War II cruisers.

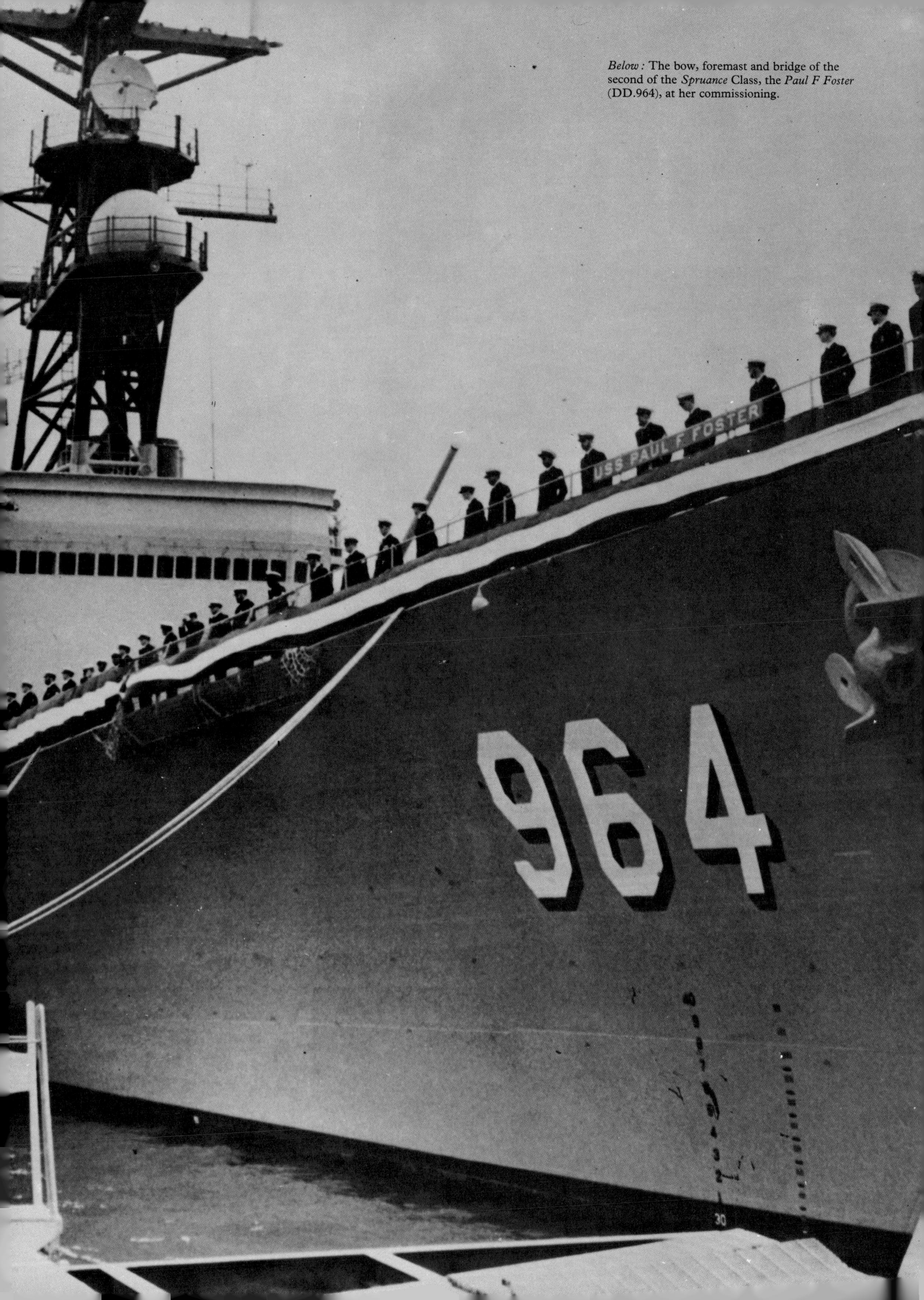

Below: The bow, foremast and bridge of the second of the *Spruance* Class, the *Paul F Foster* (DD.964), at her commissioning.

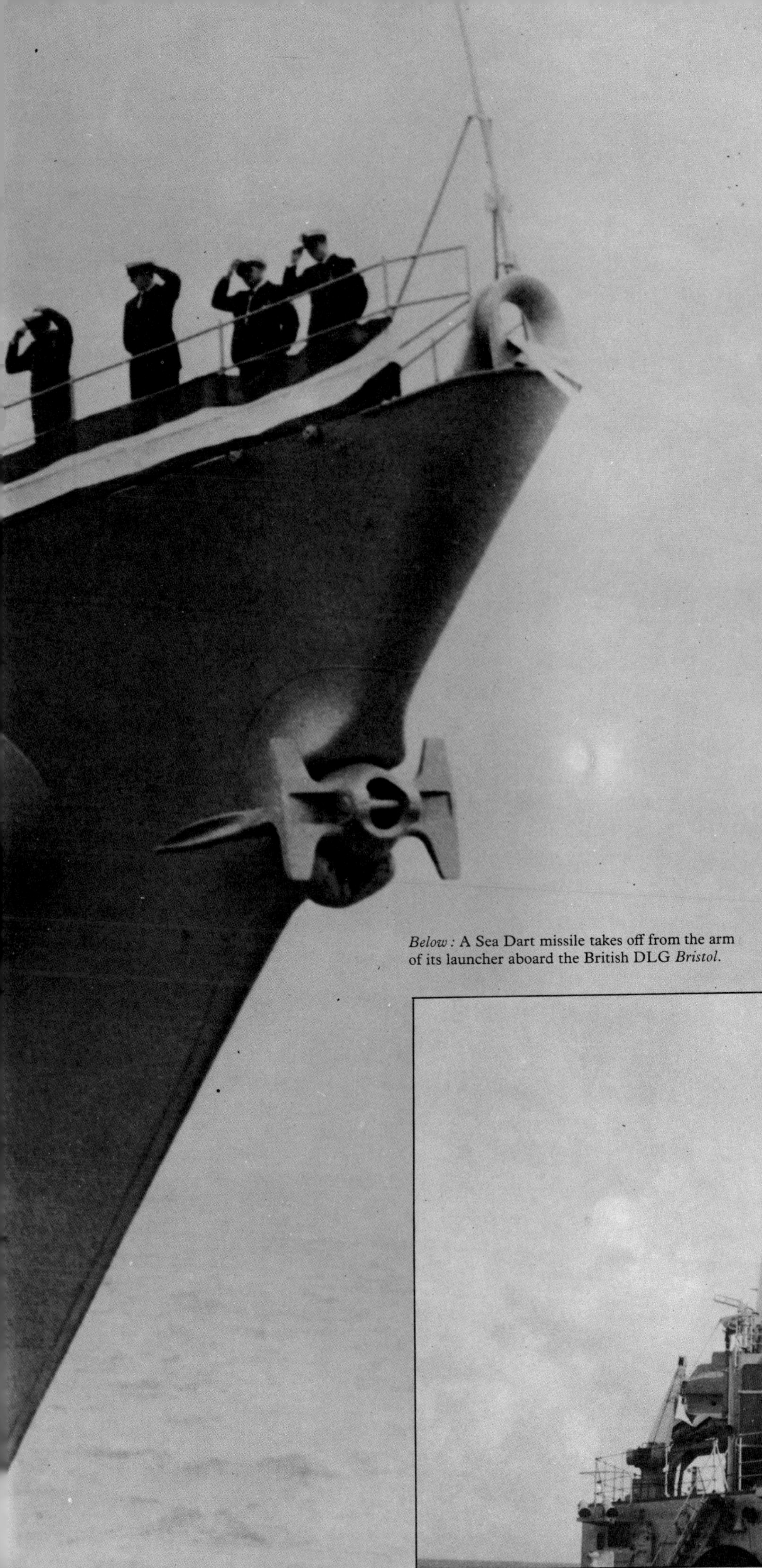

a 'wall of lead' to shoot them down or trigger off the warhead prematurely. If ever the destroyer changed from the 'hunter' category to the 'hunted', it was now. And her cost is exorbitant. However, there has never been a destroyer or any other warship before, in which bulkier equipment will be able to be installed at a later date. It has already been stated that the final ships of the class will probably have a different armament.

The long history of unsuccessful attempts to give destroyers heavy guns has been discussed earlier, but in 1975 the *Forrest Sherman* Class *Hull* appeared with a new eight-inch/55 calibre gun in place of the forward five-inch. This made an important difference as this gun is a lightweight weapon designed for simple loading. The need for a gun of this sort was highlighted during the Vietnam War when the lack of heavy gun armed ships put the burden of fire-support on destroyers and their five-inch guns which lacked the range and weight to do sufficient damage to most shore targets. The only disadvantage to the new eight-inch gun would seem to be the problem of how to carry enough shells to sustain fire for any length of time. But having a range of 30 miles (with rocket assistance) is a significant improvement in performance and the accuracy of laser-guided shells will reduce the need for firing too many ranging rounds.

So far the story of modern destroyers has been nothing but growth in size and complexity. But for many years the bulk of Western naval strength was made up of the older, 'traditional' type of World War II destroyer. At the time of the Washington Treaty the hull-life of a

Below: A Sea Dart missile takes off from the arm of its launcher aboard the British DLG *Bristol.*

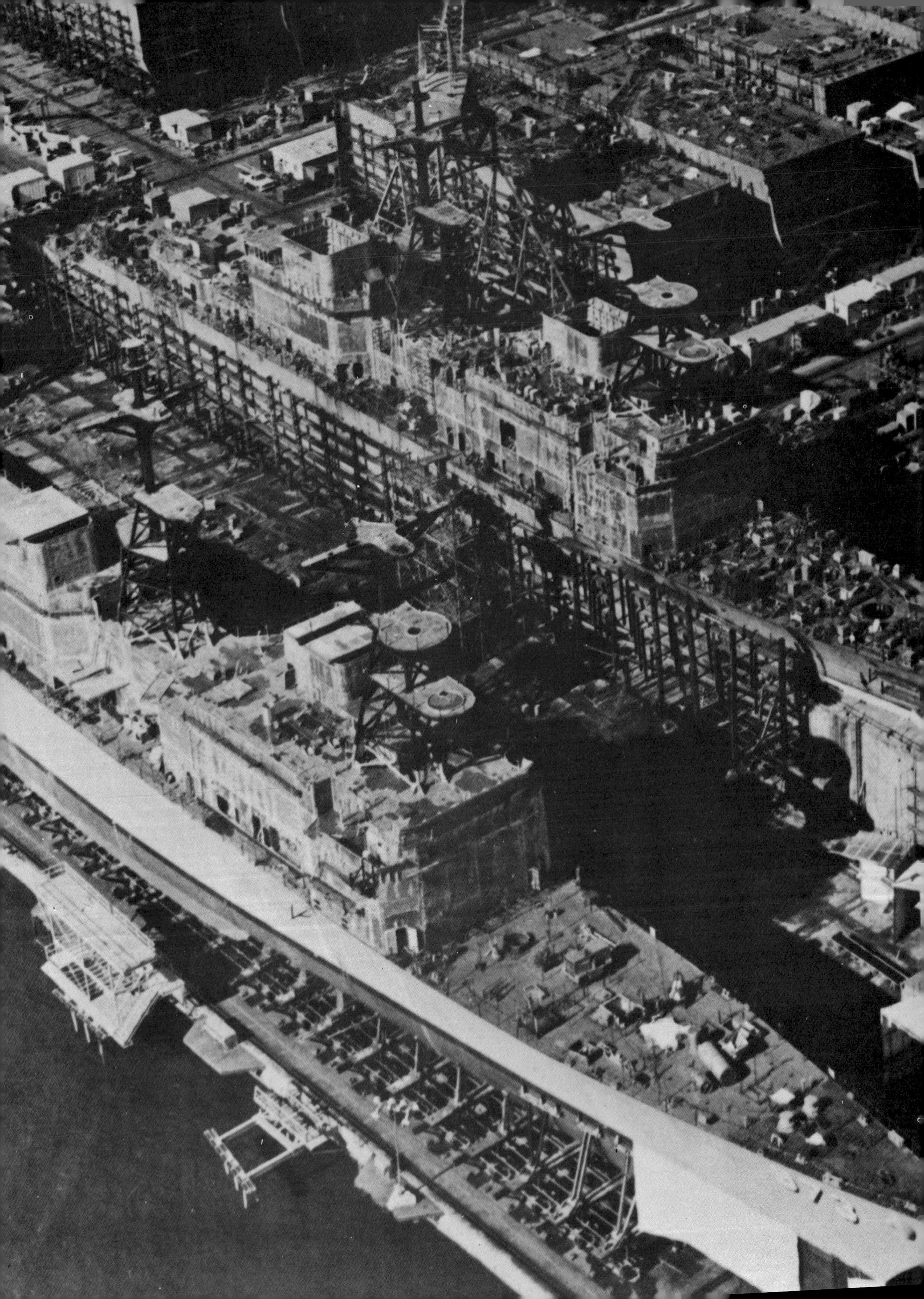

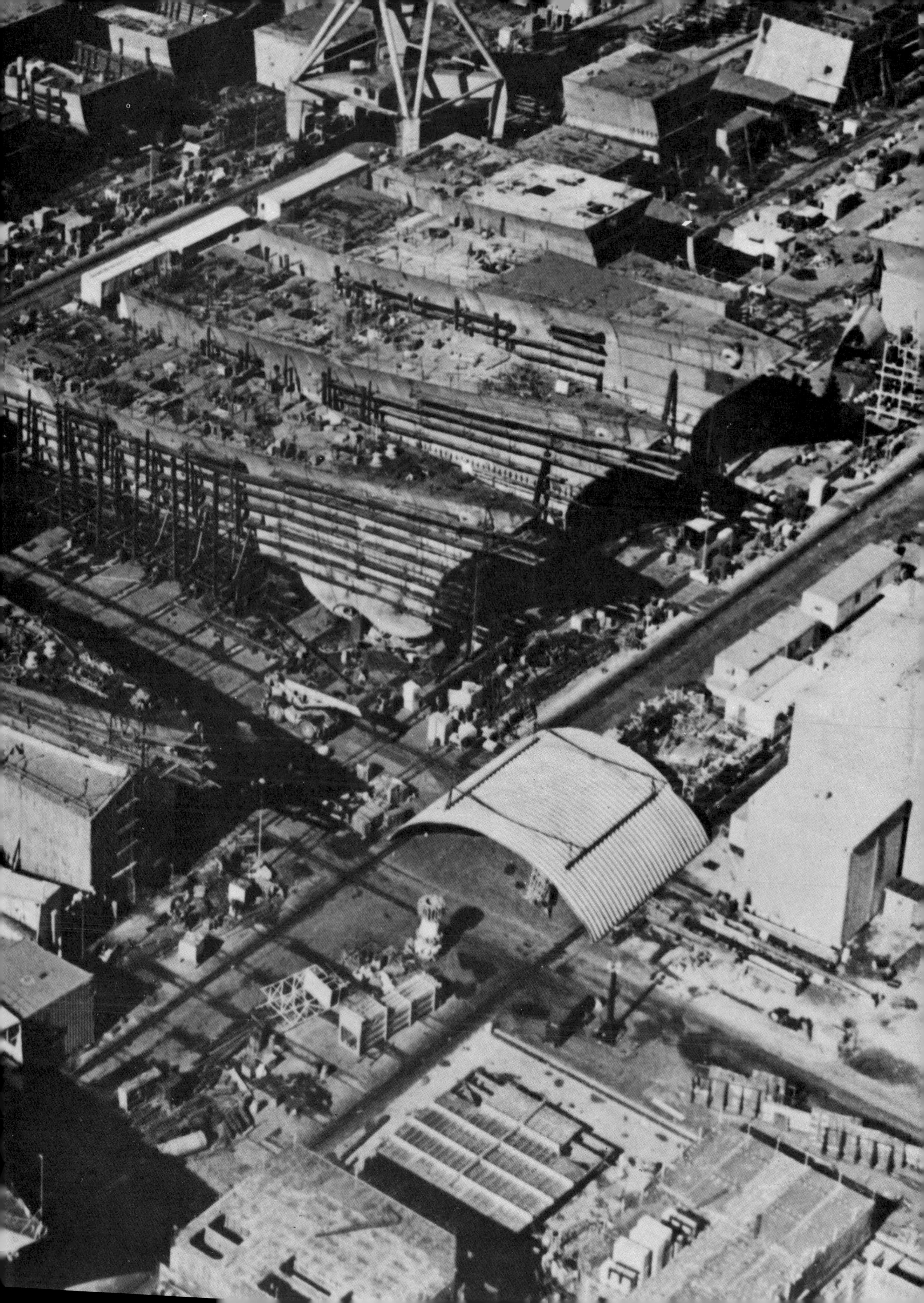

destroyer had been assessed at 15 years, with one year's war service to count as two. This meant that a destroyer commissioned in 1942 would be ready for scrapping in 1954, and if this had been adhered to rigidly the US Navy would have scrapped some 300 destroyers by 1957. This did not happen, partly because improved techniques of dehumidifying ships laid up in the 'mothball fleet' preserved them better than before, but mainly because of timely action by Congress in authorizing a big repair programme.

Between 1959 and 1964 a massive Fleet Rehabilitation and Modernization (FRAM) programme resulted in the overhaul and updating of 131 destroyers as well as other ships. The essentials of the FRAM programme were renewal of wiring, improvement of anti-submarine armament and overhaul of boilers and machinery. Two types of overhaul were planned, FRAM I for the more modern destroyers, extending hull-life by eight to ten years, and FRAM II, extending the life of the older destroyers by at least five years. Between 1960 and 1964 Congress authorized FRAM I overhauls for 79 *Gearing*s and FRAM II overhauls for 52 *Gearing*s, *Sumner*s and *Fletcher*s. The work was done by the naval shipyards in addition to their normal workload, and the work took six years. The first FRAM I was the *Perry*, which entered Boston Naval Shipyard in May 1959 and emerged in April 1960; the last was the *Herbert J Thomas* completed by Mare Island Naval Shipyard in August 1965. The conversion of a further 17 *Fletcher*s and *Sumner*s was vetoed as the work could not have been started until 1965, by which time the hulls would be nearly 20 years old.

Naturally the FRAM overhaul was not restricted to the hulls; the chance was taken to modernize the armament. The main role for the destroyers was anti-submarine warfare and to that purpose three new weapons were available: the triple Mk.32 torpedo-tube for launching Mk.44 acoustic torpedoes, the ASROC eight-barrelled missile launcher and an unmanned helicopter. The bulky ASROC launcher was fitted between the funnels, but only in FRAM I conversions. The FRAM I conversions were also the only ones to receive the hangar and flight deck for operating helicopters. The reason for this was that the installation of ASROC fire-control, improved sonars and the control gear for the drone helicopters called for a much more comprehensive overhaul of the power-supply than the FRAM II budget allowed.

In many ways the FRAM programme was a success, but it was also an expensive failure. Its main virtue was the extension of the useful life of so many destroyers at a time when replacement on a ship-for-ship basis was impossible (as it had been with the flush-deckers in the early 1930s). Its failure was in the trust put in the totally untried concept of the Drone Anti-Submarine Helicopter (DASH) system. In theory the expensive and vulnerable human pilot could be replaced at equal cost and less risk by a sophisticated auto-pilot and remote guidance but in practice the state of the art did not permit the sort of delicate control needed to put a light helicopter down on the pitching and rolling deck of a destroyer. Nor was the command-link reliable. It was not unknown for a DASH drone with a pair of armed homing torpedoes slung underneath, to run wild and fly upside down over its parent ship. By December 1969 746 drones had been delivered to the Fleet but 416 had crashed, a failure of nearly 70 per cent.

The failure of DASH had two regrettable side-effects. First, a large percentage of the cost of each FRAM conversion was taken up by the provision of the hangar and flight deck, money which could have been put to better use in converting more destroyers. Second, it gave light shipborne helicopters a poor reputation and delayed the introduction of the Light Airborne Multi-Purpose System (LAMPS) helicopter. Only now (1977)

are US Navy destroyers reaping the benefit of shipborne helicopters as hunters of submarines whereas other navies have already developed a second generation of light helicopters.

Other navies carried out their own refurbishing of old destroyers, but nothing as ambitious as the FRAM programme. The British frigate programme of the 1950s has already been mentioned. An additional programme to update a group of destroyers for service on foreign stations was implemented on the 'CA' Class, all eight of which had been completed in 1944–45 and then put into reserve after only a year-and-a-half of service. Between 1952 and 1963 they were rebuilt with new fire-control, new bridges and a modern anti-submarine armament. The last two, HMS *Caprice* and HMS *Cavalier*, were armed with a short-range guided missile system, and in July 1972 the *Cavalier* had the distinction of being the Royal Navy's last operational destroyer. She and the *Caprice* were the last of more than a thousand Royal Navy destroyers built since the *Havock* and *Hornet* in 1893, eighty years before.

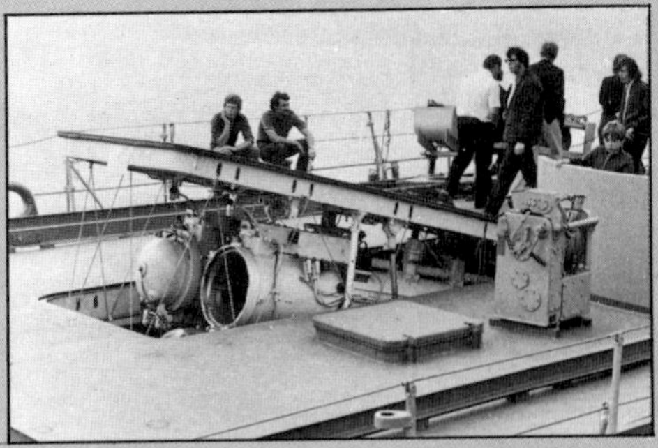

Top left and right: Two types of anti-submarine torpedo-tubes aboard the German destroyer *Hessen*: left, single on deck; and right, deck-loaded firing through stern.
Above: The *Audace* is the lightest Italian destroyer armed with US missiles and Italian guns.
Below: The Chilean *Ministro Portales* was originally named the *Douglas H Fox* (DD.779) of the *Allen M Sumner* Class II Version and was transferred in 1974.

Epilogue

We have seen the destroyer grow from a frail craft into the enormous and costly multi-purpose warship of today, with little but the name to connect her to the old torpedo boats. It can be argued that the navies which have dropped the name have at least recognized that the destroyer, like the dinosaur, has outlived her usefulness by growing too big.

If any warship-type today bears any resemblance to the original torpedo boat destroyer it is probably the fast patrol boat with her missiles and torpedoes. If expendability was a criterion of the destroyer, FPBs meet it, and if weight of punch is a yardstick the FPB has more of that than many warships. It is interesting to compare the Federal German Navy's Type 143 or *S.61* Class FPBs with HMS *Havock*:

	Havock (1893)	*S.61* (1973)
Length	195ft	200ft
Beam	18·5ft	24·6ft
Draft	6·4ft	8·5ft
Horsepower	3500	16,000
Speed	26·5 knots	38 knots
Guns	one 3-inch, three 57mm	two 3-inch DP, one 40mm AA
Torpedoes	three 18-inch	two 21-inch (wire-guided)
Missiles	—	four Exocet SSMs
Complement	42	40

Of course a direct comparison between the two ships is pointless, but the relationship between them and their potential opponents is comparable. The torpedo was in its day as lethal a weapon to its victims as the guided missile, and indeed it *was* a guided weapon, relying on its gyroscopes to ensure straight running. Both ships rely on speed and a small silhouette to reduce the risk of damage, and both can be built in large numbers because the unit cost is relatively low. It is also arguable that the crews of modern fast patrol boats are hardly more comfortable than the destroyermen of yesterday. The vibration of fast running and the cramped quarters strike a familiar echo, but the big FPBs are regarded with the same affection by their crews as any destroyer. And nothing can compare with the sight of a group of FPBs sweeping into action at high speed, the only modern equivalent of an old-fashioned mass attack by destroyers.

It is interesting to see that even the fast patrol boat is growing too big for its role. The Swedish and Danish Navies, both of which rely heavily on gas turbine-driven FPBs to guard the exit to the Baltic, have discovered the need for 'flotilla leaders' to back up their light craft. They are intended to provide superior gunpower, communications and radar cover to assist the FPBs to locate and destroy their targets. The Swedes are still studying the problem but the Danes have ordered three 1000-ton corvettes for completion in 1980. A combination of gas turbines and diesels will drive them at over 30

Below: An appeal has been launched to preserve the USS *The Sullivans* (DD.537) as the sole example of a USN destroyer of World War II. She is seen here at sea in October 1962.

knots, and 60-mile range surface-to-surface missiles will make them tough opponents for any larger ship.

With no modern destroyer bearing any resemblance to the destroyers which made the breed famous, how many of the oldtimers survive? The answer is, surprisingly, many, for the US Navy in particular has been generous in transferring *Fletcher*s, *Sumner*s and *Gearing*s to friendly navies. This has its risks, and in July 1974 during the Turkish invasion of Cyprus, Turkish Super Sabre jets attacked and sank their own destroyer *Kocatepe*. The confusion is understandable, for the opposing Greek Navy owns four ex-*Gearing* FRAM destroyers of almost identical appearance. The current issue of *Jane's Fighting Ships* lists a total of 288 'conventional' destroyers, some of them built as long ago as 1940 and long overdue for scrapping. When these pass from the scene there will be little enough to remember them by, apart from their achievements.

The thin steel hull of a destroyer does not stand up well to corrosion, and so very few have been chosen for preservation as museum-ships. The most successful attempt has been the Canadian scheme to run the old 'Tribal' Class HMCS *Haida* as a floating museum at Toronto. Despite

Below: A similar appeal has been launched to save destroyer HMS *Cavalier* as a representative of British wartime destroyers. She is seen here on completion in November 1944.

the distance from the sea she has proved a popular attraction to visitors and pays her way. An important reason for the *Haida*'s success is the fact that she and her sisters had distinguished war careers, both in World War II and in Korea. Fired by this example the British launched an appeal to save their last destroyer, HMS *Cavalier*, as a museum devoted to destroyers. The 'Laughing Cavalier' had been completed in 1944, and although most of her life was spent in a world officially at peace, she had her fair share of excitement. After nearly ten years in the Far East she returned home for a last commission, during which she was challenged by the frigate *Rapid* (with identical machinery) to a race for the title of 'Fastest Ship of the Fleet'. In July 1971 the *Cavalier* beat the *Rapid* in a 64-mile run with an average speed of 31.8 knots, a stout performance for a ship launched in 1944. Always a happy ship, the officers and men of the *Cavalier* felt that she ought to survive as a memorial to the rest of the breed. At the time of writing a trust has been formed to run her as a museum at Southampton.

People in the United States seem to have come to the same conclusion, and now an association is trying to save the USS *The Sullivans* (DD.537). This *Fletcher* Class destroyer owes her unusual name to the fact that five brothers from Iowa were killed in the cruiser *Juneau* at the Battle of Guadalcanal in November 1942. The nation was so horrified at this heavy sacrifice made by one family that President Roosevelt ordered a new destroyer to be named *The Sullivans*. Like HMS *Cavalier* she had a humdrum but active career spanning nearly 30 years. In some ways it is more appropriate to choose workhorse destroyers for preservation, rather than battle-scarred veterans. Many hundreds of destroyers

Below: HMS *Cavalier* in 1971 during her final action-packed commission. She underwent several reconstructions in her 28-year life but in 1971 still reached an average speed of 31.8 knots, earning her the title of 'Fastest Ship of the Fleet'.

did nothing more than routine patrolling for years on end, part of the larger pattern of sea power.

Another destroyer preserved for her war record is the Polish *Blyskawica*. She and her sister *Grom* were built in Britain before World War II, and with the French-built *Burza* made a dash for freedom when the Nazis invaded Poland in 1939. Despite heavy air attacks they made their way from Gdynia (Danzig) out through the Kattegat and across the North Sea. The *Grom* was sunk by dive-bombing off Norway in 1940 but the *Blyskawica* and *Burza* survived a score of actions. After some argument with the Communist regime the two destroyers finally returned to Poland in 1951, and in memory of her wartime exploits the *Burza* was laid up as a war memorial at Gdynia. When her hull deteriorated beyond repair she was replaced by the renowned *Blyskawica*, which is there today.

Although not a preserved destroyer the old Thai Navy destroyer *Phra Ruang* can claim the record for longevity. Built as HMS *Radiant* in 1916 she survived a tragic loss in December 1917 when she was the only one of four Harwich Force destroyers to escape from a minefield, and was sold to Thailand in 1920. In August 1944, while under Japanese control she sank the US submarine *Harder*. By February 1966 she had been stricken but her bare hull was still afloat in the Chao Praya River, South of Bangkok.

Whether or not destroyers are preserved, as long as naval history is read the word 'destroyer' will be synonymous with speed, hard-fought actions and endurance. Countless battles and stirring deeds are their real memorial, and whatever shape the destroyer of the future takes, she will be hard put to match past achievements or the dedication of the men who manned her.

Index

General

Ships

Acknowledgments

The author would like to thank Janet MacLennan for her editorial assistance on this book and David Eldred for designing it as well as Richard Natkiel of *The Economist* for providing the maps, Helen Downton, who provided the technical drawings, and Charles Haberlein, who provided invaluable assistance in picture research in the United States. He would especially also like to thank Mr S. Fukui for his help in captioning many rare pictures of Japanese destroyers which he supplied.

Picture Credits

Imperial War Museum: 18/19 (bottom), 26 (top), 35 (both), 40/41 (bottom), 41 (top), 60/61 (centre), 63 (top), 80/81, 92/93 (bottom), 126/127 (both), 203 (top).
Novosti Press Agency: 193 (top).
Robert Hunt Library: 6/7 (bottom), 14 (top), 15 (centre), 16/17 (all 3–17 top IWM), 19 (top), 20, 21, 22/23 (all 3), 24/25 (all 3), 26/27, 27 (top), 28/29 (all 3), 30 (centre), 32/33 (all 3), 36/37 (bottom), 38/39 (all 3), 65 (centre), 82/83 (all 3), 84 (top), 92 (top), 94 (top), 97 (centre), 106 (top right), 106/107 (bottom), 108/109 (all but top centre), 110/111 (bottom), 111 (centre), 116 (top), 122/123 (bottom), 124 (top), 129 (all 3), 130/131 (bottom), 140/141 (bottom), 144 (top), 146 (top), 147 (top), 148 (top), 152, 159 (top), 168/169, 180 (bottom), 188 (top), 188/189 (bottom), 190 (top).
National Maritime Museum: 31 (top), 34, 40 (centre), 91 (centre), 95 (top left), 103 (top), 189 (top).
Science Museum: 7 (centre), 8/9 (bottom), 9 (top), 10 (top and bottom), 12/13 (both).
Photo Mayo Ltd: 7 (top).
US Navy: 36 (top 2), 37 (top), 48/49 (bottom), 50 (top), 54/55 (bottom), 56 (top), 58/59 (top), 70 (bottom), 71 (both), 72/73 (top 2), 74/75 (top 3), 77 (bottom 2), 96, 97 (top), 98/99 (bottom), 102 (top), 104/105, 132/133 (both), 134/135 (bottom), 136/137 (all 3), 138/139 (bottom), 142, 144/145 (bottom), 145 (top), 146 (centre), 146/147 (bottom), 148 (bottom), 149 (top right), 150/151 (bottom), 154/155 (all 3), 156 (top), 158/159, 160/161 (both), 162/163 (bottom), 166, 170/171, 172/173 (bottom), 174/175 (bottom), 176/177 (all 3), 178 (centre), 178/179 (top), 181 (bottom 2), 183 (top), 184/185 (bottom), 185 (top), 190/191, 202 (top), 203 (centre), 208/209, 211, 212/213, 218/219 (bottom).
Foto Drüppel: 42 (centre), 43 (top), 52/53 (bottom), 58/59 (bottom), 62/63 (bottom), 100/101 (all 4), 106 (centre), 107 (centre right), 108/109 (top), 112/113 (bottom), 118 (top 2), 120 (top centre), 128 (top), 134 (top), 187 (top).
Wright and Logan: 42/43 (bottom), 56/57 (bottom), 201 (top).
Orbis: 53 (centre), 62 (top).
National Archives: 47 (top 2), 68/69 (all 3), 70 (top left), 72/73 (bottom), 74/75 (bottom), 76 (bottom), 76/77 (top), 98/99 (top 3), 102 (centre), 130 (top), 131 (top), 135 (top), 151 (top), 156/157 (bottom), 163 (top), 165, 167 (top), 170 (top left), 172 (top), 178/179 (bottom), 180/181 (top), 182/183.
P A Vicary: 44/45, 58 (centre).
Bundesarchiv: 102/103 (bottom).
Mainichi: 46 (centre), 66 (both), 67 (top 2), 167 (bottom), 175 (top), 184 (top).
S Fukui: 49 (top), 50 (bottom), 51, 52 (centre), 52/53 (top), 67 (bottom), 139 (centre), 141 (top 2), 194 (centre), 195 (centre).
Gaston Bereleurant: 198/199 (top centre).
John I Thornycroft: 56 (centre), 193 (bottom).
Ministry of Defence: 81 (top), 84/85 (bottom), 45 (top 2), 46/47, 86/87, 88/89, 90/91 (bottom), 93 (top 2), 94/95 (bottom), 95 (top right and centre right), 106 (top left), 107 (top), 121 (top and bottom), 124/125 (bottom), 186/187 (bottom), 206/207 (bottom), 207 (top), 209 (top), 210 (centre left), 213 (bottom right), 219 (centre).
Conway Picture Library: 86 (top), 87 (top), 88 (all 3), 89 (top), 90 (top 2), 91 (top), 111 (top right).
Swedish Navy: 202 (centre).
Ted Stone Collection: 97 (bottom).
Relações Publicas da Marinha: 202/203 (bottom).
Marius Bar: 204/205 (bottom).
PPL: 10 (centre), 14/15 (bottom), 55 (top), 57 (centre), 64 (top), 65 (top), 78/79, 86/87, 201 (centre), 207 (bottom), 216/217 (bottom).
Litton Industries: 214/215.
Upper Clyde Shipbuilders: 121 (centre).
R M Scott: 200/201 (bottom).
NMM/Vosper-Thornycroft Collection: 30/31 (bottom), 44 (top).
Musée de la Marine: 123 (top).
H C Willis: 55 (centre).
C & S Taylor: 210 (bottom), 217 (top 2), 220/221.
Navpic: 107 (centre left), 205 (top right).
Naval photograph: 210/211 (centre).
Collezione Aldo Fraccarole: 8 (top), 111 (top left), 112 (top), 113 (top 2), 114/115 (both), 116 (bottom and centre), 117, 118/119 (bottom), 204 (top), 205 (centre), 208 (top), 217 (centre).